Primrose Hill remembered

by Residents Past and Present

foreword by Simon Jenkins

The Friends of Chalk Farm Library

Published
March 2001
ISBN 0-9540074-0-9

The Reminiscence Group

Editor
Caroline Read

Art Editor
Jo Killip

Compiled by
Sieska Cowdrey
Celia Kelly
Jo Killip
Myra Newman
Caroline Read
Jean Rossiter

Cover illustration
David Holmes

Designed by
Ivor Kamlish FCSD
Printed by
Witley Press, Hunstanton

Published by
The Friends of Chalk Farm Library

Introduction

The idea for this book grew out of the programme of talks for older people arranged by Chalk Farm Library: and a Reminiscence Group was formed.

The contributions have been divided into two broad sections: the first contains reminiscences, the second tells the history of individual places and organisations.

Volunteers did the preliminary work but when we needed money for design and printing, we made an appeal to local residents and businesses: the response was truly generous.

An application was also made – in co-operation with Primrose Hill Primary School and supported by Age Concern – for a grant from the Millennium Commission. The awards, which are run by Age Concern and funded by the Millennium Commission with proceeds from the National Lottery, are designed for projects which bring different generations together. This application was successful.

The views expressed in the articles are entirely those of the individual writers.

The Reminiscence Group have received help from many quarters and would like to thank the following in particular:

Camden Leisure and Community Services Department
Malcolm J Holmes and Staff at Camden Local Studies and Archives Centre and Chalk Farm Library, London Borough of Camden
Camden History Society and Robert Leon
Camden Civic Society
Primrose Hill School
Age Concern

A full list of acknowledgements is on page 170.

funded by Age Concern Millennium Awards

AGE Concern

THE MILLENNIUM COMMISSION

THE MILLENNIUM Awards

Camden LEISURE & COMMUNITY

Simon Jenkins *Foreword*

What makes a London neighbourhood? It may have roots in an ancient village or geographical feature. More likely it has evolved over time from a group of streets and squares that felt some bond of history, commerce and community. Primrose Hill is such a place. It is defined only by the rise of the Hill, the curve of Regent's Park Road, and the great railway cutting down to Euston. Yet it has a fierce and growing sense of its own identity, as evidenced in the loyalties and memories of its inhabitants. This is the book of that identity.

Rising beyond the old Regent's Canal, the sloping Hill with its celebrated view over the metropolis was long a place of recreation. From the eighteenth century until well into the nineteenth, the Chalk Farm Tavern was the only structure in the area. It is now the Lemonia restaurant. In the 1840s the building of the Fitzroy estate farmland rapidly joined the terraces of Regent's Park to the Eton College lands to the north. The Primrose Hill enclave was at first intended as a suburb of stately villas, like Maida Vale. The market dictated otherwise, producing the present attractive layout of humbler houses, with small gardens and mews, sandwiched between the smarter residences of Regent's Park, Belsize Park and the Eton College Estate.

London is not and never has been a 'city of villages' A village is a rural place, in which everyone does indeed know everyone else. London is a city of neighbourhoods. Here bonds of neighbourliness are more complex. Friendship may straddle streets and squares, yet not extend to the family next door. Primrose Hill is a classic neighbourhood. Its nearness to the West End and the suitability of its houses for families has long attracted newcomers, commuters into town, and a ration of celebrities. Some are transient. Despite their desire for attachment to a 'real village', these transients know few local people, and few local people get to know them. Others put down roots, which nothing will induce them to tear up. I have lived in or near Primrose Hill for almost all my life, and at its heart for a quarter of a century. I cannot pretend to know more than a few dozen local people, yet the community of local acquaintanceship is wide. It can leap into action when required, whether to celebrate a local occasion or resist an unwelcome threat.

This volume records the vitality of our corner of London. Its memories are primarily those of long-standing residents, of the trauma of the war and bombing and the more drastic changes brought by the property boom of the past two decades. The latter has transformed Regent's Park Road from a mostly working-class high street to rows of specialist shops and restaurants of wider than local appeal. Pavements have become boulevards and parking has felt the backwash of the adjacent Camden Market. Yet the scale of the houses and absence of large blocks of flats has kept Primrose Hill true to much of its past. It retains low-cost properties and an astonishing mixture of uses in the alleys and mews of its hinterland. Pubs, churches, schools, shops may have altered their character, to an extent much bewailed by established residents. But they still serve their purpose. I cannot believe that Primrose Hill in a hundred years time will look much different from that of today. What we have now will remain, as long as we defend it.

This is still a place of families and thus of the attachments born of childhood and adolescence. Primrose Hill memories are overwhelmingly those of 'growing up'. This book is crowded with the insights of youth, matured by the recollection of age. Reading them brings home what an extraordinary richness of experience lurks behind these old buildings and sits in these windows and cafés. It is good for any neighbourhood to stop occasionally on a milestone, rest and look back. Here is the view from the hill.....

Contents

The Histories

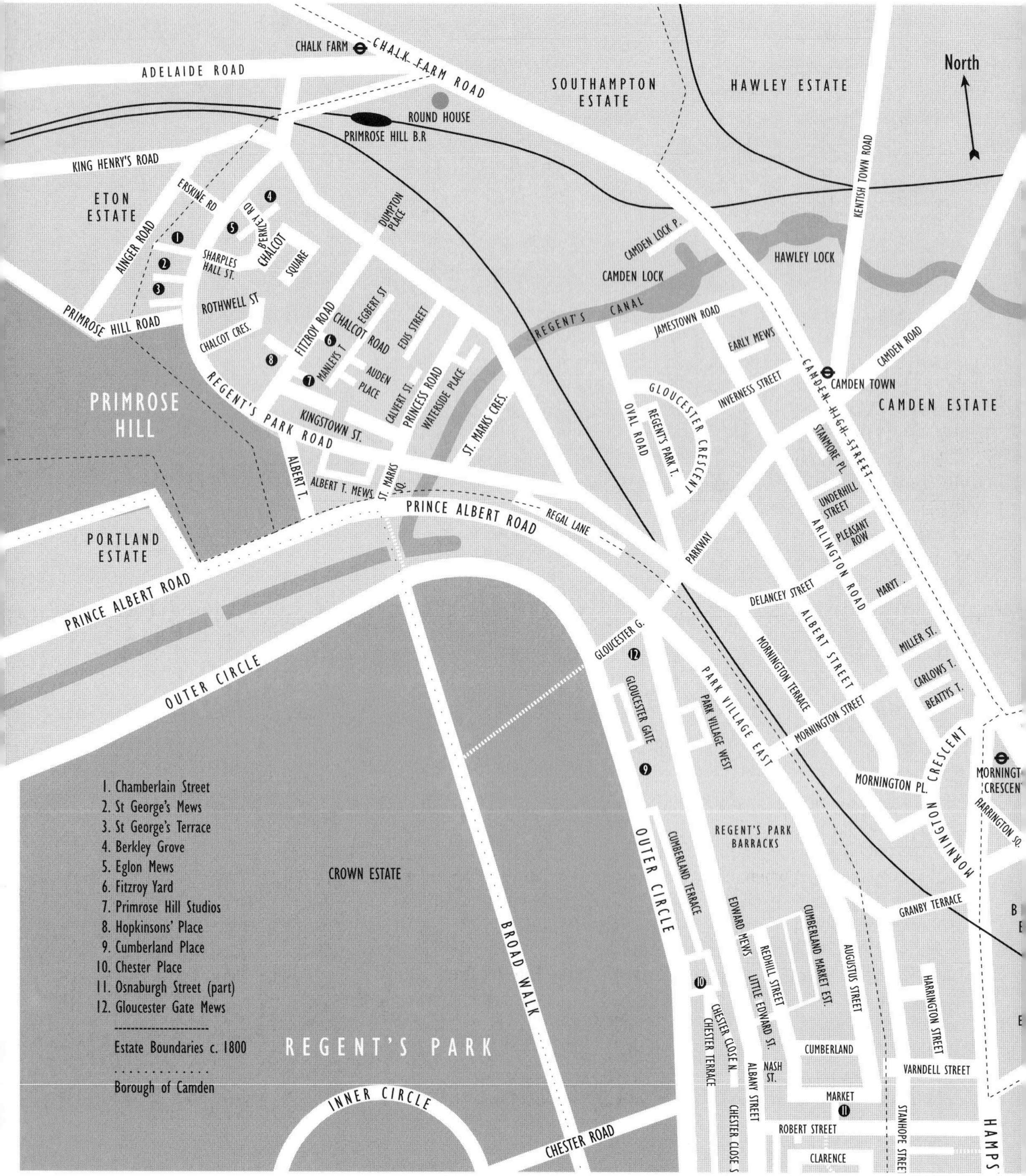

Map showing Eton, Portland and Southampton Estates *CHS Stephen Kamlish*

Roger Cline *Setting the scene: The History of Primrose Hill to 1900*

Primrose Hill has never been an official entity. The green area of the Hill itself has stone boundary markers which show the eastern border in St Pancras, the western part in Marylebone and the northern edge in Hampstead. The 1964 local government reorganisation combined St Pancras and Hampstead into the London Borough of Camden but the tidy minds of local government officers have neatened up the borough boundaries to follow paths and roads, with the result that Westminster, the successor to Marylebone, lost its share of the Hill, all of which now lies in Camden. In the same way the tidy minds have moved the borough boundary from the middle of the Zoo to the Broad Walk in Regent's Park, so that the Zoo is now entirely in Westminster.

The old local boroughs were derived from the parishes, but as housing was built round the Hill, new parishes were carved out of St Pancras, St Marylebone and Hampstead at a time when church-going was an important social obligation, giving us St Mark's in NW1 and St Mary's in NW3. Even today the postal districts divide up the Hill, NW1, NW3 and NW8 corresponding roughly but not exactly to the pre-1965 borough boundaries.

Ownership of the land has played a significant role in the development of the area. Over the centuries it had passed through many hands but, by the nineteenth century, had become divided between two extensive holdings - the Chalcot and Southampton Estates - each with its own distinctive history.

In Domesday times, when most land was held in manors, Primrose Hill, originally part of Middlesex Forest, had been part of Rugmere Manor, in the possession of St Paul's Cathedral. That part of the land in Hampstead parish had been given to endow first St James's Leper Hospital in the thirteenth century, and second Eton College by Henry VI in 1449. Henry VIII closed down the Hospital and built his St James's Palace on the site: he carved out his new hunting park, Marylebone Park (see later), from other land in the manor of Rugmere, which lay in the Parish of St Pancras and was still owned by the Cathedral. The Cathedral was compensated for the loss by the gift of an advowson elsewhere, while their tenant received in compensation the freehold of the part of Rugmere Manor not required for the park

Over the years the compensation land has had several owners. In 1668, Charles II granted its lease to the Earl of Arlington, a personal favourite and father-in-law of Charles's illegitimate son, Henry Fitzroy. Three generations later in 1769 Henry's great grandson acquired its freehold. He was created Baron Southampton in 1780, and shortly afterwards bought further land that lay adjacent - the whole then forming the Southampton Estate to the north and east of the Hill.

Henry's hunting park was later used by Charles I to reward his supporters in the Civil War and they, seeing that their tenure was likely to be short, stripped the park of its main asset, its trees, in order to realise their holding before the land was confiscated by the Commonwealth. The Eton College land was similarly cleared, and all the land was thereafter farmland, which attracted walkers from London, and local farmers would supplement their income by providing refreshment and entertainment.

The owner of Lower Chalcot Farm opened the Chalk Farm Tavern, with an assembly room at the back, and semicircular 'gardens' at the front, an outline still defined by Berkley Street and Sharpleshall Street. Nearby on the slopes archery practice took place: butts were dug into the Hill, with a Target Cottage close by. The Hill also provided a suitably secluded site for duels or even murders, the victims usually being brought to the Tavern for treatment or identification. The notorious murder in 1678 of a JP, Sir Edmund Berry Godfrey, whose body was left in a ditch on the Hill, gave the Hill the temporary name of Green Berry Hill, after the three men hanged for the murder, but the name Primrose Hill has continued in general use from the fifteenth century. Once the area was developed with houses, the rustic character of the tavern was unsuitable and the present building was erected in 1864: today once more providing refreshment and entertainment to a wide area of London. The farmland of Marylebone Park was converted nearly 200 years ago to the 'garden city' housing estate of Regent's Park and its adjacent service area, now part of the Regent's Park Estate.

Landholding history gives us a clue to the prevalence of leasehold properties in NW3 and freehold ones in NW1. Lord Southampton was fairly quick off the mark to develop his fields, setting out the area in building plots big enough for large semi-detached villas in 1840. He clearly wished to take the money and run, so the plots were sold freehold. The presence of the London to Birmingham railway at the back of his estate meant that potential owners of large villas were only interested in Regent's Park Road: thus, in other streets, we have short strips of terraces, each strip on one of the original building plots. Numbers 1 and 3 Fitzroy are an exception, being an early semi-detached project. In spite of the terrace development appealing to a less discriminating client, some of the plots took time to sell, the Primrose Hill Studios and their fronting terraces in Fitzroy Road being developed only in 1886.

It is the nature of trustees to be conservative, which may account for the delay of the Eton College trustees in following Lord Southampton in developing the fields for housing and their wish, when they did so, to retain some control over the development by selling only leasehold plots in the 1860s. This limited holding lent itself to comprehensive re-development over the Chalcot Estate in the 1960s when the 99 year leases fell in, whereas development of the Southampton Estate has been sporadic and piecemeal.

The College landholding included a large part of the Hill itself, and in the early nineteenth century it was a customary haunt of Londoners from the increasingly crowded West End, seeking recreation. Even if the shape and geology of the Hill made it unsuitable for housing, the redevelopment schemes proposed by the College did not allow for public access. One such scheme was to build a massive mausoleum with catacombs to house the coffins recently diverted from inner city churchyards, which had been closed for health and safety reasons in 1835. The Select Commission on Public Walks of 1833 put in a plea for the public to be given access to the private areas of Regent's Park (which they were progressively in the years 1835-41), and for Primrose Hill to be secured for public access in perpetuity. This object was achieved by the green area of the Hill in the Chalcot Estate being acquired by the Crown, which gave some land near Windsor to the College in exchange.

The area of the Hill along the western edges of Albert Terrace and Regent's Park Road was part of the Southampton Estate and was offered as building plots for sale by Lord Southampton in 1841. Had these plots been sold to local builders, we would have ended up with the Hill being hidden away by houses in NW1 just as it is today behind Elsworthy Road and Avenue Road. The reason why this did not happen is yet another benefit we derive from proximity to the Crown Estate, because its agent (who had already been negotiating to buy the Eton College holding on Primrose Hill to ensure its preservation as an open space) managed to persuade the Southampton Estate Auctioneers to sell him all the plots bordering the Hill before the auction took place, even though he had to pay what he considered an exorbitant price per acre. These plots were then added to the Crown holding, so that the area of the Hill open to the public comes right up to the pavements of Albert Terrace and Regent's Park Road, thus making those roads so desirable.

Before the houses were built, Primrose Hill

was cut through by two transport systems. The Regent's Canal was built at the same time that Marylebone Park became Regent's Park, around its northern perimeter, with the connection to Limehouse extending across the first lock at Hampstead Road (now Camden Lock). The London and Birmingham Railway came some 20 years later, passing under the Chalcot estate in a tunnel, so that the College trustees would not lose too much good house-building land. Before the line opened, an extension had been authorised to take it over the canal and then steeply down to a grand terminus at Euston, (named after a Suffolk village on one of the Southampton estates). The original terminus site was used for locomotive and goods sheds, and smoke from the locomotives lowered the tone of the eastern fringe of the Southampton land. As late as 1958 housewives in Fitzroy Road petitioned against the smoke which made clothes hung out to dry dirtier in minutes than before washing.

The railway was always greedy for land and even while Gloucester Avenue (then Gloucester Road) was being laid out the Railway caused it to be moved a little west and houses at the northern end of Regent's Park Road were demolished almost as soon as they were built. Later railway expansion caused the loss of houses on the southern side of Adelaide Road and the rebuilding of Regent's Park Road bridge as a girder bridge in place of the original brick arch.

By 1900 the area had become much as we see it today, apart from a few developments in the gardens of older houses and on bomb sites. Since the terraces did not need such large gardens as the semi-detached villas originally planned, the internal areas were used for industry - particularly piano-making. On the site now occupied by Auden Place there were densely packed streets of railway cottages for workers at the depots and even there a livery stable was fitted in behind Primrose Hill Studios: this became the Fitzroy Garage in the twentieth century.

We owe our many public houses on the Southampton Estate to the thirsty railway workers, and the London School Board Princess Road School to their many children – the College estate houses sent their children to private establishments on the Hampstead slopes and drank at home, if at all! Since most office jobs were in the city, the Primrose Hill to Broad Street line was the main transport route, although a few horse buses ran to the West End, and horse trams as far as the Euston Road. The tube was yet to come (1907): the canal was still used for goods transport - though Parliamentary Bills had been lodged in the 1880s for its conversion to a railway and the building of a station to occupy almost the whole block between Albert Terrace and St Mark's Square – a narrow escape!

Now in 1900 we end our history derived from dusty old records and look forward to more recent history from personal memories. . . .

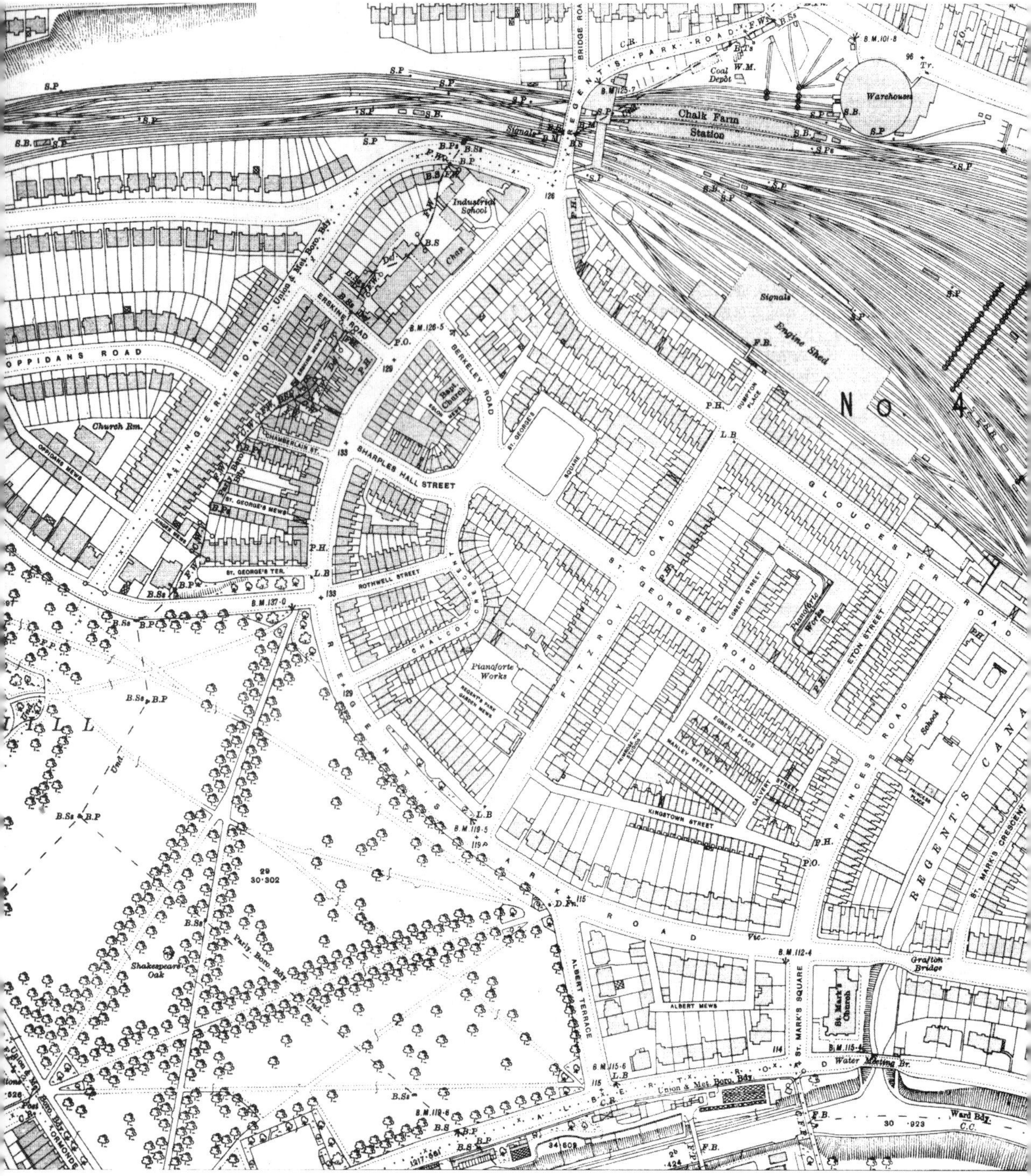

Reproduced from the Godfrey Edition (1986) of OS Map of Kentish Town and Camden Town, 1913

Ernest Albert Hart
Princess Road School 1914–1923

On reaching the age of five years on 27th March, 1914, my mother took me to Princess Road School. My two older brothers were already pupils in the school. I was taken to Miss Thomas who was headmistress of the infants. I remember her as a stout lady with a very clear complexion and a head of white hair...After my particulars had been taken, my mother left me. The headmistress took me to a classroom and handed me over to the teacher, a Miss Fisher. She introduced me to the class. I felt rather lonely, but I know I did not cry.

While in the infants I had two other teachers, Miss Hyde and Miss Dench. I liked Miss Hyde, but Miss Dench I liked better because, to me at my early age, she seemed a kind motherly person (but make no mistake she was the boss) and during the whole time I was in her class I cannot remember her striking any of her pupils.

During the summer holidays of 1914 the First World War was declared. When the Germans started dropping bombs on London during the daylight hours, we had to take cover under our desks. During night air raids the arches of the school were used by the local residents as air raid shelters. If there had been a direct hit on the school the casualties would have been very heavy.

At the age of seven I was sent to the Boys' Department. I should point out that there were no mixed classes at the time I am writing about – mixed classes were introduced towards the end of my schooling. As previously stated Miss Thomas was in charge of the infants. Mr Orchard was headmaster of the boys, and Miss Winterton was headmistress of the girls. My wife (maiden name Maud Willey) was at Princess Road School for three years, and her teacher was Miss Gadbury.

In the boys my life changed. The masters

Princess Road School, later Primrose Hill School *Virginia Smith*

and mistresses were very strict and pupils were caned for any infringement of school or class discipline. My first teacher in the boys was Mrs Riley. She taught the Standard 1 boys every subject. There was no teacher for any special subject other than woodwork, which was taught at Haverstock School. The teachers had in some classes as many as 45 boys, and they taught the three Rs as well as history, geography and English.

My second teacher was Mr Cole. He was a lover of music. He trained my class in singing and we represented Princess Road School at a singing contest for a further appearance at the Royal Albert Hall. We did very well, but were not good enough to qualify. He was also very keen on science and was always carrying out experiments. He had two accidents and was stopped from doing any further experiments.

I feel I must tell of an incident concerning me while I was in Mr Cole's class. He always had his dinner (it wasn't called lunch) from the cookery. The children's parents who could afford it paid for their children to have school dinners. The cookery mistress was Miss Hookendor, and her assistant was Mrs Sawyer. One day Mr Cole instructed me to collect his dinner from the cookery and take it to him in the masters' room. I collected his dinner and sweet, put the plates on a tray, and took them to the masters' room.

On my way to the masters' room I stopped and put the tray down to rest my arms. Being curious, I lifted the covers of the plates to see what was on them. The dinner was a roast and the sweet was prunes and custard, and looked very nice and made my mouth water. I'm afraid temptation got the better of me and I did a very naughty thing. I ate the sweet and left the plates and spoon in the wash house, where the ink-wells were cleaned.

When I gave Mr Cole his dinner he asked me about the sweet and I told him that I had not been given one. When I returned to school in the afternoon, Mr. Cole confronted me about the sweet. I told him I had eaten it and where I had left the plates. He took me to the headmaster, Mr Orchard, and told him what I had done. The headmaster took his cane from a drawer and gave me three strokes on each hand.

When Mr Orchard caned a boy, he was not allowed to stretch his arms out sideways so that the cane struck the palm of his hands, but he had to extend his arm forward so that his fingers were pointing to the headmaster's nose, and, if the hand was not up high enough, he would bring his cane up under the hand with a swish to raise it up to the required height. His cane was rather thin, so when it came in contact with the hand, the tip of the cane cut or bruised the wrist. This punishment taught me a lesson: 'never take anything that is not your own and always tell the truth'. The only other severe punishment I received was a caning for swimming in the canal without any clothes on. Not only was I punished at school but also at home, because my sister had seen me and told mother.

My sister was in Miss King's class. I remember her coming home and telling mother Miss King had told the girls where babies came from. Other girls had told their parents and this resulted in the mothers marching to the school and complaining about Miss King.

Empire Day was held on 24th May. The whole school, weather permitting, was assembled in the girls' playground, this being the biggest playground in the school. A piano was placed in the centre of the assembly, and a boy, whose name I believe was Edwards, played various traditional songs of the then Empire. Parents attended. This function was completed about 1.00 p.m. and school was finished for the day.

Sports day was also held in the girls' playground. Classes competed against each other. If my memory is correct, I believe the class winning most events was, every Friday for a month, allowed to leave school at 4.00 p.m. instead of 4.30 p.m.

Swimming lessons were taught at the Prince of Wales Road Baths. My class, under the supervision of Mr Bradbury, had 30 minutes swimming tuition. After dressing, we were lined up in twos and marched back to school. On the way back we were allowed to stop near a baker's in Prince of Wales Crescent, named Streetons, to buy rolls. Not all the boys (and I was one of them) had money, but those that did bought rolls and shared them with their classmates. Those rolls or half rolls were delicious.

There was a sweet shop opposite the school on the right hand corner of St George's Road, (now Chalcot Road) owned by two sisters named Thomas. I sometimes went in there for halfpenny-worth of toffee known as Stick Jaw

Toffee. I was fascinated to watch the lady break the toffee with a small hammer. During very cold weather the toffee had to be prised out of the tray with a large knife.

On the left hand corner was a baker's named Bates. Not only did the owners sell bread and cakes, they also sold chocolate. One of my teachers, Miss Evans, used to send me to the shop every morning to buy her a bar of Cadbury's chocolate, price one penny, and a plain penny-halfpenny bun (no – I did not eat any of them!). She put them in her desk drawer, and then when her afternoon cup of tea was brought to her, she would walk round the classroom, drinking her cup of tea and eating her chocolate and bun.

A bit further along the road was a dairy owned by a Mr Carrington. Mr Nelson, another of my teachers, always had a glass of milk from there, price one penny. Believe me, it was a work of art trying to carry a glass of milk from the dairy to Mr Nelson without spilling any of it.

A music teacher called at the school every Thursday and taught boys how to play the violin. He charged threepence for each boy. The violin class was made up of about 20 boys. They were all very good players. Two boys I remember were outstanding. One was named Kakanco. He left the school before I did. He lived in Oppidans Road up to the time he left school, after which he left the district. The other boy was named Crane, and he, after he left school, had an audition and was successful in playing in Jack Hilton's orchestra.

The teacher who was in charge of amateur dramatics was Mr Ball. He selected a number of boys and after he had rehearsed them, he staged *The Merchant of Venice*. It was a great success, so much so that the teachers decided to invite the parents in to see it. Regarding this venture, there was the problem of having a proper stage. This was overcome by having collections over a period of time to raise the money. I cannot remember how much the stage and trestles cost, but I know when Mr Orchard told us at morning assembly that the stage could be bought, there was an almighty cheer. I might add that there were at the school boys, whose parents owned businesses and they gave generously. The play was shown to the parents for one week, and was a great success.

Wynne Creighton Davies

Raspberry Jam by Gaslight

I was born in 1914, the beginning of the First World War. The first zeppelin fell near our house. I saw one of these great balls of fire falling out of the sky and remember being taken several times to the cellar in the middle of the night to be safe from them. It was terrifying. We had ration cards and I remember that what was called raspberry jam was really made with turnips and colouring. My father trained disabled men, and as there was no plastic in those days he used real skeletons in his work. His students hung our three skeletons out on the balcony on Armistice Day which caused a great furore! One of my earliest memories of infant school was our procession on Empire Day. Specially chosen children dressed in the national costumes of the countries and waved Union Jacks.

I had two sisters and we three were always dressed alike. A needlewoman made our clothes and we once had blue satin party dresses with little roses and wide sashes. I loved sewing myself and I was allowed to use the sewing machine to make simple dresses. My most special Christmas present was a tiny sewing machine with which I made clothes for our dolls. We had beautiful dolls with china heads which sometimes broke and could be mended at a dolls' hospital.

Our home was lit by gaslight then. The gas mantles were frail and easily broke. Cooking was done on a kitchen range which was black with brass knobs and had to be lead polished. The front doorstep was whitened daily.

Washday was momentous as it started very early in the morning with lighting the fire under the copper already filled with water. Sheets were put in when the water was warm and a 'posh' was used to pummel them. They were taken out by a strong stick and rinsed in the zinc bath full of cold water, and then put through the mangle to squeeze out the water. Then they went into a bath of blue to improve their whiteness and through the mangle again: drying was a nightmare on a wet day. The laundry was eventually ironed using a flat iron heated on the kitchen range.

We always had cold meat on washday.

Food was delivered by horse and van, milk came in a churn and we bought it by the jugful. Coal came in sacks delivered by a horse and cart. The brewer used large carts drawn by shire horses for the barrels of beer.

Easter and Whitsun were very exciting, as there were parades of the horses and carts in Regent's Park. The tradesmen took great pride in their horses and on these days they were groomed and decorated and there were prizes for the best.

In those days we rarely travelled far but I can remember occasional trips by charabanc to the seaside. I remember sandcastle competitions, Punch and Judy shows, and a puppet theatre at Hastings. My first trip in a motor car was in 1926 – an open Morris Oxford, a very comfortable ride. In 1928 we had a Morris saloon. It started by the driver winding the crank (a handle at the front) and it was a real problem to keep it going, especially in the winter.

Margery Napier
Boys don't talk to Girls

I first came to Primrose Hill when in the early 1920s my father kept a butcher's shop in Delancey Street, and, from the age of seven to about eleven, I went to Princess Road School. My older brother, Phil, went there too, but he always went in at a separate boys' entrance, and would say to me: 'Don't speak to me: boys don't talk to girls.'

I was taught by two teachers, Miss Chew and Miss Dench. Miss Chew was very strict and not particularly attractive with straight hair and a bit of a moustache. She threatened us with dire consequences – a Fault Mark at least – if we got a blot on our book in dictation, and I can remember being quite scared when, using a lovely Jay nib, I saw a big blob developing. This type of nib wrote more thickly and held more ink. I was petrified of her. We would sit in double desks in rows, facing the teacher and the blackboard. At one time I was an ink monitor, when I would spend my playtime or dinner-time washing out the china inkwells, many of them blocked up with bits of blotting paper. This was quite an honour and we would fight to do it.

Princess Road Infants Class with Miss Hyde 1920s *John Grosse*

Miss Dench was quite different, rather motherly, and we all liked her. She would often ask me to bring her some meat from my father's shop, and one day she asked me to get her a shillingsworth of steak, giving me a florin to pay for it. Just outside the school, however, clutching the meat and the shilling change, I dropped the coin and watched spellbound as it rolled and rolled across the pavement, into the gutter and down a drain. There was nothing I could do and I was so upset that Miss Dench took it in good part, I often wonder now whether she could have been an elderly relative of Dame Judy.

On 24 May each year, Empire Day, we would all gather in the playground and sing 'The Maple Leaf for Ever' and other patriotic songs.

The Dinner Room was in the little house across the playground and as we went down the steps we could smell the gravy. School dinners cost fivepence and I was supposed to have them on most days. Sometimes, however, I would keep the money and spend it in the sweetshop opposite the school, on the corner of Chalcot Road, that is now a house. I would buy four farthing bags of popcorn, but there was also stick jaw toffee, pretend tobacco and sherbet dabs.

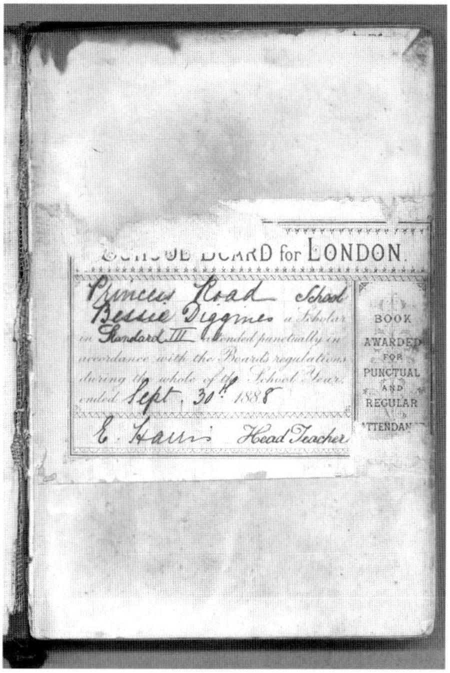

Bessie Diggines went to Princess Road School. She won *The Cuckoo Clock* by Mrs Molesworth for punctual and good attendance *Jenny Wallis*

John Grosse
A London Childhood in the Twenties

I was born 2 August 1920 into a family which consisted of Ma and Pa, two sisters and four brothers, who all lived at 48 Gloucester Road, occupying four rooms, two in the basement and two on the ground floor. The two rooms on the first or balcony floor were occupied by a Mrs Pearce and her companion, whilst the top two rooms housed Mr and Mrs Ascot and their teenage son Jimmy.

Number 46 housed four families, and number 50 several likewise, the Varleys amongst them. Mrs Varley was in the habit of standing on the front steps chatting to neighbours with her babe suckling at her wholly exposed and ample bosom. This was a then not uncommon sight.

On the first floor of this house dwelt a man,his wife and their adult son. The parents quarrelled frequently and violently. On one occasion, after the usual shouting and hurling of crockery, the wife, a large obese lady, clambered out of the back window, displaying her enormous bloomers, in full view of the assembled neighbours who watched her fall about 30 feet to the paved area below. Her fall was partly broken by the clothes-line stretched the length of the backyard, which snapped like a fiddle string.

There were only two WCs in our house, one in the basement and one on the first floor landing. My family used both. Newspaper and interesting publications like the Sears Roebuck catalogue were used as toilet paper.

A paved area at basement level, not accessible from the street, separated the house from the coal cellars which were beneath the pavement. Behind the area lay our kitchen/dining-room/lounge and 'rumpus room'. It measured about 20 feet deep, front to back, about 16 feet wide, and some 10 feet floor to ceiling. From the front to the coal cellar was about six feet.

The kitchen was where we lived. It contained a very fine ogee shaped rosewood dining table with hand carved claw and ball feet at the end of ivy leaved legs, again hand carved. This stood beneath the window which opened on to the area. My father was a master wood carver, and among his works is the wording on the original Cenotaph, the choir stalls in Lichfield Cathedral, the dining suite in Buckingham Palace, and a vast amount of the hand carved decorations on the *Titanic.* A couple of years ago some remnants from this vessel were recovered and amongst them was a cherub's head from a newel post on the grand staircase. This was a piece of dad's work.

There was also a standard pine kitchen table in the middle of the room. To the right of the window stood a sofa where my cousin, Freddy, and I slept. We were two years old. We wore matching pinafores with hems decorated with baby animals.

Opposite was the fireplace and cooking range. Of cast iron, it was coal-fired, and needed blackleading at least once a week. It had to be cleared of ash and re-lit every day. All the cooking was done here, the only addition being a small gas ring of very limited capacity.

The right hand alcove formed by the chimney breast was dad's workplace, where, amongst other things, he mended our boots, shoes, toys and whatever else needed his skilled attention. He was very good at sharpening knives and taught me how to sharpen a pencil properly. The left hand alcove was one large cupboard which I was barred from even looking into. And I never did. And I never did discover why. On its door hung the mirror used by my brothers when shaving.

John Grosse, 1920s Studio portrait, aged 4 *John Grosse*

Along the wall between this cupboard and the kitchen door stood the dresser. Crockery hung, was propped or stood there, whilst the three large drawers housed cutlery as well as the thousand other kitchen appurtenances of those days. Beneath these drawers was a large space, at the left hand end of which was the toybox, 'the' not 'my' since it had been used by my siblings for several years before me. It had originally been a Hudson's Soap box. At the other end nearest the cupboard stood dad's small tool chest. It housed only his carving chisels and there were dozens, all carefully laid out in their appointed position, nestling in specially shaped velvet lined recesses. Between the toy box and the tool chest we kept shoes, boots, boxes and bags, and the cat's bed.

Space was limited, which meant that we all read or wrote or drew in solo pastimes, or played only games suited to a table top. But in the holidays, when my sister, nine years my senior, did not have to go to school, she would play shops and explorers with me. For the latter, the sofa became a canoe in which we paddled past the crocodiles and sharks which swam in the deep, deep waters where the lino was, or we shot arrows at nasty people on the banks, and, if we felt very brave, would go and rescue my sister's teddy bear from the savages who wanted to eat him.

'Shops' was fun. We would monopolise the kitchen or 'best' table, and lay things out with prices written on scraps of paper pinned to them: mum's needle work box was a treasure trove for this game. Then Phyllis would walk in and walk around and ask me about this or that, and I would wrap it up and take her money – buttons or counters – write out a bill, count out her change, and off she would go. Then it would be my turn.

By now Freddy had gone to live in Albany Street where his parents had found rooms: his father had been discharged from the Army after spending four years as a P.O.W. (Prisoner of War) in Germany. Burned into my memory is bath night with Freddy on a Saturday evening in front of the kitchen fire. Neither of us liked this, and we howled when our heads were washed – fleas, lice and other nasties were prevalent then. Finally dad would stand us up and pour a jug of cold water over us! Brutal? No! To come out of a hot bath in front of a hot fire into a cold room, whilst the pores were wide open was asking for trouble, but Freddy and I did not appreciate this at the time.

I started school at three. To begin with Phyllis took me, but within a week or so I could go by myself. It was, after all, only about 150 yards from door to door. We had free milk daily, a cot for our afternoon nap, small wheelback armchairs in which we sat, four to a circular table, where we learnt our numbers, letters, prayers, songs, nursery rhymes, times tables, and elements of reading: three letter words and hyphenated two-syllable words for those who learnt easily. I was one of these, thanks to the kitchen table, and the help and encouragement of Mum, Phyllis and Noel, eleven years older than I, who taught me to draw.

The streets were my playground and I was never short of someone to play with – nor was there any lack of games to play: mostly very energetic, frequently noisy, occasionally annoying to neighbours, and sometimes mildly destructive.

At five I became an infant proper in the eyes of the L.C.C. (London County Council) and life changed. No afternoon naps but chastisement for being naughty: a freer rein in the playground and hence more occasion for squabbling. But now we had to learn about multiplying as well as adding, and dividing as well as subtracting: spelling and reading were harder, and we had to learn to recite proper poetry. But it was worth it because now we could read comics.

Our playing became more competitive and girls, hitherto accepted, began to be barred or avoided. But there were exceptions. Both boys and girls were becoming curious about each other. I suspect that the curiosity was greater among the boys, but I could have been wrong. We played a game called 'Release'. We would form two teams, one of which would stay at 'base', a corner of the playground or some mews or other, whilst the other team scattered over a pre-agreed area. If we were lucky the teams would be girls v boys. Leaving one member in charge of base, the others would go a-hunting. If a 'freeman' got touched, he was honour bound to go to base. It then became the task of the other freeman to 'Release' him/her by approaching the base and touching him/her without being touched by the 'warden'. A little imagination will show that there is room for a variety of strategies

John Grosse and cousin, 48 Gloucester Road *John Grosse*

here. But, this is where, with puberty knocking at the door, things may get interesting. It was the prerogative of the 'warden' to inflict upon the prisoner whatever discomfort he/she chose. It could be torture, a 'Chinese burn' for example, or a command to repeat what the 'warden' said: for example 'My friend, Billy, is fat and ugly' or a demand to 'reveal all'. Sometimes this was demanded in a reciprocal form – 'Show me yours and I'll show you mine' sort of thing. Naturally this led inevitably to bragging amongst boys, a practice that persisted for years and still does, I have no doubt.

School became more demanding as the 'Eleven Plus' approached. This then was the defining moment for most schoolchildren, since upon the result depended their future schooling and to a great degree their future prospects in employment. But until then there was so much to find out, to experience, delights to be savoured, places to be discovered and explored.

Empty houses gave shelter to vagrants who could not even afford the couple of pence needed to get a place in Rowton House. Heartless little brutes that we were, these poor souls were fair game for any sort of name-calling, teasing and derision and no difference was made between the sexes. If one such unfortunate was discovered defecating in the gutter or over a drain, or staggering from the effects of cheap liquor, the taunts and scornful remarks hurled must have been devastating. The morbid and explicit curiosity about a malformed limb, scarred face or physical deformity was cruel in the extreme, but one has to remember that among the poorer classes Life was often very cruel.

Sometimes, however, our mischief backfired. Cars were a rarity on Gloucester Road. Opposite us lived a chauffeur. He drove a Stutz Straight Eight, a magnificent vehicle, which he tended with great care. One summer day it was parked outside his home. I crept to it and with my finger wrote in the inevitable dust that gathered on the boot lid – 'WASH ME'. Mr Stewart came upon me and with a large and very heavy hand belted me across the side of my head and sent me flying – and bawling. I ran squealing to Mum who had no sympathy. Having told me off, she waited for me to recover and then told me why Mr Stewart had been so mad. In those days the polishing of such a car was a long, hard and difficult job, and dust was very abrasive, like the sand on sand-paper. She then took me across to Mr Stewart and made me apologise.

The traffic was principally horse-drawn and slow: cars were few, lorries, both petrol and steam driven, only slightly less so, hence the streets were great places for wheeled items such as roller skates, trolleys and scooters. Dumpton Place used to be the delivery point for Scottish herrings destined to be turned into kippers. The fish were carried in wooden boxes by overnight long distance lorries and off-loaded into the huge yard at the left hand end of Dumpton. There the boxes were broken open and the fish transferred to the long smoking shed that ran down the backs of numbers 88 to 46 Gloucester Avenue, covering the area now known as the Courtyard.

The wood was of great value to us boys. We would find an almost whole box and fill it with chopped and broken-up wood suitable for fire-lighting. We would then drag it round the streets, selling a pennyworth here, and another there, until all the small wood was sold. Then we would go back and repeat the process – unless, that is, we wanted the wood for some other purpose – to make a trolley or a scooter. The trolley base was a single plank, across the back end of which was nailed a square bar. At each end was fitted either a pram wheel or a ball-bearing wheel, according to preference. At the front was a similar bar fixed to the plank in the middle with a circular bolt. This allowed the vehicle to be steered with one's feet. A single rope or stout string was tied to each end of the front bar: and the middle grasped in the hands to hang on by as the thing hurtled from the high end of the road faster and faster towards the Post Office building and the bridge over the canal.

By the time I was nine or ten I was able safely to wander further afield – wherever I could walk in fact. There were ways of getting in and out of the Zoo without paying. Fruit could be stolen from the stalls in Wellington Street; there was a door through which one could enter the Camden Hippodrome Cinema without paying. Thanks to Mum I knew my way around quite a large area, including the far side of Regent's Park, and Hampstead Heath, Kentish Town and Mornington Crescent were all familiar territory. The library was near Mornington Crescent for a start and I was already a voracious reader.

Mum had come from a small village in Shropshire to work as a housemaid in some of the wealthier households in London, and had become very fond of the big city. She had worked in the service of several of the 'Quality', and would take me to the Levees held at Buckingham Palace when the Debutantes were presented at Court. The Mall was lined with coaches principally, with coachmen and tigers (footmen who rode on a step at the back of the coach). Mum knew many of them and would exchange a greeting. Sometimes a lady or gent would lean out and ask 'How are you, Annie?', and Mum would curtsey and respond, at the same time telling me to take my cap off.

Food was, as far as I knew, good. I had nothing to compare it with, and like all small boys I was always ready for my food. Every morning we had porridge, a cup of tea, and a slice of bread and margarine. For lunch at playtime my favourite was a buttered roll, but more often it was a jam sandwich – jam only – not jam and marge both. On Saturday night we went to Camden Town shopping. The butchers then hadn't the cold storage they have now, and they used to auction off the meat to a small crowd of housewives surrounding the shop. Mum would buy a piece of roasting beef.

Every Sunday we had roast beef at lunch (then called dinner) with cabbage or sprouts, potatoes and such, followed by the inevitable stewed apples and rice pudding made by Phyllis and Lily (my eldest sister, and the oldest child). Sometimes we had custard as well, which I loved. Monday we had cold beef: Tuesday it was minced and curried: Wednesday we had corned beef or six pennyworth of scrag end of mutton: Thursday, stew and Friday, whatever could be found. If we were lucky we would have steak and kidney pie, and Phyllis would make the crust. On Saturday, it was liver and bacon. I hated liver. And cabbage. Chicken we only saw at Christmas.

I wore almost always the common grey flannel trousers and shirt, sometimes a jacket, grey woollen socks, boots in winter and cheap, black canvas plimsolls in summer. My boots were always reinforced with Blakeys, metal spikes with large flat hatched heads, which kept the leather from wearing out, made a satisfactory noise on steel covers of coal cellars, and other metal surfaces, and greatly facilitated sliding across the playground.

At seven years of age all children were examined medically and most were sent off to have their tonsils and adenoids removed. By dint of massive story telling I was persuaded by my siblings that this was a real treat, and I was eagerly looking forward toit. It was not until I was laid on a board, enveloped by a pink and white striped sack from my neck to my feet that I began to wonder. Then the mask was placed over my mouth and nose, and I woke up in a tiny canvas hammock, with a metal bowl full of blood by my face and a very sore throat. I felt terrible and scared. What had happened? Taken home in an ambulance a couple of hours later, I was fed ice-cream, but it did not do much to alleviate the situation. A short while later I suffered the removal of a few teeth, because 'my mouth was overcrowded'. This was not so traumatic.

By the time I was 11, I was earning one shilling and sixpence a week delivering repaired shoes for Albert W. Ladbrook and Son, Bespoke Boot and Shoe Makers and Repairers, whose shop was on the corner of Eton (now Edis) Street and Gloucester Road. I also used to be given the odd penny by the customer, so that although I was obliged to give Mum a shilling of my earnings, I contrived to get by as far as sweets and sticky drinks went.

Dad died when I was six, despite my tearful and urgent pleas to God not to let him die. And despite everything the Sunday School teacher could say, I could not after that take God seriously. Nor could I believe in Him when, as my life broadened, I encountered other faiths and found they fared no better when it came to the crunch.

In 1931 I won a scholarship and started at Haverstock Central School, so my life changed markedly as the thirties began.

Reg Pleeth
The Primrose Hill Connection

Before the 1914–18 War, my parents lived at 23, Princess Road, Primrose Hill, where my father, John, had a ladies' hairdressing salon. My two elder brothers, Sidney and William, were born there.

A little later on the family moved to 55, Park Street (now Parkway) in Camden Town, where I was born in 1922.

Our house there, and the next door one, were on the exact site later occupied by the cinema. It is hard to believe that at number 55, we had a very long garden, and what today would be called a patio.

In 1927 I started at Primrose Hill School in Princess Road, and although there were several other schools nearer to where I lived, my mother thought they were a little too rough for her youngest if not dearest son. I recall very vividly being taken there on an open 74 bus by my mother.

I was not very happy at the prospect of school and saw no need for it. I wasn't a very bright child, but I could already read well, and I was quite happy with that.

When we arrived at the school, my mother had to more or less drag me over the threshold. A sweet little girl with a fringe asked my mother why I was so upset. My mother explained that I didn't want to go to school, adding that she thought I was a bit frightened.

'Oh, he'll be alright', the little girl said, taking hold of my hand: 'I'll look after him: my name is Elizabeth Fry.'

I soon stopped snivelling, and the three of us went into the school together.

Elizabeth and I became firm friends; we were in the same class and shared our plasticine at playtime. Is she still around, I wonder? My guardian angel!

I certainly remember our headmistress, Miss Cockington, a tall stern-faced lady. – No 'luvey duvey' relationship with us! Later

Sheep grazed on Primrose Hill until 1940 *CLSAC*

on, when I moved up to the Boys' School, the headmaster was a quietly spoken man from Yorkshire, Mr Arundel. He had a broad, but very clear accent, and wore a high stiff wing collar.

When I was at school in Princess Road, I used to enjoy walking along Kingstown Street, which at that time was rather like walking along a country lane, with tiny cottages on either side: I would notice the women chatting to their neighbours on the front steps. Now, as one can observe, the road has been altered out of recognition. Very up-market indeed!

After we moved to Camden Town, my father's hairdressing salon at 23 Princess Road was taken over by his brother-in-law, married to my mother's sister, Cecily. They had three daughters and three sons.

Quite often we (the 'Camden Town mob'), would descend upon the 'Primrose Hill Gang' for musical evenings – very much 'on the go' in those days! There was a piano on the top floor. My eldest brother was a good pianist, and one of our cousins, Michael, played the violin, and another cousin, Maurice, helped out on his harmonica. The rest of us would gather round the piano to provide moral support and belt out the equivalent of the present day 'Top of the Pops'.

On warm summer evenings, we would often get away from the noisy trams and bustle of Camden Town, and walk to the top of Primrose Hill. I enjoyed being there, watching the stars and lights; on the way back, I had much fun sliding down the pathways at great speed, which sometimes caused sparks to fly from the heels of my shoes.

There were sad occasions too. During the 1939 War, an air-raid shelter was built under Primrose Hill. On top of the Hill, an anti-aircraft gun-emplacement was positioned.

One night, during the 'blitz', my mother's sister, Cecily, decided to go to the air-raid shelter. That very night, the shelter received a direct hit from one of the bombs dropped by the Nazi 'planes attacking the gun-site.

Aunt Cecily was one of the casualties killed outright. Not a good place for an air-raid shelter, was it?

Although I was born in Camden Town and spent my childhood there, and have lived here in South Hampstead for nearly 60 years, there is still something that draws me to Primrose Hill, which is about two miles from where my wife and I live.

Could it have been the connection between the sheep grazing peacefully on Primrose Hill, and those I used to see trotting down Park Street to their doom in Lidstone's butcher shop opposite 55 Park Street where I lived? Maybe – who knows?

Not long ago, whilst wandering around Primrose Hill, I found myself in St George's Mews, off Regent's Park Road. There I was astonished to come across an office, which inside displayed a large wooden board on the back wall bearing the words:

BUCKNELLS Ltd
Electricians,
55, Park St NW1

I entered and found myself speaking to Mr Jonny Bucknell, and explained that many years ago, his family and mine were practically next door business neighbours. How intrigued I was to see the Bucknell shop sign after all these years. The family business is still very active in St George's Mews, but now into estate management rather than electrical work.

I still 'nose around' the Primrose Hill end of Regent's Park Road – can't keep away from it! It would be nice to end up there. Here's hoping.

Winifred Coulter
Schooldays between the Wars

I was born in Rothwell Street – where individual houses were occupied by as many as three or four families – almost entirely working class. The breadwinners were postmen, busmen, workers on the underground and so forth. We all got on nicely together and respected each other. People lived at close quarters and there was a sense of community.

Primrose Hill was our playground, as it was my children's, and now my grandchildren's when they visit. We all gathered there to climb trees, go on swings, or skip – eight to twelve at a time.

Cricket games were played in the road. The stumps were drawn on the side of 118 Regent's Park Road. As a girl I was not allowed to bat, but fielded at the junction of Primrose Hill Road and Regent's Park Road. Play occasionally stopped to let a horse and cart pass.

My father's sister was already living in Rothwell Street, which is why my parents came to live there on their marriage in 1918. I lived there, even after my own marriage, until 1989. I had two brothers, one older, one younger.

One of my earliest memories is of the General Strike in 1926, when Chalk Farm Tube Station was shut. It then had two exits, one on Haverstock Hill, and it was a short cut on the way to Haverstock Infants. To a five-year-old the long way round seemed truly long.

I can also remember my first day at school: I was smacked by a teacher: I had never been smacked in my life before! I'd done a little scribble on what I thought was folded brown paper - a new exercise book in fact. I was not upset - just very cross: 'What a nasty person!' I thought, but I think if you have been loved by your parents, you can rise above things like that.

From the Juniors I went on to Haverstock Central School. There we wore uniform, and

Rothwell Street in the snow, 1913 *Winifred Coulter*

I remember it well: a square-necked navy blue tunic, three-pleated back and front, buttoned on the shoulder (also called a gym slip), with a roll-neck, long-sleeved jumper in a beautiful dark red. I inherited the outfit from a Rothwell Street cousin who had just left. Her gym slip was a nice one, but her jumper was darned! I was the only one in the class with darns on the elbows! We did not wear socks of any kind, but black stockings, kept up by a suspender belt, with four dangling suspenders, worn round the tummy. I used to sit and mend these stockings in the evening.

In summer we had swimming at the baths in Prince of Wales Road, and we were lined up in twos for inspection to see if we were decent enough to go out. We were all working class girls, but if you didn't have a pair of white gloves you could not go! My mother at first refused to buy any such thing, but when I convinced her that I could not go without them, she gave way and bought me a pair – price one shilling and sixpence – at Mrs Green's haberdashery shop on the corner of Chamberlain Street (where the Betting Shop now is).

Classes were not mixed: girls were on the ground floor and boys upstairs, but notes were thrown and there was a certain amount of mixing on the pavement outside.

I certainly got a good education there, and so did my children who have all done well. I think now that I did not take enough advantage of it. My parents did not push me in any way – they felt that as long as you went to school and behaved yourself that was all that was required. 'Just do your best' was the most they would say. My father had many interests, particularly London's history: but, looking back, I realise now that just earning to put food on the table took up almost all his energy.

When I left school at the age of 16, however, I was able to build on Haverstock's business training at evening school, and find interesting work that gave me responsibility as well.

War brought its many changes: my father worked long hours in an aircraft factory: my elder brother was taken at Dunkirk in 1940 on his twenty-first birthday and spent the war a prisoner in the Danzig Corridor.

My husband too was captured when we

Chalk Farm Library, 109 Regent's Park Road, 1947 *CLSAC*

lost Tobruk in 1942. I used to say we'd had no quarrels for three years – the years he spent as a prisoner!

We married four days before his leave ended and spent our last evening at the Odeon Cinema (opposite Belsize Park Station where Screen on the Hill is now). It was the Odeon's last evening too – that night after the show, a bomb destroyed it.

The bombing had already started when we left, and the guns were going – including Matthew, Mark, Luke and John – my husband's nickname for our guns on Primrose Hill. This became my code – letters to prisoners were censored – but I could safely say 'Matthew, Mark, Luke and John were very busy . . .'.

As I saw him off, I had a premonition – I thought – 'It will be three years before I see you again!' – and so it happened.

Peter Bond
Chimney sweeper, Carpet beater

Old photo of no. 87: – My uncle Albert, who lived in Eglon Mews, round the back of the shops opposite with Peter the pony, who was stabled in Chalcot Mews. I am told that I was in the pram, just visible under the pony trap, which would put the date at around 1931–34. Next door says 'Decorators' over the top, but my recollection is that it was 'Ruffles' laundry not where laundry was done but stored and distributed. On the other side was the Chalk Farm Tavern where, on Saturday afternoons these painted garish 'women' smoked cigarettes, and, in long black dresses, danced to a barrel organ. I did not find out until years after that these were drag artists! Over the other side an uncle Len managed a hardware shop. Next to him was Wilson's, a radio shop (and TV shop – I saw my first TV in the

87 Regent's Park Road; Uncle Albert the Sweep with Peter the pony, early 30s *Peter Bond*

window in 1938) where they used to charge up the accumulators for our wirelesses. My grandfather owned 87 and my dad and uncle Albert worked for him as chimney sweeps, on percentage I guess. They would start at 4 a.m., work through until about 2 p.m., and then beat carpets, which they 'finished' by dragging them face down, over the grass on Primrose Hill. They worked so hard.

Grandad was a drunk, gambler, bookmaker and fight promoter. He never worked if he could help it, and got himself a cushy job as Quartermaster during the 1914–18 war, when, I am told, he proceeded to make his fortune out of diverting stores! He was also a wife beater. Just before I was born, he escaped to a small village in Cambridgeshire called Cumberton, where he bought some properties. The escape was from the law, people whom he had upset and also alcohol. He was not very successful. He subsequently bought a pub and ended up potless and friendless. The village kids called him 'bleeding David' because of his continuous use of the 'London' expletive! I used to spend summer holidays there before the war. They were idyllic days. Roaming the countryside with the village kids; fishing for minnows and newts; water from the village pump; oil lamplight; sitting on the fence around the pump in the dark, scaring the life out of each other with ghost stories, no street lighting, no cars, no TV.

There is another photo of him off to the races with his cronies. It is typical of him ... he holds the reins. I am told it is my Gran looking out of the window of their house in Ainger Road. The stories are that if he won, he would come home drunk and dish out a few bob to his wife and kids. If he lost, he would come home drunk and beat the wife and kids!

It was a time of some open buses and motor transport, but still plenty of horse-drawn vehicles, especially at the LMS Railway at Chalk Farm. Dad and Albert used the pony and trap, a three wheeler van and a hand cart. I was 10 when war broke out and my father got us to stay with my Grandparents in Cambridgeshire until he bought a bungalow in King's Langley, near Watford/St Albans in1940. My Aunt Daisy remained at 87 then moved to Chamberlain Street before coming to Hertfordshire in 1941–2.

Hilda Fox

Picking up the Threads

I worked as a dressmaker for a firm which made exclusive underwear. I would walk to work through the park to save the penny fare. I also used to dressmake from home, making anything from items for trousseaux to christening robes – often sitting up all night to finish an item – my clients would come through word of mouth.

I began my working life in a hostel in Fitzroy Street and then went to live in an unfurnished room in Crowndale Road where the rent was seven shillings and sixpence a week. After two years, a friend living in Chalcot Road persuaded me to move there. I paid twelve shillings a week for two unfurnished rooms. There was a gas stove on the landing and down another eight stairs there was a tiny sink. As I could not afford two rooms, I left the second room empty. I paid one shilling and sixpence for half a ton of coal which I bought from Wallace Spiers from near the Roundhouse. He came into the streets shouting 'Coal'.

I led a busy life, walking most evenings, visiting friends and going to the Gaumont on Saturday afternoons to keep warm. We sat where we liked for sixpence from 2.00–6.00 p.m. Bridge Radio – now gone – were already in Gloucester Road (now Gloucester Avenue) and I took my wireless accumulators there to be recharged. I bought oil at Welsh's. There were plenty of noises at night – the lions roaring at the Zoo and the cleaning of engines in Dumpton Place.

Early in the war I remember passing the Black Cat factory where a bus had been blown up and was pushed in front of the building. People slept in Chalk Farm tube and when fire wardens ordered me into the shelters I would say 'no fear!'.

The Salvation Army ran a Red Shield Club at King's Cross and I used to make sandwiches, tea and coffee for soldiers arriving at the Station. Troops came in all night – sometimes 400 at a time. I particularly liked the Yanks who would arrive chewing gum. I met people there who are friends to this day.

I remember seeing Tessie O'Shea at the Bedford Theatre in Camden Town. It was then a variety Music Hall. Everyone dressed up and it was always a Full House.

Fred Taylor
Horse Power

This area before the war had a great railway connection: Dumpton Place was the entrance for drivers' and firemen's access to the engine sheds located behind the Pembroke Castle public house.

Many years back, Mac Fisheries had the premises now occupied by Volvo. Their lorries would distribute fish. They subsequently moved to Finsbury Park adjoining railway premises.

At the end of Oval Road there was a very big railway goods depot known as Camden Goods Yard. The goods were brought in by rail and collections were also made for dispatch up country. Everything pre-war was done by horses, hence Oval Road and the Mornington area was all cobblestone roads. There was no such thing as one-way traffic.

The goods depot required a large number of horses. There were stalls just prior to the canal bridge. During the war when the area was bombed, there was a fire and the horses were let out: they were running round the neighbourhood until they were rounded up.

There was also a stables entrance in Princess Road, just past the Engineer pub, where there is now a row of houses adjoining the canal. This entrance in those days had quite a slope and was cobblestones.

Daily there was a manure cart to clear the stables each morning. This required a third horse at the front to pull the cart up the slopes. It was quite a sight to see the sparks flying off the horses' hooves.

There was a tunnel from the Gloucester Road entrance leading to Chalk Farm Road where there were more stables. It was all railway lands with Gilbey's having a part for their gin distillery and distribution operation.

The neighbourhood was troubled by dirt and smoke from the railway. There was thick fog at times, and car drivers would use the kerb to navigate – a thing that would be impossible today! At the top of Gloucester Road there was a big wood depot – they had several fires there.

Chalcot Road, formerly known as St George's Road had some excellent shops: on the corner of Manley Street there was a superb dairy, Griffiths, and on the opposite corner a very good butcher named Reading. There was also a very good Baker, Beischer, where the Black Truffle is now, and another butcher opposite – Turner. On the Fitzroy Road corner, opposite to the Princess Pub, was W.H. Cullen, an excellent grocery shop for bacon and cheese.

It was possible to get deliveries from most of the shops: they had order boys who delivered to the home by bicycle, with a basket at the front of the handlebars.

Left: Rear view Princess Road Stables Right; Goods Depot Warehouse, Gloucester Avenue, demolished, 2000 *Diana Gurney*

Virginia Edwards
Henry Handel Richardson

Before Oldfield Estate was built there was a lovely terrace of houses – the distinguished ones typical of this area, in Regent's Park Road, taking the same area as the frontage of Oldfield. As I remember they had gardens facing the street, and a lot of greenery that gave it a dark mysterious air. One of them was the home of a famous Australian author, Henry Handel Richardson. She had chosen that as her pen name. Her real name was Ethel Henrietta Richardson. She was born in Melbourne, Victoria, Australia, in 1880 and died in 1946. She left Australia when she was 18 and lived abroad subsequently. The most famous of her works is a trilogy – *The Fortunes of Richard Mahoney* which was based on her father's life.

A blue plaque (from the London County Council) commemorated her life there until the buildings were demolished to make way for Oldfield.

Dorothy Gwen Starling
Name Dropping here and there

Life started for me in the Albany Street of the 1920s: it consisted then of three-storey terraces, a few shops, several public houses, a Police Station, a school, a church and Army Barracks, all within sound of brass bands, and the Household Cavalry. Our home was a gas-lit tenement, once lived in by Edward Lear and his sister, Ann. All the land was owned by the Crown Commissioners

Beyond were the Nash Terraces, and these housed the Aristocracy or the Landed Gentry. Ladies in fine clothes were a familiar sight and sometimes we would see a red carpet rolled out under a canopy. Princess Elizabeth – today our Queen – would now and then appear riding in an open horse-drawn carriage with her grandmother, Queen Mary, and Princess Margaret, then a little girl.

I remember as a child when sheep safely grazed on Primrose Hill, on the upper slopes. Uniformed gatekeepers patrolled the Park and the Hill daily, and at dusk they would blow on a whistle, giving you minutes to hurry out

Coronation Party Rothwell Street, 1953, Winifred Coulter foreground *Winifred Coulter*

or be locked in for the night.

The year 1939 changed this scene: ack ack guns replaced the sundial on top of the Hill: air raid shelters were dug out on the far side and the gates and iron railings all taken to make weapons for the war effort. New features in our lives were gas masks, identity cards, clothing coupons, food rationing, coal rationing … and conscription for girls reaching the age of 17, which drafted me into the ATS.

Peace in 1945 saw most of the aristocracy gone – either to war or to their country houses. Some of us returning from the Services came home penniless; but St Pancras Council had been quick to snap up abandoned houses (at least 10 to our knowledge) and, while my husband was still serving in the Pacific, I was offered one in Prince Albert Road, one in Prince Albert Terrace, and number 54 Fitzroy Road. This and its adjoining house, along with the mews, and the elegant terrace in Regent's Park Road were demolished about 1959 to build the Oldfield Estate.

I had some knowledge of the previous history of number 54, one reason why I chose it. In the late nineteenth century it had housed William Galloway, the first vicar of St Mark's. Professor J.B.S.Haldane had also lived there until 1939. In his absence on war work, his wife took in displaced persons in search of refuge. Even when my husband and I lived there, misdirected letters still arrived, some addressed to Albert Einstein! These were duly returned to our postman.

Our neighbour was Charlie Meadows, World War I veteran and Secretary of the Old Contemptibles, an Over the Top survivor. He and his wife went several times to Buckingham Palace, and each time Bette wore her peach plume hat with feathers.

Next to our two houses came a cul-de-sac, a mews, which in its heyday had been a cobblestone yard with stables – horse boxes and a carriage house with large wooden doors. By 1945 the mews had been made over into small houses with garages – there remained only one horsebox, and the large doors. The Wheeler brothers, later BBC foreign correspondents, lived there at one time.

A few houses, which still survive on that side of Fitzroy Road, were once known as 'servitude houses' that is, quarters for chauffeurs, house-keepers, butlers, boilermen and so forth. Beyond these was a piano factory (no home without a piano once upon a time), and this is now Hopkinsons' Place.

Where flats are now, there was also once a large depository. In this the household possessions of deceased persons were stored, for St Pancras Borough to distribute to the needy. For many years, until the flats were built, it was a well-known tale that the ghosts of two of the deceased would stamp the floor at night in protest, should their belongings be touched. The Vicar from St Mark's came in to lay these ghosts to rest.

The bitterest winter on record, 1947, we spent there: snow, ice and fog: standpipes in the street for water: no food deliveries – horses could not get through: little fuel – no central heating in those days! We slept in our overcoats that 1947 winter.

In Coronation Year, 1953, my husband canvassed Fitzroy Road for donations towards a street party. Everyone pitched in to make it a memorable day – including the proprietors of the Queen's, the Lansdowne, and the Princess of Wales' Darts Team. Street parties brought a feeling of community and the friendly spirit that still exists today.

Well known people lived here then: Jacquetta Hawkes, archaeologist and author, would fly along Fitzroy Road, as if on wings, with cloak streaming out behind, and Primrose Hill Studios was home to other famous people. These included the artist, Montague Smythe, dapper in spats and fedora, never without a fresh carnation in his buttonhole, and Martita Hunt, Grande Dame of stage and screen: star in *Great Expectations* and *The Madwoman of Chaillot*.

She employed a cook, a housemaid, a lady's maid, a secretary, (Lena Ramsden) and a daily hairdresser. I was her dressmaker: in her heyday her clothes had been made by Worth, Givenchy and Balenciaga. Their patterns I had to copy twice over in silk tussore, for fear something might happen to the originals. She kept everything from her stage and screen career, which I fastidiously packed and unpacked for over 10 years. She was the height of eccentricity down to the last folded handkerchief.

Long gone now are horse-drawn vehicles, and deliveries of shopping to the door. No longer do we see men in spats and bowler hats or pin-striped suits: the 1960s changed all that.

One thing, though, we do have now is cleaner air – gone is the *Foggy Day in London Town*!

Lily Parish
The Butcher's Boy

We rented a butcher's shop from Goodmans the greengrocer from 1935 to '46 or '47. We were next door to them, and United Dairies were on the other side of Goodmans.

Our shop front said 'H.W. Parish Butchers and Poulterers' and our phone number.

We had two delivery boys on bikes with a large basket over the front wheel. They took orders all over Primrose Hill, from Ormonde Terrace and Elsworthy Road to Steeles Road as well as the roads round Regent's Park Road.

One day one of the boys was helping in the shop on the mincing machine. Suddenly there was a shriek – he'd sliced off the top of his middle finger, because he'd forgotten to put on the guard. There was quite a to-do. The man from the mincing machine company had to come and dismantle and check the machine to see it was working properly. Before the war we sold a lot of mince, especially to customers who bought pound packets for their cats. Of course that stopped once rationing began.

During the war we had suppliers in Scotland who sent us rabbits, hares, pheasants, chickens and turkeys (at Christmas). As they weren't rationed, it was a way to get extra meat – if you could afford it. We closed every afternoon once meat became rationed, as there wasn't anything left to sell by lunchtime. On Mondays we closed all day, so we could clean the shop thoroughly and go to Smithfield.

Delivery boy's bicycle *Jack Wilby*

Mary Johnson
The Chalcot Road Bakery

I was one of five children, and lived with my parents in the basement of 13 Fitzroy Road: my aunt and uncle lived in the same house with their seven children. There were other tenants as well – railwaymen, mostly single men from the Midlands, who cleaned engines in Dumpton Place. I think our rent was about seven shillings and sixpence a week. We were a happy family with a good mother: our father was a telephone engineer.

We were not allowed to play in the road, but the house had a long garden, and the older ones would take us to Primrose Hill to play in the sandpit in the playground. We also went to church at St Mark's, and to Sunday School. When we heard banns read out at services, we made sure to go and watch the weddings they announced.

When I was nine or ten years old I contracted diphtheria, and spent 10 weeks in the isolation hospital in Lawn Road in Hampstead. The nurses were very kind to me, but no visitors were allowed and I was very homesick.

At the age of 11, I had my first little job. It was to collect two ladies each day at 8 a.m. from Turner House, a home for the blind in Chalcot Square, and take them to the Mother Shipton, where they caught a bus. I collected them again at 5 in the evening: each lady paid me one shilling and sixpence.

When St Mark's was bombed in the war and no services could be held there, the chapel in Turner House was used by the parishioners. Later it became a home for wayward girls!

I also used to help at the Beischer Bakery on the corner at 40 Chalcot Road and when I was 14, Mrs Beischer asked me to work in the shop. I was paid 10 shillings a week, 8 a.m. to 6 p.m., half day Thursday and all day Saturday. I was given breakfast, dinner and tea. My mother offered a ration book, but Mrs Beischer said it wasn't necessary.

Mr Beischer's father had come to England at the turn of the century: he was married and had three sons and a daughter. During the First World War, he was interned and his wife ran away with another baker called Bateman.

Albert and Muriel Beischer had married in 1936, and in the Second World War, Albert tried to join the army, but they would not take him because his work was a 'reserved occupation' – important for the war effort.

Bread was made seven days a week. The shop was on the corner and there were two ovens, one under Chalcot Road, and one under Fitzroy Road. They burned Welsh nub from Wallace Spiers coal-yard by the bridge.

They made round white rolls, whole-meal rolls, Hovis, Vitbe, bloomers, farmhouse, sandwich, and quartern loaves, as well as buns and cakes – doughnuts, swiss buns, scones, sheets of chocolate sponge, iced and cut into portions sold for threepence – and seven pound fruit cakes sold for twopence and threepence a slice. Mr Beischer's wedding cakes were chocolate iced. He made bread at night and cakes in the morning. If they sold out on Saturdays, he would make up more dough in a large drum with a steel arm, which was driven electrically. He tried to sleep in the afternoons. When left in charge on Wednesdays, I was instructed to go into the bakehouse at certain times as dough had to rise twice. My hours were long at first, but later it was agreed that they should be reduced to 9 a.m. to 5.30 p.m. I often looked after the shop alone and the children on Wednesday afternoons, so that the Beischers could go into the West End. A glass door separated the parlour from the shop, so I could see when a customer came into the shop. Ladies came from the Council to check on my hours and see that I was well-treated. In five years my wages went up to £5 a week.

During the war large loaves cost fourpence halfpenny, small loaves were twopence, Hovis and Vitbe were fourpence dearer. Rolls were seven for threepence: loaves were reduced in weight. Hovis always tasted slightly wet: I believe bakers used to mix mashed potato in the dough as a preservative.

I loved bakeries. The shop changed hands several times before it closed in 1970.

Fitzroy Road with Druce's Repository in background *CLSAC*

Gerald Eve
Rabbit Stew and Brylcreem

I was born in Gloucester Road, now Gloucester Avenue in 1928. My father was in the Police, stationed at Albany Street, and my mother worked in Camden High Street, where her parents had a bakery. They were German and arrived in this country sometime before the First World War. Their shop was next to Pages the butcher, and they used to provide them with bread for their sausages. These loaves lay all the way up their stairs until they matured! My mum specialised in pastry and I can remember her helping out there and at another German baker's. I remember visiting the grandparents but later they moved to Neasden. There my grandfather trod on a nail in his bakehouse and died of it in the Whittington: both of them lie in the cemetery at Finchley.

I went to school at Princess Road and then to Haverstock. I do not remember much about Princess Road. I was monitor in charge of ink, and clearing up the room after art on Friday afternoons. We had a good teacher – Miss Hyde with a large flat bun. I remember another master, a vicious guy, who used to push you hard against the radiator till it hurt. He wouldn't get away with that today!

I used to go around with Deubelbeiss: his family were Swiss and lived in Regent's Park Road. They sold car batteries. We were both runners – we used the track in Regent's Park and at Parliament Hill, and ran for our school – but he could leave me standing.

In 1939 when war came I was evacuated to St Alban's with my younger brother. We were billeted with two others on a maiden lady. I was the eldest and responsible for all. We had two half-days schooling a week at a local school but my chief memory is of gang fights. We soon got fed up with St Alban's, and got on a bus – the 84, which ran into Golders Green. We easily made our way home from there.

My mum could not believe her eyes. She took us back and they put us in what they called the camp – near a stocking factory that was doing war-work – I don't know what. We were then settled with another family – but it was not what I was used to! We had rabbit stew one day – but I don't think they had skinned it properly – it was all hairs – ugh! I said to my brother 'pack your bag – we're going home – we're not having this!' We ran away again and came home. This time they did not send us back.

That was in the early days – 1940 – and we were here all through the war. By now we were living at the top end of Ainger Road – 41 – ground floor and basement. In August – September that year when the Battle of Britain took place we used to watch the dog-fights between fighter planes over the City and East London from the attic.

My father being in the Police was not called up, and he had an allotment over the back of Primrose Hill, which we called the football field. The top of the Hill had been flattened to make a gun emplacement, and the trees up there cut down, and that area fenced off by a perimeter fence. The gun was a huge naval gun: I can only remember it going off once, and the whole house shook. We used to lie along the perimeter fence, watching. Beyond the water-works there was a block of flats full of Maltese children evacuated from Malta, and we used to mix with them.

Ainger Road was a mixed road: 'good' people lived at the top with the 'rogues' at the bottom: and if there was any trouble – and there was now and again –my father would be asked to identify the culprits. This made me seem a traitor to the rest. It was difficult being a policeman's son! There was another police family nearby – my friend Bashford's. His father was a mounted officer based at Rosslyn Hill. He later left the Police Force and worked for the Blue Cross – the animals' Red Cross – at Kilburn.

Not many bombs fell in the Primrose Hill area: we were just fortunate I suppose. The most devastating was the land-mine that destroyed sections of Oppidans and King Henry's Road – the area now occupied by Primrose Hill Court. A land-mine floated down on a parachute and exploded just above the ground, releasing a tremendous blast. This one came down about 4.30 a.m. I was asleep on the ground floor of 41: the partition separating the front from back room was blown on top of me, my eardrum was blown out and my hearing damaged for life.

By now I had left school – Haverstock – of which I have no memories to speak of –

and begun my working life. I have not kept in touch with any friends – in fact everyone seemed to move away about this time. The Deubelbeiss family left: my friend Norman Wood, son of a railwayman, was drafted down the mines as a Bevin Boy: he absconded but was later picked up.

I had already had some work experience. Boys in those days used to work after school and all day Saturday for a 'dollar' (i.e. five shillings) a week. And I used to deliver dry-cleaning, carrying it on hangers over my arm, mostly to Eton Rise, Eton Place, and Eton Hall, where large numbers of Polish and Czech officers lived with their families – refugees from their own countries.

Deubelbeiss, Regent's Park Road, supplied car batteries *PHCAAC*

The dry-cleaning shop was the last shop in Regent's Park Road (now David Birkett's). Next to it was a tobacconist, run by a big Irishman, said to have fought with the Black and Tans: then the garage, and a factory that provided balsa-wood used in building Mustangs (fighter planes): next to that the stationery shop, where I bought my lead soldiers: then Mansi, the greengrocer – the same family as ran Marine Ices: the Café, The Hole in the Wall, with high-backed benches each side: a bagwash: the doctor's surgery: the dairy with cows' heads on the wall, where you took your own jug and paid twopence or whatever for a pint of milk: then a confectioner, which made high class chocolates (then rationed) next to the Post Office.

On the even-numbers side I remember the United Dairy: a butcher's shop that sold pease pudding on Wednesday or Thursday nights – one night a week anyway: a draper's: a 'teashop' run by a mother and daughter – where bags of broken biscuits were on offer – we'd rush in and ask if we could mend them! Alderson's, the chemist's, where they made their own Brylcreem during the war – from liquid paraffin and some unknown whitening substance! Yeoman's – who used to supply all the fruit and greenstuff for the Zoo animals: Welsh's: an electrical shop that charged accumulator batteries you used to run radios: a butcher's: a baker's: a shoe shop: a grocer's that roasted coffee beans – a gorgeous smell!

For some 18 months, when I was 16–17 I had a job at the Zoo. There had been two overseers: one was killed by the Oppidans landmine, but the other, Bowman, was a friend of Sid Webb, the local bookie, a friend of my family, and this got me the job there.

I worked on the Mappin Terrace, looking after goats and polar bears including Brumas, the celebrity cub, the first to be born in captivity. I also had to break in a camel for camel rides. The place was packed on holidays – we were pushing them through the turnstiles to get more in. Nowadays prices are so high that it makes an expensive day out for a family. This was 1945 – the war in Europe was finishing – and the place was floodlit once a week.

When I reached the age of 17 that year I volunteered for the army and they put me in the Coldstream Guards because of my height – 6 ft. 4. I've shrunk a bit now, I think.

I found myself doing Public Duties – guard at Buck Palace, St James's Palace, Picket Duty at the Bank of England: we done all the strikes too – Dock Strike, Covent Garden Strike, Smithfield Strike – you name it. They put us in the Deep Shelters on Clapham Common. I was on the VE Day Parade. The day before, they had us cutting sandwiches: we melted all the margarine in a big tea vat, took our shaving brushes and painted it on the bread.

After four years I bought myself out. At the time I was living in Princess Road, and cycling in uniform to Wellington Barracks every day, having to salute officers on the way. I had married a war widow with a little boy and we had one room, with a wash basin and cooker on the landing. My daughter was born there, and when the boy contracted polio, I went to the Council to find better accommodation. Their response was 'While you're in the Army, you're adequately housed'.

We were eventually rehoused on the middle floor of a requisitioned property in Priory Road, West Hampstead, so I never lived in the Primrose Hill area again. However my contacts with the neighbourhood did not end. I went back to the Regent's Park Road dry-cleaning shop where I had had my evening and Saturday delivery job, serving my apprenticeship there.

When I look back, I see great changes, not all for the better. Take Regent's Park Road. Restaurants or cafes have taken the place of shops. Tenement living of the kind I have described – living at close quarters – bred consideration and respect for other people. We used to know one another and the next door neighbours, but now care and neighbourly feeling seem to have gone.

Mary Aherne

Jellied Eels

I have lived in Primrose Hill more than 50 years, but I was born in Co. Tipperary, in 1912, a girl with eight brothers. The only work in Ireland was labouring on the land, and times were hard. As the saying goes – 'we were ready to eat the heels off each other'.

It was in London that I found work, where I followed two brothers: first at Mansi's serving the eels – a good meal and a cheap meal!

Later I worked at the White House Hotel for 13 years – running the Breakfast Room and also the Still Room. The residents there each had their apartment, as I did myself – a place of my own.

During the war, when space in barracks was short, the hotel filled sometimes with soldiers in transit – and I used to cry when I saw from my window at the back these hundreds of young men marching to Euston.

I married in 1941, but I only left my work when I was starting a family – the Manager said 'There's a flat for you here – you've been a good worker and loyal – until you find somewhere outside'. I thanked him – but I'd found one already – a basement flat in Edis Street – unfurnished, two bedrooms – no bathroom: a galvanized iron tub instead!

And that is how I came to Primrose Hill!

Spreading margarine on bread for sandwiches for the VE Day parade *Celia Kelly*

Christine Finn
A Primrose Hill Quartet: some writers in their landscape

3 Chalcot Square: Frieda and Nicholas Hughes unveiled a plaque commemorating Sylvia Plath, July 2000 *Malcolm Fowler*

> When I have been working late on a summer night, I like to go out and lie on a patch of grass in our back garden. This garden is a square of about twenty feet, so that to lie in it is like exposing oneself in an open box or tray. Not far below the topsoil is the London Clay which, as Primrose Hill, humps up conspicuously at the end of the road...(From *A Land*, by Jacquetta Hawkes, published in 1951)

A sense of place has inspired writers over generations, and across cultures. Primrose Hill is a place which holds a certain fascination. This essay pulls together four writers connected by geography, none of them born at Primrose Hill, and one or two just passing through; but all have acknowledged the area in their memories.

The writer Jacquetta Hawkes moved to number 39 Fitzroy Road, as a young mother with a promising career as an archaeologist. It was an obvious choice: her then husband was the distinguished archaeologist, Christopher Hawkes, who was working at the British Museum. The proximity of the Hill and Regent's Park boded well for bringing up their son Nicolas, and the landscape was especially appealing to Jacquetta's vivid imagination. Her musings on the transformation of Britain flowed out from, and returned to, the author's vista of Primrose Hill. It was probably her best work, and this 'prophetic book of weird beauty' as Harold Nicolson described it in review, helped to make Jacquetta Hawkes's name. Its combination of poetry, geology, social history and archaeology, with colour plates by Henry Moore, was a brilliant synthesis inspired by such sensations as the sounds of the distant trains, and the night sky over the Hill.

And Hawkes, passionate about literature as much as archaeology, included a nod to the distant presence of another writer, the poet William Butler Yeats, who lived at 23 Fitzroy Road, from 1867 until 1874. He was a child of two when he arrived there with his parents, uprooted from Ireland with his father doggedly trying to pursue a career as an artist. Three of W.B. Yeats's siblings were born at the house – Robert, who died in 1873, Jack, who achieved prominence as an artist, and Elizabeth, who with her sister Lily, worked as needlewomen in William Morris's workshop.

W.B. Yeats was to spend much of his life between London and Ireland. As a child of seven or eight, and embarking on one of his many Irish Sea crossings, his aunt had told him: 'You are going to London. Here you are somebody. There you will be nobody at all.' Although not fond of the urban life, Yeats was sustained by the treasures of the British Library in Bloomsbury, where he often researched. The family moved several times in London and little is known of his time in Primrose Hill, but what he professed to be his earliest ever memory is recalled in *Reveries over Childhood and Youth:*

> I am looking out of a window in London. It is in Fitzroy Road. Some people are playing in the road and among them a boy in uniform, a telegraph-boy perhaps. When I ask who the boy is, a servant tells me that he is going to blow the town up, and I go to sleep in terror.

Rather more positive memories of the area are contained in a letter, written on 26 April , 1961 by the poet, Sylvia Plath. She had moved to number 3 Chalcot Square, with her husband, Ted Hughes. The letter was written to the critic Alfred Kazin. Plath had asked him to referee her application for the Eugene F. Saxton grant, to enable her to complete *The Bell Jar*, her first novel.

> We live here in north London, on the brim of Primrose Hill and Regent's Park and I never want to move, except into a house of our own in the neighbourhood some day in the distance. Our first baby daughter Freda Rebecca, was delivered in our flat by an Indian midwife for free a year ago April Fool's Day and her pen is the centre of everything. I write seven mornings a week at a borrowed study up the street which is so beautifully padded with dust that even a dropped pencil makes no sound....

The move to England had been eagerly anticipated. Writing her journal in America on 23 October, 1959, she noted a 'fine welcoming letter from an editor at Heinemann on seeing my *London Magazine* poems...England offers new comforts. I could write a novel there...without this commercial American superego'. The birth of her first child at Chalcot Square in April 1960, and the publication of her first collection of poems, *The Colossus* in the October, was followed the next year by a miscarriage and an appendectomy; the turn in fortunes is reflected in Plath's journal: 'Last night I got lost in the wet black Sunday streets of Camden Town, walking resolutely in the wrong direction...'.

Plath's growing acclaim as a poet was overshadowed by her increasing mental instability. As her marriage to Hughes foundered, she threw herself into her creative work, writing to her mother in the autumn of 1962: 'I am a genius of a writer. I have it in me. I am writing the best poems of my life; they will make my name.' She continued to live in Primrose Hill and from her study produced the collection *Ariel*. A fellow poet, Robert Lowell, wrote:

> In these poems, written in the last months of her life and often rushed out at the rate of two or three a day, Sylvia Plath becomes herself, becomes something imaginary, newly, wildly and subtly created – hardly a person at all, or a woman, certainly not another 'poetess', but one of those super-real, hypnotic, great classical heroines.

On 11 February 1963, aged 30, Plath committed suicide at her flat in Yeats' former home at Fitzroy Road.

Another poet, Louis MacNeice, moved from Ireland to number 16a, Primrose Hill Road, in May 1938. He was a contemporary of Ted Hughes and Sylvia Plath, wrote on Yeats, and knew Jacquetta Hawkes and her second husband, the playwright J.B.Priestley.

With MacNeice after the breakdown of his marriage was his young son, Dan. The child would be walked over the Hill by his nanny to meet his father as he returned from work at Bedford College. MacNeice had written of his imminent departure for London: 'I think I am going to live in an upper maisonette overlooking Primrose Hill (therefore very near the Zoo) with amazing views from the windows. Five rooms lots of sun.'

The Zoo was an important feature in the poet's life at Primrose Hill and he was commissioned to write a popular book on the subject for Michael Joseph. Jon Stallworthy, MacNeice's biographer, has written that the poet was fascinated by zoos since his first visit as a schoolboy on holiday. He thought of the place as 'a cross between a music hall and a museum' and it allowed him to observe people as well as animals. On 1 June 1938 MacNeice had been back to London Zoo, and later that evening had observed a courting couple from the window of his Primrose Hill flat, writing later:

> They lay facing each other, caressing, she with

her hand on his hair, he with his hand in her bosom – for a long time lay there entranced and I could not see their faces. Then both sat up like puppets pulled by strings, their faces unflushed, perfectly matter-of-fact. He took out a cigarette, lit it, threw away the match like a man perfectly in control; she patted her hair, looked silently away into space. Spirals of blue smoke, ash tapped off into the grass, then Bang – both flopped down on the ground and resumed their loving. And all within earshot of the lions.

MacNeice's summer spent researching *Zoo* was in idyllic contrast to the years ahead for London. At the end of September, 1938, a squad of Territorial soldiers cut down the ring of trees on the brow of the Hill to make room for an anti-aircraft gun-emplacement. This depressing event was included by MacNeice in his acclaimed narrative poem *Autumn Journal*, a work rich with the poet's memories of life at Primrose Hill:

...Hitler yells on the wireless,
The night is damp and still
And I hear dull blows on wood
  outside my window;
They are cutting down the trees
  on Primrose Hill.
The wood is white like the roast flesh
  of chicken,
Each tree falling like a closing fan;
No more looking at the view
  from seats beneath the branches,
Everything is going to plan;
They want the crest of this hill for anti-aircraft,
The guns will take the view
And searchlights probe the heavens for bacilli
With narrow bands of blue.
And the rain came on as I watched
  the territorials
Sawing and chopping and pulling
  on ropes like a team
In a village tug-of-war; and I found
  my old dog had vanished
And thought 'This is the end of
  the old regime.
(From *Autumn Journal* VII)

More than 50 years on, and Primrose Hill retains its sense of place and inspiration. It stands rounded and resolute in the midst of changes in its semi-urban landscape of homes, shops and cafes. And when the weekend crowds disperse, the locals regain their conspicuous hump of London Clay, and the Hill evoked in Hawkes's reverie remains.

Grace & Bill Nowak
The Railway Connection

This house, we believe, was built in 1860, and we have been living in Fitzroy Road for 53 years. At first we lived in the same house as Dorothy Starling on the site of the Oldfield flats. Where you see an opening now opposite, there was an entrance to a mews, with cottages at the back. This was a service area for a huge terrace of fine houses, with their own close and gardens, fronting Regent's Park Road. They were superb and should never have been demolished: it would not have been allowed today. But someone then had the power and exercised it.

Bill and I met at Gordon Mansions on the corner of Tottenham Court Road. Our families had been made homeless by enemy action and accommodated in flats there. When we married and moved here the ack ack guns and barrage balloons were still in position on the Hill, and the piano factory, now Hopkinsons' Place, was still making pianos. It was later occupied by Osram Lamps, and then empty for quite a while. There was talk of demolition, but it was designated 'a significant building'. This saved it, and it was converted into flats. Had this happened earlier, the beautiful terrace would have survived.

There have been big changes in population here: first there was an influx of Irish – then an influx of Cypriots. We can remember the Greek Church being built at the top of Arlington Road. The original Duchess of Kent, Princess Marina, used to go there quite often. She was Greek.

There was work here in those days – the Railway. All down Kingstown Street there were rows of two-up, two-down railway workers' cottages. You could walk right through to Princess Road to catch the 74 bus. They overdid the demolition – they were lovely little houses and everybody knew everybody. They were nearly all older people who worked on the railway.

In those days they used to have the shunting at the end of Fitzroy Road: they used to do it at night down to Euston. A shunting engine did the work. The Roundhouse originally housed a turntable – an engine used to go in on to a rail and be turned round. Then Gilbey's took the building over. My grandfather and my uncle worked in the distillery – the gin factory in other words.

The 68 bus used to terminate at the Adelaide, and wait on the hard-standing at the corner of Adelaide Road and Chalk Farm Road and the London Transport garage was in Harmood Street. My uncle was doing night work there, when a bomb went down and killed most of my family at the end of Grafton Road.

Dad worked at Euston for 40-odd years, and he was very proud of being LMS (London Midland and Scottish). Then there was LNER – London North Eastern Railway: GWR – Great Western Railway and Southern. The pride that railwaymen took in their own company!

We'd had long connections with the railway. Dad's dad, my other grandfather, was a platelayer, and he was killed on the Watford line. As a train was signalled, a friend went to cross the line. He was just that bit late: they pulled the signals over – the two rails caught and his foot was trapped. Granddad went back to help him and they both were killed. We got his Death Certificate a long time after and it made him quite a hero. Before that he had been a platelayer on the Canadian Pacific Railway.

Grandmother was given compensation: she had the choice of a lump sum or a pension. She was in her late forties, and she chose the lump sum, but she lived to be 98, so she could have had a pension for life. She bought a house in Grafton Terrace with the money.

Bill was born in Huntley Street, and I in Arlington Road, both in the old borough of St Pancras, which was later merged with Holborn and Hampstead to form Camden. Between us we can notch up some 155 years of life in Camden.

Irene Demetriou (Sharpe)

Buried Treasures

I have spent most of my life in Primrose Hill. I was born in 1940 at 143 Gloucester Avenue where my parents had rented rooms. My maternal grandmother lived around the corner in Fitzroy Road, next to the Princess pub – she had bought the house for £200 in 1932. My father worked on the railway as an engineer, and eventually driver, for the LMS (London Midland Scottish Railway) and went to work via Dumpton Place.

My great-grandfather had been a coachman working in the mews at the top of Fitzroy Road which is now Oldfield Estate – a private road ran alongside Regent's Park Road with its entrance in Fitzroy Road, and the mews behind it housed the horses and carriages. My grandmother was a housekeeper at Tower House – now Cecil Sharpe House – which

Fitzroy Road air-raid shelter: Irene Sharpe foreground
Irene Demetriou

housed refugees. My mother's elder sister was born there in 1916 (I have the Birth Certificate).

My mother had fears that my father would be called up to serve in the Second World War so they eventually moved back to my grandmother's house when I was very young. My mother had two sisters who also lived in the house with their families – we lived on the top floor. My grandmother kept chickens in a run in the garden and I remember trays of new-born chicks on the boiler in the scullery.

On top of Primrose Hill was a gun emplacement – after the war we children used to have great fun playing in the little 'rooms'. There were no railings round the Hill, these having gone to the war effort. There was a bank of searchlights on the Outer Circle above the canal bank where the two park-keepers' houses are now (opposite the floating Chinese restaurant). I can remember being taken to watch the searchlights operating. We were very fortunate to have a brick air-raid shelter in the middle of Fitzroy Road and also one in Chalcot Square. As far as I remember, the one in the Square was made of black metal and covered the whole of the grassed area. As you approached from Fitzroy Road it rose quite steeply to about six foot and gradually sloped down to the opposite side where there was a central entrance. When I was about seven or eight, a few of us were wiggling upwards on our bottoms to get to the top when I disappeared down a manhole or air vent – legs and arms upright, bottom down! Fortunately, one of my friends had an older brother who eventually dragged me out – the only damage was a small cut on my ear!

The shops have changed a great deal since my youth. Mrs Lees ran the Post Office in Princess Road – now the video rental shop. There was a hairdressing salon run by Debbie and Harry, the barber shop in front, Debbie in a back room with her Marcel wave machine. The Primrose Dairy was here until about ten years ago. Ian was a greengrocer (but years later he changed his profession and became a betting shop manager on the same site) and the corner shop was always a newsagent's. Opposite the school – Princess Road School – on the other corner was Wagstaff's, another sweetshop which sold ice-cream. We would be sent to this shop with a pudding basin to get scoops of ice-cream and would have to run home before it melted! At the other end of Princess Road, on the corner of Gloucester Avenue, was a grocer's shop run by Ben. He sold me my first ice-lolly: an ice block with half a plum inside. He also sold penny bags of broken Smiths Crisps which were incredibly greasy. He must have been a very kind man because he allowed people to put things on the 'slate', my mother told me, after he was found hanged because of money problems. Round the corner in Gloucester Avenue was another newsagent's, Westlake's – my sister is still in touch with the family – where the Curly Dog is now. Ladbrook the cobbler was on the corner of Edis Street, the shop set back from the road. We didn't go there very often as my father had a cobbler's foot and used to mend our shoes himself. There were so many newsagents – there was another one past the Lansdowne – the last shop – Scott's.

In Chalcot Road, on the corner of Manley Street where the housing office is, was Griffith's Dairy. They had a bottling plant for milk where the big silver chimney is now. The glass milk bottles would roll along their metal channels and we would watch through the open door – not very hygienic but very interesting! On the opposite corner was the butcher and next was the dry-cleaner/cobbler which later turned into a café. Harvey Johns the photographer lived along here for a number of years before moving to Parkway. There was a small printer's shop and then the greengrocer, May Hunt, who ran the shop until she was extremely old! Next to that was Miss Cole's shop, a tobacconist and sweetshop. It was extremely dark in there and most children I knew wouldn't go in. Miss Cole wore long black dresses and weighed sweets out on tiny gold-coloured scales – I used to love Embassy Assortment and would ask for mainly fondants. She sold tobacco and snuff mostly. The next shop was the 'oilshop', Mr Puddifoot. You could take a bottle and he would pump vinegar up through the floor! It was an Aladdin's cave for me. The dairy was next and I can remember my mother sending me back with a bad egg to be changed! This is still a dairy, Nisha's. Mr Solender had the next shop. He was a tailor, and, if we were very lucky, he would give us a piece of his special marking chalk for our hopscotch. The last shop on the corner of Fitzroy Road was the baker's where Mary used to sell us ha'penny rolls and stale cream cakes for a penny. There was a window in Fitzroy Road where you could look down into the basement and see the baker preparing the bread and cakes. On the corner of Fitzroy Road, opposite the pub, was an off-licence – another one was opposite the Queens pub, by the telephone box. Utopia Village in those days housed Westminster Laboratories.

The fish and chip shop in Regent's Park Road was run by the Jacobs family and a bag of chips cost 3d. The shop on the corner of Sharpleshall Street was Alderson's chemist. His assistant was a very stern lady who insisted that I ask for purchases instead of offering a note from my mother – this when I was about seven or eight. Our family doctor was Dr Eli Copeland whose surgery was on the corner of Fitzroy Road and Regent's Park Road and we'd make our way from there to Alderson's to get our medicine. Opposite Alderson's is a narrow alley at the top of which was a workshop where, if my memory serves me, two brothers called Deubelbeiss supplied and charged car batteries. A little further along, where the Retsina Taverna is now, was Andy's Taverna run by a Greek-Cypriot family who had a window open to the street where the visitors to London Zoo, making their way from Chalk Farm Underground, could buy Marine Ices. Yeoman the greengrocer is still there, as is Welsh's hardware store. Between these last two shops was a dry-cleaner's where a sewing machinist sat making repairs in the window. The only other place I went to in Regent's Park Road when I was young was the library. The last shop in the parade before Bibendum (in my youth this was Chesterfield Motors with a petrol forecourt) was the library with two large rooms full of books. This eventually became Ron Weldon's antique shop. A row of two-up, two-down houses were pulled down to house the present library – much more spacious than the old library. On the corner of Gloucester Avenue and King Henry's Road was another dry-cleaner. At the top of Gloucester Avenue, next to the Pembroke Castle, was the electrical shop of Mr Gwinn, who hired out television sets more often than repairing them.

As children, we spent a lot of time playing on the streets and on Primrose Hill. The streets were mostly empty of cars. Every day the milkman called –my mother used the Co-op milkman, her 'divi' number was 794067 and when you had enough points you could go to the Co-operative Store in Camden High Street and get a discount off goods. The coalman delivered by horse and cart and I would be told to stand and count the hundredweight (1 cwt) bags as they were shot into the cellar. If my grandmother noticed that a horse had left a 'deposit' in the vicinity we would be sent out with a bucket and spade to collect this for the roses in her garden! The two houses behind the Lansdowne pub had been bombed and we also enjoyed playing in there but mainly we played hopscotch, skipped or played on home-made scooters. We didn't seem to play in each other's gardens, only the street or the Hill.

We went to Sunday School at St Mark's and were occasionally taken to see the bombed part. I also went to Sunday School at the convent, Holyrood House – the nuns gave chocolate cake and milk, a great incentive. The Salvation Army played regularly in the streets on a Sunday Morning and we would sometimes follow the band back to the Citadel in Chalk Farm Road. We went to the Girls' Brigade, which was held in the chapel in Berkley Road and to Brownies at the school.

Quite a few of the zoo-keepers lived in the area. Mr Orbell, next door, was a senior keeper and his son and daughter-in-law also worked in the Zoo. She looked after the Shetland ponies in the Children's Zoo. In the next house was the keeper of Dixie the elephant, Mr Jones. He would sometimes take us with him and we would watch while he washed the elephants. The Zoo used to give a Christmas party for children which we often attended. In those days also, the railwaymen had a club adjacent to Primrose Hill Station and every Christmas a party was held for the railwaymen's children; one of the high points of the year, as we were all given a present!

It wasn't an affluent area, most families living on one floor of a house, but we had a glorious childhood – always out in the open air. In the early fifties my father was allocated a house in Egbert Place – now Auden Place. It was two-up, two-down, with a small back yard – with its own air-raid shelter – and an alley running between the backs of the houses in Egbert Place and Manley Street. (If you ever saw the film *Those Dangerous Years* with Frankie Vaughan, he ran up that alley.) It was a very close community – everyone working on the railway – and we used to hire a charabanc for day trips to the coast during the summer. Most people were upset when told that it was to be demolished and new housing built there but people were promised that they would be given the chance to move back when the scheme was finished. Alas, the community was dispersed throughout Camden and (as far as I know) only one person from the original community managed to get housed in Auden Place.

On the way to play on Primrose Hill, the houses with the small front gardens in Fitzroy Road almost all had laburnum trees hanging over their front walls – it was beautiful at blossom time. These trees are long since gone – laburnum are poisonous I believe. This reminds me that Mr Press lived along here. His daughter Jennifer was at school with us and he was a Punch and Judy man.

Once on the Hill we had our favourite climbing trees and we would sit in the branches for what seemed like hours. Over the back of the Hill, by Ormonde Terrace, was a long clump of bushes where we would fashion our 'houses'. We spent hours on the Hill, sometimes taking a picnic, and were completely safe. We would play on the swings and, sometimes, manage to creep into the boys' gym and have a go on the parallel bars if the keeper wasn't looking! Girls weren't allowed in there! On the edge of Primrose Hill, in Prince Albert Road, opposite what was then the Zoo entrance, was a police box like Dr Who's Tardis. There seemed to be many more park keepers about then.

Primrose Hill has changed greatly since I was a child. Most of the houses are single family occupancy whereas then there would be three families or more to one house! The shops sold the basic necessities and we would have to go to Camden Town, Kentish Town or Holloway only to get footwear and clothing. Things are certainly very different, nowadays.

Lillah Warner
Seeing it through

WINDY they used to call me – because my name was Gale: 'Come on, Windy' they used to say. Thank you very much! That was at school – Gisborne House, Watford. I often wonder if it's still there.

I was born in Gloucester Road – Gloucester Avenue now – into a big family – and at one time my mother couldn't look after us all – so I went away to school. I was about eight then. I had a lovely teacher, Miss Carter. She said to me, 'Do you want to learn to read and write?', 'Yes please' I said: and she taught me to read and write and to speak properly. I always say that was the best thing that ever happened to me. Not to be able to read and write is the worst thing in the world. I've had jobs where you've had to use this up here – your brain – being a waitress, a chamber maid and a petrol pump attendant – remember what customers want and do figures.

As I say, I was born here and I never moved out. I loved it round here, and when I married my husband, was a local boy: it was local boy marries local girl! We were married for 40 years and were very happy together. We moved into this house in 1939 and I've never moved out.

We went through all the war together – bombs dropping and the old guns on the Hill blaring away – when they went off the windows used to come in! I've often wondered why we tried to shoot these planes down – they were full of bombs – and if they'd come down on the houses! They used to get rid of their bombs before they went home and drop them anywhere.

My husband wanted to join up, but he was an invalid. When he was a young man, he had pyaemia and there were great big scars on his back, where they'd taken part of his lungs out. He could never do heavy work.

I enjoyed myself during the war – I shouldn't say that! I was in a local factory doing war work – making bombs and dummy bombs as well for the boys to practice with: we also made markers – things to aim at. I liked the job, but not factory work – being shut in all day long – so when the war was over, I worked in the open, as a petrol pump attendant on Haverstock Hill.

Another thing about the war – people were much more friendly: even strangers would say good-morning to you on your way to work – like they do in the country. In a raid, the other people in this house would come down to shelter in the basement where we lived. We had an Anderson shelter at the bottom of the garden, but we used to stay in the house, under a table. Of course the whole house would have come down on top of us! I sometimes went into the cellars under the road. If you were caught in the street you were advised to sit in the gutter!

It was a terrible time, but you took things as they came – you did not worry about tomorrow – because there might not be one! I never thought we'd lose the war: I always had confidence, but I used to feel scared: it was a frightening time – especially when you heard the bombs coming down – they used to whistle. The landmines that you couldn't hear did more damage – they floated down on a parachute. Later on came the flying bombs – they chugged along – but when the engine stopped – that was the warning they were coming down. Bombs fell all around us here, after the railway or those guns perhaps – but we were lucky!

Peter Toms

A Wartime Childhood

I have known the area since my birth in 1938. Physically very little has changed. However, when I was a child, generally speaking, looking north from Princess Road, along Chalcot Road to Regent's Park Road, the residents were divided by class. To the east of Chalcot Road (going towards Primrose Hill) the residents tended to be more middle class. While on the opposite side running towards Gloucester Avenue, the residents were all working class, and all those large houses were occupied by at least three families. The only exception to this was an enclosure bounded by Kingstown Street, Calvert Street, and Manley Street. These were two-up, two-down houses for railway workers. In fact the area I described as being populated by working class families was dominated by the railway which was the major employer.

I lived at 44 Princess Road, which was a three-storey house between Princess Road

Inter-Station Horse Parade, London Goods District. Prizewinners: Carters E. Jordan and F. N. Dunbar. Right: Stable Foreman Toms *PeterToms*

School and The Engineer public house. Behind my house were stables for the shire horses that were used for the delivery of goods for the railway. My father was a stable-man.

If you walk down where the town houses are now and turn left, you will come to a wall where, in the past, there was the entrance to a tunnel: this went under the canal to Oval Road and Chalk Farm Road. It was used by the horses returning back to the stables at the end of the day.

I'll now describe other shops and businesses in the area. All the public houses remain. The Lansdowne public house used to open in the early hours of the morning for railway workers coming off their shift through Dumpton Place. The Mac Fisheries Depot was also there and this employed many people.

The school was then called Princess Road School. The headmaster was a Mr Mason. The school had a bell on the roof which rang morning and evenings. During the war anyone could go to the school and get a meal for one shilling (1/–). On the corner of Chalcot Road and Princess Road, looking north, was Wagstaffe's – a sweetshop that made their own ice-cream, opposite a newsagent which is still there. Next door was a greengrocer, off-licence, a grocer, a barber, and a haberdasher. On the corner of Kingstown Street was a Post Office.

Local industries included Westminster Laboratories making the well-advertised laxatives Sennacot and Ex-Lax (chocolate flavoured) in what is today Utopia Village: Osram light bulbs in the former piano factory, now Hopkinsons' Place, Chappell's piano factory in Berkley Road, and in Erskine Road, Ultra Radio. In a former shop in Regent's Park Road (next to what is now Bibendum) was a library. I remember it being opened after the war.

My earliest memory of the war was being pushed in a pram through Regent's Park and the 'bushes' standing up and walking away! Of course they were soldiers in camouflage, training! The part of Regent's Park at the back of London Zoo was out-of-bounds to civilians as it was used for training exercises. A Flying Fortress crashed into the pavilion in Regent's Park, killing several people.

Beside the swings in Primrose Hill a barrage balloon was tethered: and an underground air-raid shelter built close by. On top of Primrose Hill there was a large naval gun, and, at the back of the Hill, army barracks, bounded by Elsworthy Road.

Chalcot Square was totally covered in tarmac, underneath which was another air-raid shelter. There was yet another at the bottom of Chalcot Road, and beneath our house a shelter that held about 20 people.

A fire-bomb hit the stables one night. The horses had to be let out and were running round the streets for several hours.

On VE (Victory in Europe) night and VJ (Victory over Japan) night at the junction of Princess Road and Gloucester Avenue we had huge bonfires. This continued for some years after the war until the Police stopped it.

The Grand Union Canal was not open to the public and we, as children, were forbidden by our parents to swim there. This was because of infantile paralysis (polio). But we did! On the bridge opposite Princess Road, when people were coming from London Zoo, we used to jump off for money.

My memories of my childhood in that area were of feeling secure. Regent's Park, Primrose Hill, and the streets I have mentioned were our playground.

In many ways it was like a northern town, dominated by the railway and a strong bond between the working-class people living there. I remember charabanc (coach) outings, for adults only, to Southend – organised by my mother – firework nights on Primrose Hill and street parties.

One big event every year for my family was the Horse Show in Regent's Park. This took place on the Outer Circle. At Easter, the show was for shire horses and at Whitsun for 'light' horses. During the Easter weekend we prepared the horse brasses and leather reins etc. We also groomed the horses. On Easter Monday we paraded around the Outer Circle to be judged. We were on the cart behind with our parents and a picnic.

We always seemed to come home with plenty of rosettes. There was always a huge crowd and we used to wave to them, like royalty!

Helen Newbound
Times they are a-changin'

I came to the 'Island', as it is so called, in the forties; living first in St Mark's Crescent, then moving to Princess Road, St Mark's Square and then to a flat in Chalcot Square. We had quite a few influential people living around – politicians, actors, musicians – Hutch lived up the hill and the late Peter Finch used to visit friends in the Square. Most of the residents owned their own houses. We also had little shops – bakers, grocers, dairies, butchers, hardware store, bootmender cobblers, café, sweet and paper shop, greengrocers, a Post Office and a haberdashers. We were a close knit community – there were children around but most of them went over the Hill to play. If you had the money the houses were going for around £3000 to £4000. As my husband was in the forces I couldn't get a mortgage. A lot of the gentry left their big houses and went into the country.

Alas, times have changed, and not for the better. We have to go to Camden Town or far afield for whatever we want as all we have now are bistros and small eating places. We missed Dr Stoll when he retired; he was a father figure – nothing too much for him. We now have a few nice doctors in our surgery. We also missed our chemist Mr Alderson and his staff – all gone and sadly missed.

P.S. Got to say Mr Lelani and staff in Chemist are very helpful.

Maureen Hawes
A Journey into the Past

I'd always dreamed of going back to the house, my first home, in which I'd lived as a child in the early thirties, but with all the former tenants gone, I knew it was an impossibility. Then, one day, more than 50 years later, almost by chance I found myself back in the area and discovered that the shop had become the Primrose Hill Bookshop. A thrill of delight went through me; I can't resist bookshops and libraries wherever they are. I went in and almost immediately found myself standing at the top of a small spiral staircase leading down to the second-hand department in the basement. I realised I was about to take a journey into the past….

At first I was completely disorientated. There was no window, no heating, and it felt cold and damp. The walls were lined with somewhat rickety bookshelves and there were piles of books everywhere. (The basement had not yet been refurbished. It has since been transformed.) A shiver went through me; I felt confused and bewildered. Then gradually I was able to make out the chimney breast and with some considerable excitement the space at its side where I was sure I could remember a built-in cupboard. It felt as if almost 60 years of my life had fallen away. I wanted to sink to the floor right there and then as I had done as a child of four or five years old.

In those days, the basement was the home of the Merediths, a lovely family whose two children must have been almost young adults at that time. Their home was always warm and welcoming – it still evokes images of Badger's house in *The Wind in the Willows*. Their simple furniture fitted it as if it had been made to measure and the range was always gleaming. Occasionally my mother would leave me in the care of Mrs Meredith whilst she went off on some important piece of adult business. Despite my intense shyness, I always felt secure and at ease there. Mrs Meredith's ample figure and slow steady gait inspired confidence. I thought of her as a grandmother. For perhaps a couple of hours I would sit contentedly playing on the floor often not with toys but with Mrs Meredith's kitchen scales and jars of real foodstuffs brought down from that very cupboard. How she indulged me! Even when I mixed things up – the rice with the beans for example – she never grumbled! Of course there was no radio or television, only the singing of the pot on the hob and our occasional chatter.

Mid-afternoon she'd lovingly prepare a special treat for me: the peeled segments of an orange arranged like a flower on a white saucer and sprinkled with sugar that gleamed like drops of dew. It was a dish fit for a princess! 'Has she been good?' my mum would ask on her return. Then after profuse thanks and a fond farewell we'd start to climb the 60 stairs that took us home to our flat upstairs.

Our flat was, in fact, three unfurnished rooms at the top of the house. The larger top landing with two built-in cupboards became a sort of kitchenette, housing the gas cooker and the large iron mangle – later replaced by a smaller modern version, the 'Acme'. On a landing five to six steps below was a minute corner sink, cold water only of course, but at least it was for our use only. There was no hot water and no bathroom and heating enough water for the zinc bath was a lengthy business. There was a communal toilet on the ground floor, the cleaning of which was shared between the three families that used it.

The shop on the ground floor then housed the offices of Bucknells, a well-respected firm of local builders and decorators. Mr Bucknell was not only our landlord, but until 1937 also my father's employer.

There were well over 50 stairs between the ground floor and our rooms at the top… I used to help my mother clean the brass stair-rods.

Whoever picked up the mail left it on the first post of the lower banisters, a very pleasing flat wooden spiral, rather like a Danish pastry; so one could look over the banisters from the upstairs flats to see if there was any mail, but of course there was no way of knowing who it was for, except by going down. The wooden banisters were always kept well polished. In fact, the three families took a real pride in the house and had great respect for each other's privacy.

The small backyard housed the dustbin and the dustmen had to traipse down into the basement to collect it.

Heating was by coal fires. The horse-drawn coal wagons came up the hill from the coal yards at Chalk Farm – close by the Roundhouse. Sometimes, when there was snow and ice on the road, the horses simply couldn't make the climb under the weight of their heavy loads, and many households would have to go cold. Some houses had the coal delivered through the manholes in the street into basement coal cellars, but others had it delivered even upstairs in the house. What a wretched job the coal-men had heaving those shiny black half hundredweight sacks of fuel about all day!

When the pipes froze up in winter, standpipes would be set up in the street. There was usually one on the corner of Sharpleshall Street, in front of the off-licence.

Much to our sorrow, in 1937 or '38 – I'm not sure of the exact date – we had to move away from Primrose Hill, but to our great joy came back into the district and I continued living there until I married in 1952.

It was 1939 or '40, during the war years when we moved back to Regent's Park Road into No. 140. The shop at 140 was then a draper's. Once again we rented the three top rooms. Coming back was really like coming home.

Then evacuation came along. My brother and I, and my mother were all going. We were up at what seemed like the crack of dawn and breakfasted sadly with my dad. Gas mask boxes on our shoulders, labels on our coats (just like Paddington Bear!), sandwiches and our bags of belongings in our hands we set off tearfully down the stairs. A couple of flights down my mother changed her mind; the separation from husband and her beloved Primrose Hill was just too much for her. So back we climbed and that was the last of evacuation. We stayed in London for the duration.

I'm really glad we never went because, although we didn't know it, my dad had only three or four more years to live. He was a victim, not of World War II but of World War I and the trenches. His wounds had left him permanently lame and gas warfare had wrecked his lungs. He died aged 49 of TB.

Primrose Hill was our garden, our playground and our picnic place … but suddenly it was being 'mobilised' for war. It was disturbing to see the Hill being ravaged but, nonetheless, we were intrigued to watch the preparations. Of course, in the beginning, we children had no idea what war really meant, but we were soon to learn – especially those of us who stayed in London.

The summit of the Hill was a natural position for an ack ack gun site. Gun-fire and searchlights lit the night skies – 'son et lumière' – but not for entertainment! A barrage balloon was 'stationed' somewhere near to the children's swings and sandpit. (At the end of the war the creamy white silk of which these were made was, I believe, much sought after by home dressmakers!)

Ground was ploughed up both at the back of the Hill and on the front, just below the gun site, for allotments. 'Dig For Victory' was one of the many wartime slogans... 'Careless Talk Costs Lives'; 'Be Like Dad – Keep Mum' etc.

A large water tank was erected just inside the gate at the bottom of Primrose Hill Road for use by the ARP's fire fighters – though I never saw it used. An underground air-raid shelter was tunnelled into the lower part of the Hill facing what I believe in those days was called Regent's Park Gardens, a terrace of lovely houses. Even the Hill's iron railings were requisitioned. Some houses lost their railings too, and the public was asked to donate any old pots and pans or other scrap metal for the war effort.

Sheltering from the air-raids was a grisly business though the sense of community, and good cheer – stiff upper lip etc. was tremendous and there were plenty of laughs. A basement room at 140 had been reinforced with iron posts and at first we spent the air-raid nights down there. Two or three neighbours joined us and we played children's card and board games to take our minds off the bombardment. It was rather like camping: flasks of hot drinks, sandwiches, and makeshift beds. But it was freezing cold and very damp.

Then we started going to the underground shelter on Primrose Hill, a labyrinth of passages, wooden duckboards on the floor. There were some bunks but many people, us included, had to spend the night on the narrow benches which lined the walls. It was wonderful to hear the all-clear siren and we'd emerge in the early morning blinking like animals coming out of hibernation. News came down to us one night that some nearby stables had been hit and the horses were running wild through the streets. The raid that night had been horrendous.

I hated all these shelters but was relieved that we never went 'down the tube' (the underground) to sleep on the platforms. There were, of course, periods of the war without air-raids when we all slept in our beds.

The V1 and V2 attacks of 1944 really demoralised the country. There wasn't time to shelter from them; they were sinister and caused immense damage.

This was the Hill in wartime. However, despite all the upheavals and new installations, substantial areas of open space did remain.

Collecting shrapnel, ugly jagged chunks of spent artillery shells, had been a new hobby for the boys. Remembering my brother's collection and its rich rusting colour reminds me now of a beautiful Anthony Caro sculpture. Plane spotting was also popular. My brother spent hours making model aeroplanes from balsa wood, paper, and dope, a type of varnish used in aeroplane manufacture – the toxic fumes of which used to make my poor dad cough alarmingly. These models were really splendid and hung from the ceiling of my brother's room as if in flight. His war scrapbooks, volumes of newspaper cuttings and a history in themselves, have sadly not survived.

After the Raid "Is it all right now, Henry?" "Yes, not even scratched."
Sidney Strube, 1941

Winifred & Nora Benson
Wartime Memories

Our father worked at Chalk Farm Bus Garage, and as a bus driver he also drove ambulances. At the time we lived near the bus garage at the bottom of Hartland Road/Harmood Street.

Chalk Farm was where the trains ran, and the bombers were after the trains – bombs would drop, and when we heard the ack ack guns, we would shelter next door to 'The Load of Hay', Haverstock Hill. We were bombed so the Council rehoused us in an empty house in Chalcot Square. Our brother who lived in Chalcot Crescent worked at Bowmans in Camden Town.

When we heard the ack ack guns, we would shelter underneath the table. The siren gave us a warning. Air Raid Wardens in tin hats went round to see if all was well and if there were any fires. We would remain under the table until the all-clear siren went off.

We went from firebombs to doodlebugs – that was awful. The silent bombs were the worst – setting fire to places as they dropped. The ARP would warn us to turn the lights off when there was a warning. We had blackout curtains at the windows. The first thing we did when we got home was to change clothes and get ready to go to the air-raid shelters.

Men and women in the ATS did the land work. Nora volunteered for land work – you weren't allowed a holiday – instead you could spend a fortnight picking fruit and potatoes in Tilehurst near Reading.

Win worked in Mansells factory in Cressy Road, – making hand grenades and mortar carriers. We'd get a bonus if we did a lot – it was called a rat race – you had to work so hard to get your money!

Jonny Bucknell
Bucknell's D.I.Y.

Great Grandfather, Bob, came down here in 1885 from Devon – he'd heard of a building boom in London, and did a Dick Whittington – he had a pound in his pocket and his brickie's trowel – and he wrote back to his friends – reputedly excellent craftsmen – 'Come to London the pickings are good'. He started a building company, which earned a good reputation.

His successor, Arthur, my grandfather, was a staunch Baptist and later became a Conservative Councillor in Hampstead, at the same time as my father, Barry, was a Labour Councillor and Chair of Housing in Holborn and St Pancras. It was Arthur who opened Primrose Hill Court, as recorded on a plaque there, though Bucknells were not its builders.

The family home was in King Henry's Road, and during the war it received a direct hit in an air-raid. My father's brother was killed and my grandmother, Dora Bucknell, was buried for some 12 hours or more in the rubble. When eventually she was pulled out, her face was bright red from inhaling brick dust, and her injuries so bad that it was thought she would never walk again. However, thanks to her determination, she recovered and survived into her nineties, independent to the end, outliving my grandfather, whose premature death was put down to the shock of that night.

After the war ended, Barry Bucknell, my dad, started the D.I.Y. (DO IT YOURSELF) movement. He first broadcast little talks on how to help the war effort: and one thing led to another, in this case the TV series after the war, on which he did all kinds of household repairs and building work. Bucknell's House Project, in which he demonstrated how to refurbish an old house was the peak of the whole thing.

When these programmes started, you could not call in a local builder – every tradesman in the country was repairing bomb damage. Domestic repairs were at

Entrance to former garage, c.1938 – now Shepherd Foods *Bucknell's Ltd*

Regent's Park Road, 1976 *Painting by Timothy Jaques*

View from Primrose Hill, 1992 *Painting by Simon Dobbs*

Dancing round the Maypole, late 1980s *PHS*

Community Festival, early 1980s *Betty Bird*

Lost in a book, 1999 *Nora Holder*

Fireworks on the Hill, November 1999 *John Donat*

The Rolling Stones, on Primrose Hill early one November morning in 1966 for the cover shoot of their legendary album 'Between the Buttons' *Gered Mankowitz*

Away we go ! early 1980s *Ronald Hooberman*

a standstill, but he inspired people to do little jobs for themselves. This also brought into being a new industry manufacturing D.I.Y. products!

He did always urge caution, and advised people when a professional should be called in. However some enthusiasts started tackling major things which were beyond their capacity, and disillusion set in. You could say D.I.Y. was the victim of its own success, but he was the catalyst for certain innovative ideas.

His new career, the consequences of the bomb, and my grandfather's death hastened the end of the building firm, which at one time employed virtually the whole family. It had been a fairly substantial organisation – a building business, an electrical business, properties and a garage: but the building and electrical business was wound up, the garage too, leaving only the property rental business which remains to this day.

Bonzo often rolled in sheep droppings on the Hill *Sylvia Ballerini*

Sylvia Ballerini
World War II

Soon after the war started I was in Pentonville Road on my way home from work, waiting for the bus. I remember seeing troops of children carrying gas masks going towards King's Cross and St Pancras Station. I thought it was the most dreadfully sad moment. My friend Kathleen's eyes were full of tears and I felt the same.

I was living at 20 Albert Road, now Prince Albert Road, in my grandmother's family house. We looked out over the nearest parts of the Zoo. We all wondered what would happen to the animals. Some people were worried about ferocious animals getting loose if the Zoo was bombed. And being British they were worried about the animals as well. So when the animals were evacuated to Whipsnade we certainly missed the barking of the sea lions and the roaring of the lions. All the big animals were evacuated to Whipsnade, but they killed all the poisonous snakes and insects.

The Aquarium was drained, which was a good thing as it had a direct hit. Thousands of people asked what had happened to the animals. Mr Clark, the time-keeper at the Zoo, had told us they were being evacuated. Afterwards it was in the papers.

There was no thought of any member of my family going away or being evacuated. My father was a clinical thermometer maker and had a workshop at home. My sister Dolores and I worked in Lilley's (Lilley and Skinner, the shoe firm) offices in King's Cross. My mother looked after us and her mother. In the lower part of the house lived my father's mother and her two daughters – my aunts – who were dressmakers and worked at home.

There was great excitement with the arrival of three huge guns on top of the Hill. They were christened 'Primrose' by all and sundry. At the base of the Hill, near the drinking fountain, some public air-raid shelters were built. They were made of bricks, with electricity, but no running water. The shelters looked like long corridors with benches around the walls.

We reckoned the sirens would go off about 5.30 – 6.00 p.m. After that, people would choose whether to remain all night at home or go to one of the tube stations (either Chalk Farm or Camden Town). People took their own food and met up with friends they knew every night.

I knew of several people who went to the underground. On the whole, people didn't go to the public shelter on Primrose Hill at night. It was a grim place to go into, especially at night. There was a lot of noise from the guns and the underground shelter was a warmer and friendlier place. As far as I remember the public shelters on the Hill were the only ones built in this area. People preferred the sociability and safety of the underground stations. They really enjoyed being together and the feeling that if something was going to happen, it would affect everyone. Later on in the war there were tea trolleys on the stations.

But, in my grandmother's house it was quite a different cup of tea. We all hoped to be in for the early evening meal. Then we all assembled in my grandmother's drawing room, which was a huge room on the ground floor – we didn't go to the basement, because this held everyone in some comfort. We often played cards, rummy, seven of diamonds and had whatever sweet things someone had managed to get during the day.

One grandmother slept on the sofa with the other one in a big armchair next to her. My mother had an armchair, my sister and I had a mattress on the floor with our heads under the piano. One aunt would have a deckchair. My future husband, Ugo, arrived about 7.00 and had a chair by the door, so he could be first out! He often brought us something good to eat.

In 1939 I was 21 and my sister Dolores was 23. We answered the call for young alert people to help with firewatching in their locality. My father let us go because it was near to home. We went to Kentish Town for a short course on how to use fire-fighting equipment. We were given helmets but there was no uniform. In due course we were supplied with a timetable. When on duty, if we spotted something or saw something, we informed the Fire Warden. But this never occurred. Dolores and I would be on the 5 to 8 or 8 to midnight shift. The men did the later ones. Usually my father joined us to keep an eye on us. We were on the lookout for incendiaries which started fires when they landed. We wandered around the public shelter area (at the bottom of the Hill) in all weathers, always on the look out. But we saw no action. Fire-watching for us ceased when soldiers took over in 1940–41.

We'd already witnessed the bombing of St Mark's before the Blitz was in full swing. I remember my father saying he was going up the Hill as far as he could to see London burning. Many people went up the Hill to see the sky ablaze. They seemed to leave us alone that night. There was a feeling of unity, like there is now when everyone goes to see the fireworks, except we were full of sorrow and fury at the sight of the City and the old parts of London burning.

There was a barrage balloon tethered at the bottom of the Hill. Then one day we had a bomb in Prince Albert Road. We had no gas, electricity or water. Doors and windows were blown out, but no one thankfully was hurt. The wardens came round knocking, to see how we were placed. The following morning we went to Princess Road where the nearest water hydrant was and joined the queue for water. I remember when we got back we only had half a pail each because we'd slopped it. Auntie said that's why women carry water on their heads in hot countries. She made us laugh.

We were refitted with windows and doors and to celebrate, a doodlebug arrived a few weeks later, and we were faced with the same situation once again. It seemed a long time from those days when Bonzo our dog used to roll in the grass on the Hill and bring sheep's droppings home in his fur.

Looking back over the years I remember clearly the sense of unity and caring for each other. There was a warmth between people. We didn't just help each other when the bombs were falling. There was a general and genuine feeling of concern, even for those you only knew casually. Towards the end of the war many of us felt pity for the ordinary German people who had been bombed just like us.

Bombed stairwell, Cecil Sharp House, 1941 *EFDSS*

Maureen Hawes
Public Libraries

There wasn't a public library in Primrose Hill before the war. Primrose Hill was then in the Borough of St Pancras, whose central library, a Carnegie building, was situated in the far corner of the borough at Chester Road – near Parliament Hill. A temporary branch had also been set up in a house in Camden Street.

However, at the rear of a stationer's at 107 Regent's Park Road there was a private subscription library. I believe its stock was mainly popular adult fiction.

The arrival in the forties of the Borough's mobile library was the cause for great excitement, though not perhaps to private entrepreneurs. But those subscription libraries ought not to be decried, for in a limited fashion they served a need and have a place in library history.

The mobile library came to Primrose Hill twice a week, and was stationed for two hours at the top of Sharpleshall Street by the side of Alderson's, the chemist. The van was driven by Mr Woods, the janitor of the Chester Road Library, who also helped Leila, the library assistant who accompanied him. Mr Woods dealt with any obstreperous youngsters in a firm but kindly fashion. The children's section, a very narrow book stack, was near the exit stairs. Despite its limitations, the service was welcomed like manna from heaven, something to lift the spirit of the community during a time of austerity. From those shelves I first discovered the delights of Arthur Ransome as well as the pleasures of non-fiction. Two tickets were issued, but only one could be used for fiction.

Then a friend and I discovered we could take our St Pancras library tickets up to the neighbouring borough of Hampstead, and we transferred our allegiance to the Antrim Road branch at Belsize Park – quite a walk for us – but we were attracted by its larger bookstock. Not surprisingly our books were sometimes overdue and fines imposed!

The Chalk Farm part-time branch at 109 Regent's Park Road was opened, I think, in 1947. Frederick Sinclair was the Borough Librarian. The first two library assistants in charge of the branch were Dennis Debell and Dennis Hawes, both recently demobbed war veterans. The shop had once been a bakery but without the ovens, the basement was a cold, dark, dingy place, which served as staffroom/office and stockroom.

I've since learned that, when working down

Phyllis Neilson Terry with Krishna Menon (St Pancras Councillor, later High Commissioner for India), and Mayor of St Pancras opening the Library at 109 Regent's Park Road, 1947 *Hulton Getty*

there, the two veterans wore their old army battle jackets for warmth – complete with medal ribbons! Both had seen a lot of action abroad, for which Dennis Debell had been awarded the Military Medal … a bit of one-upmanship. They were only at the branch a year before taking up posts elsewhere in the Borough. St Pancras had opened several other temporary branches, most of them in converted shops or houses – in Euston Road, Fortess Road, and Malden Road.

Next door to the library a small working man's café had been opened by a Canadian war veteran and his wife. 'Canadian Joe', as he became known, was a flamboyant character, and a great raconteur. Baseball soon became something of an enthusiasm in Primrose Hill!

St Pancras had a strong commitment to its junior library service and maintained close links with the schools. The Children's Book Week was an annual event in which the schools were invited to take part. Exhibitions, talks and illustrated lectures by well-known people, as well as competitions were amongst its features. I can remember my class trekking up to Chester Road Library to attend these events. I felt very envious of the children who had such a splendid library on their doorstep! It was purpose built, separate from the adults, well-stocked and with tables and chairs, where the kids could browse and even do their homework. I was greatly chuffed when I won a prize, a book token, in a Book Week diary competition.

In 1949, I joined the staff at St Pancras Library, but eventually moved on into teaching.

The thought of a community without a public library appals me. It is a focal point. Libraries aren't just about books, they're about people. How can local authorities even think about contracting the service! The level of adult literacy in this country is incredibly low and the cause of great concern. Recent statistics (c. Mar. 2000) quote seven million adults with only minimal skills, and two million totally unable to read or write. Literacy is important for social cohesion and for the success of the economy. Sixty per cent of the prison population has literacy problems. We should be extending our library services not contracting them!

Claire Daglish

Picnics in Manley Street

The only cars I can remember seeing in Manley Street in the early forties were my Aunt from Barnet's car (which she actually drove all by herself, to my amazement) and hearses: the street was bereft of any traffic which could harm us to any extent, although the dairy's delivery lad nearly killed my doll with his great iron basket holder as he rounded a corner one day. Uncle Albert had his milk barrow and on Sundays the winkle and shrimp man would come calling through the street about teatime, so we children could skip around the narrow street so long as we didn't play too near the Anderson shelters which were dotted around the area.

There was one such shelter directly outside my grandmother's cottage, and once the siren went my mother would dawdle too much for my nan's liking and although we lived so close we were always last through the door.

When the doodlebugs were flying on their deadly missions, Morrison shelters were put into the cottages, and my nan's kitchen was almost wholly filled with this rusty iron cage which doubled as dinner table with beds underneath. I used to crawl into the underneath which was surrounded with zoo-like grills and I would be allowed 'picnics' in this delightful playroom.

The cottages were very basic – two-up, two-down and no hallways or bathrooms to muddle the squareness of it all – straight into the living room from the front door and straight into the kitchen from the back door, reached from an alleyway at the end of the street. The stairs to the two bedrooms were shut away behind a door in the kitchen and under those stairs was the coal-cellar. The kitchen floor was flagstoned in red and a black-leaded range under the mantelpiece contained a two-tier oven and coal fire and on the top the 'constant hot water' bubbled in a huge kettle: the mod cons were there in the form of a Gas Light and Coke Company oven and a copper for the washing.

There were coal fires in all four rooms which necessitated the chimneys being swept quite often and it really was a messy enterprise – curtains down, ledges, skirting and picture rail cleaned, everything dusted and, of course, find the cat which always ran for its life on seeing the sweep arrive. There were one or two chimney fires which were always dealt with by the occupier and/or neighbours.

I lived with my grandmother during those years – my mother was working all day and dad was off in this place called Burma, so my nan and I were very close. I went to Princess Road School and on looking back it would probably be thought very strict for primary school children. There were prefects and head boy and head girl – nobody ran on the stairs or spoke as we came in from playtime. The punishment for that was to stand hands behind back and feet apart for half an hour after school and, if really bad, an hour. We grumbled but nevertheless most of us were crying when we left to go to other schools.

The teachers seemed quite old to us – I suppose some of them might have been taken from their retirement to fill in during the war years. We were served our regulation milk, teaspoon of cod liver oil and teaspoon of that wonderful orange juice, then put to sleep on canvas beds for two hours in the afternoon because we often lost our sleep through air-raids. We were regularly checked by doctors and a parent had to attend the medicals and of course the dreaded nit-nurse came with her dangerous steel comb – searching!

I was found to be an accommodation address for these awful creatures at one time and I remember my mother was extremely cross (embarrassed) with the nurse, accusing her of not cleaning her comb properly before attacking me. However, that did no good and she then had the added shame of going to Boots to get a bottle of something with a skull and crossbones on the label!!

After the war, I suppose to make up for the time she could not spend with me during those years, my mother would regularly come to the school, open the door and call to the teacher, 'Dentist today' or 'Eye-test today' or some other excuse and she would whisk me away to matinees at the Palladium, Victoria Palace or the Cameo Poly and I have wonderful memories of that. I should have been the child with the best looking teeth and keenest eyesight but…

There was only one very close, very small bomb near to us which demolished a bootmender's shop on the corner of Calvert Street and Kingstown Street, but there was an awful lot of noise with every air-raid. To this day I jump out of my skin at thunder or a car back-firing but all in all I and my friends had the sort of childhood that many parents would wish their children had the chance of today.

Manley Street, 1967: Emily Garland, aged 3 *Harriet Garland*

Gwyneth Williams
Allotments on the Hill

In addition to being the year of the Invasion of Europe, 1944 was the year of the flying bombs, alias buzz bombs, and the rockets, and the year I took up a post in London, and was invited by a friend to share her flat in Steeles Road. It was also the year when we had the opportunity to take over half of one of the allotments on Primrose Hill.

The allotments covered a large area, running from the top of the Hill down to a piece of flat ground as far as a footpath, in sight of Prince Albert Road, and across into Regent's Park. That was where we began.

It was not quite virgin soil, but it was very fertile, and we produced good crops of vegetables, which we, and our colleagues at work, enjoyed very much: sprouts, onions, marrows, and herbs stand out in my memory, together with quantities of good round lettuces – everything helping to enliven the sound but boring diet we were enduring.

No form of storage on the site was allowed, so bicycles were essential, and we rode or walked them along Primrose Hill Road, draped in forks, spades and trowels, returning laden with produce.

At first the WAR was with us, and we had an anxious day, my friend in the City and I in Clapham, when a rocket fell about 11.00 a.m., and judging by the direction of the sound, we both thought Primrose Hill was where it fell, as indeed it did.

Digging for victory ended with the war, but food was still needed, and at one period we found ourselves with two whole allotments. So we grew potatoes on a whole allotment, which sloped sharply, at the top of the Hill. We had a magnificent crop, dried it out on the allotment, and became known as 'the ladies with the lovely potatoes'.

Potatoes were rationed that winter, and our crop helped many friends, a fitting ending to our efforts.

The author with prize marrow from her allotment on the Hill
Gwyneth Williams

Elizabeth Horder
A Local GP's Surgery

No one nowadays would expect, when visiting the doctor, to walk into his house, sit down at his dining room table and enjoy looking at the *Tatler, Country Life*, or *Punch*, until called into the surgery for the consultation. But that was how it was at 114 Regent's Park Road until the surgery was closed in 1974.

The practice was founded by Dr James Wigg in 1897. It was at first in a shop at 112 Kentish Town Road, above which he lived. But later, when his patients increased in number, he moved to Regent's Park Road with his family and opened a second surgery there.

Dr James Wigg wore a top hat and a tailcoat. He hired a 'growler' occasionally, but mostly walked or rode a bicycle, because he was too poor to own a car.

In 1905 the practice income was £400 per annum. But in 1911 he became a 'panel doctor' under the Lloyd George scheme. This made him more affluent and enabled him to look after and treat without payment more of the very poor working population of the district.

Celia Kelly

He retired in 1935 and his son, John Wigg, took over the practice until he was called up in the Second World War, during which he served in the army as a psychiatrist.

After 1945, when he returned, the practice started to expand. Doctors, and other staff were gradually recruited to form the James Wigg group practice, which moved into the newly opened Kentish Town Health Centre, Bartholomew Road, in 1973, where it was eventually based.

The waiting room at 114 Regent's Park Road was comfortable to sit in. It was carpeted and furnished with polished Victorian furniture – a great sideboard, a large glass-fronted bookcase, dining-room table and chairs. Behind in a smaller room, was the surgery. It was relaxed and comfortable too – with a big desk, family pictures, a cosy gas-fire between two bookcases and rather simple medical equipment hidden by a screen.

The atmosphere was informal and personal. John's wife, Margot and sometimes even his young daughters, Felicity and Ann, were called down from the upper part of the house to help at exceptionally busy times, such as a 'flu epidemic or a smallpox scare. There were two surgeries each day, including Saturday, and the doctor usually had a long list of house-calls to do as well.

Although John Wigg started his medical career when medical knowledge was primitive compared with today, he was always ready to accept new ideas and to move with the times. He welcomed the National Health Service because it made medical care available to all for the first time. He came to accept that increase in technical knowledge and the recognition of social problems brought a complexity which demanded the help of other professionals, even if this might interfere with the very personal service he believed in. If he were alive today I have no doubt he would have taken up the challenge of the computer era.

Dr Lionel Stoll
Medical Practices

There were once three medical practices in Regent's Park Road.

The one now at 99 Regent's Park Road, where I practised since 1946, was originally run by Dr Joynt who was killed by a direct hit on his home in King Henry's Road. He had returned from a visit to a patient in the early hours of the morning, and was making himself a hot drink in the kitchen at the back of the house when the bomb fell. Had he been in his bedroom at the front he would have survived.

There was also the Wigg-Horder practice at 114 Regent's Park Road. This closed in 1974 and moved to the Kentish Town Health Centre.

A third practice at 70 Regent's Park Road, on the corner of Fitzroy Road, was run by Dr Swann and after him by Dr Copeland: this also closed.

Thompson's Pharmacy, now the Post Office, on the corner of Erskine Road, was at one time a veterinary chemist, providing for all the stables that once existed in the area. Cumberland Market (on the Regent's Park Estate) was once London's haymarket, and fodder for the horses stabled in Primrose Hill was conveyed by canal until that was cut short at Prince Albert Road. Carter Pattersons stabled their horses in Chalk Farm Road, and there were also stables at the end of Princess Road for horses belonging to the railway company.

Thompson's Pharmacy, at one time veterinary chemist for all the stables in the area *PHCAAC*

Noreen Cullen
From Mecca to the Zoo

I left Ireland about 1945 – not long after the war – and came here to train as a nurse, but, because I was too young to start by six months, took a job as children's nanny instead. I shared a flat with Irish friends in Adelaide Road, and to help with the rent, found employment at the Adelaide, a pub – now gone – opposite Chalk Farm Station. I liked the work and atmosphere, so I decided against nursing and learnt to be a barmaid and prepare food instead! I met my husband-to-be, an Irish building worker, who used to walk me home.

We got married in 1951, and settled in a rented flat in Chalcot Square, where our son was born and we lived there 25 years. The rent was only £5 a week, but I used to give the landlord, who lived in the basement – more: he was so good to us. When he moved, I had the chance to buy our flat for £450 and I'm sorry now I didn't, and when we were offered one in Auden Place (then newly built), we took it and moved in.

There was nothing the matter with Auden Place except some noisy neighbours but I missed my view: nothing to see but brick walls. I felt lonely and shut in and longed to move. A chance came when the Old Piano Factory in Fitzroy Road and the houses on each side were converted into Council flats. My application was successful, and I still live there quite happily, although my husband died three years ago.

I also had my jobs – two evenings a week (for two years after my son was born) at the New Inn Bar, Avenue Road, where Dylan Thomas and his wife, Caitlin, used to drink. Then I followed the managers to their new job, The Two Chairmen, in Mayfair, as a lunch-time waitress. I was never so well-off – loads of tips! It was a Mecca pub, and when these managers emigrated, I was asked to take it over. At that time a woman couldn't hold a licence, it had to be in my husband's name, and though I ran the business, the hours were long and he never liked it. Mecca then offered me a job as restaurant manageress in the City, where there would be no evening or weekend trade.

After a spell in a Notting Hill restaurant, and tired of long hours, I decided it was time to leave catering and try retailing. I applied for and was delighted to get a job as a retail supervisor at London Zoo. It was just a five-minute walk to work instead of an hour on tube and buses. I loved meeting so many different nationalities and didn't mind how busy it was. I was invited to join the pension scheme soon after I came – 'I won't be here that long' – I said, but I stayed 18 years and then retired early! One day I was putting up a display when I fell off a ladder and fractured my skull.

After retiring, I went back to my first love – catering – and worked part-time in the dining room of London University. I really did love it – catering was always good for a laugh!

I've been very happy in Primrose Hill. There is everything I want here and I have known many interesting characters and made many friends. I was very fortunate in my doctor, Dr Drummond, always very kind to me, but specially during my husband's last illness. I cried when she retired, and I miss her dreadfully.

In Princess Road I remember dear Mrs Davies of the Dairy: she worked so hard and kept her shop so clean. Her husband delivered milk first from a handcart and then from an electric float, guiding it as he walked alongside. Both he and her son have died now.

I used to help Daisy and Toddy in the Albert: when Toddy died he was laid out in the room above the bar, for us to pay our respects. The sons had stalls in Inverness Street market: many traders came to the funeral: and Princess Road was blocked with cars and flowers.

I went into the Queens too where you felt you were with friends – Sir Alexander Fleming used to go there – so did Bob Geldof and Ken Roach from Coronation Street. Another friend there was Molly, who delivered papers from her trolley, and loved all animals. By her gate in Ainger Road, she had a little hutch – a shelter for stray cats with food as well.

Primrose Hill is such a lovely place to live – I wouldn't want to be anywhere else.

Prince Albert: Toddy was the Landlord *Virginia Smith*

Caroline Cooper
A View of Primrose Hill

My architect father, Anthony Cooper, returned from war service in India in 1946, and with my mother Margery took a long lease of this house. It had been empty throughout the war but its decrepit state was offset for them by the view of Primrose Hill and the neglected garden overrun by an untamed white rambling rose.

As a small child I remember a procession of builders – no staircase – only a ladder – much talk of dry rot – and the dramatic descent of the bath from first floor to basement. Once the kitchens, larder, cellars etc., this was made a separate flat: the old food lift is still down there, fixed in position as a sort of open cupboard. Lodgers occupied two rooms on the second floor and various 'Miss So-and So's' (respectable tweedy secretary types) would creep up our stairs to their bed-sits. A third room on the top floor was occupied by a succession of German or Swiss au pairs. For a time the second floor too was a self-contained flat, my father having built an additional outside stairway.

The house was cold – my parents were always struggling with a gas poker to keep the north-facing drawing room warm enough to sit in, and it must also have been dirty: these were the days of steam trains and coal fires and mother would complain about dirty yellowy brown water when she washed the huge curtains in the bath. A 'charlady' too came in to clean.

The area was run-down, though being a child I was not really aware of such things. I was not allowed to walk down certain roads, where 'rough men' lived. My first solo outings were to buy bread from 'Mary' in the baker's on the corner of Fitzroy/Chalcot Road: and to the library, then in what is now Ian Mankin's shop. I remember the thrill of being taken there for the first time, to choose books. I also went to the sweetshop up the road – but I was rather frightened of making a fool of myself over the rationing coupons.

I played on Primrose Hill – on the swings – climbing trees – looking in the spooky gun emplacements on the summit, collecting dandelion leaves for my rabbit from the allotments, hanging over the Regent's Park canal bridge to watch the horse-drawn barges, and drinking from the fountain by Albert Terrace – forbidden to use the cup on its chain.

When I came back I had to stand opposite the house so that my mother could see me and fetch me safely across the road – though then quiet with little traffic.

My father worked as an architect in St John's Wood and soon became fascinated by the history of the area, becoming something of an expert. He campaigned against the demolition of the piano factory in Fitzroy Road, and of the Boys' Home Chapel in Regent's Park Road. After his retirement he devoted himself to bookbinding, genealogy and to local history, becoming a contributing member of the London Topographical Society and of the Camden History Society. He gave talks on the area, on the Chalk Farm Tavern, and edited the Camden History Society's booklet *Primrose Hill to Euston Road; A Survey of The Streets of West Camden (1982)*. In 1979 he and Margery moved to Waterside Place, Princess Road.

They had found the house too large and so we bought it from them at a 'family rate'. I have now been back again here for nearly 20 years and it has been through the same procedure of 'lodgers – separate flats – back to family home' as other houses in this area.

The pyracantha hedge which my mother planted in the fifties has grown into a monster, earning it the name of the Dragon Hedge House.

The author in Regent's Park Road looking at the Hill without railings
Caroline Cooper

Judy Millett
Blowing in the Wind

My husband and I came to live in Fitzroy Road just before our first child was born in 1951. At that time, the coal fired steam engines used to be fired and cleaned out at the far end of Fitzroy Road just behind a high wall. When the wind was blowing from that direction we used to get a lot of acrid smelling smoke and smuts. On those days we didn't feel like putting the pram outside. As a result, a tenants' and residents' association was formed to persuade the Council and British Rail to deal with the problem. Mr Saxon, who lived in Gloucester Avenue on the side overlooking the railway, regularly collected the soot from the window-sills and took it along to Council meetings to show what we in the area had to put up with. It would be nice to think that we hastened the change to diesel engines – a lot cleaner.

MAKE A DAMN NUISANCE OF YOURSELVES—
Says the Mayor

Councillor Tom Barker, J.P., Mayor of St. Pancras, and Mrs. Barker, Mayoress, received a warm welcome from the residents when they attended the Association's public meeting at Dumpton Place on Tuesday, July 15th. Alderman P. J. Jonas, Councillor J. J. Edwards, and Councillor A. W. Stallard were also present. Councillor T. Donovan sent his best wishes for the success of the meeting.

"You have got to fight for clean air," exclaimed the Mayor. " Make a damn nuisance of yourselves. As mayor and a J.P. I should perhaps not tell you that but you have a damn nuisance to deal with and its no use being toffee-nosed about it. You have got to fight it."

While the mayor spoke smoke poured from the Depot and in the course of the meeting, one hour, Alderman Jonas twice went into the Depot to make a complaint.

Mr. S. A. Edmonds, Association Secretary, reported on the present position and outlined the points to be raised at the meeting with the L.C.C. on the following day. **The meeting showed its support for the Association's policy.** A collection was taken of one pound, five shillings and ninepence.

From: 'The Record' 1962. Chalk Farm Residents' Association campaigned for Clean Air in the 1950s and early 1960s *CLSAC*

DISCUSSION. It is apparent that to avoid damage to curtains, clothes, etc. windows are kept shut; **this probably contributes to the high incidence of respiratory ailments complained of.** The most striking feature that emerges under other subjects of complaints, however, is the **extra work** due to the entry of smoke, dust and grit into household premises. The following quotations from questionaire replies illustrate this :—

"Impossible to leave any room uncleaned for more than one day. Curtains are always filthy and grey and require more than normal washing".
"Necessary to dust twice a day".
"It is quite impossible to cope with the dust".
"Daily cleaning of all parts is essential here".
"Extremely difficult, almost hopeless".
"Constant labour in vain. The pride of housekeeping is lost under such abominable conditions".
"The smoke and dirt are one move ahead all the time".
"The dirt is awful".
"We are never finished cleaning".
"Put clothes out and they are dirty when you bring them in again".
"Can't possibly hang out washing".
"You could be cleaning from morning to night and would still be dirty".
"I find the housework has become a drudgery".
"Endless work cleaning".
"Need to spring-clean every day".
"Never finish work".
"Never-ending work to try and keep clean".

The replies suggest that a considerable, **even intolerable burden of extra household work is caused by smoke and dust,** so much so that an element of despair is apparent in some of the replies, especially from old people and the mothers of larger families :—

"Waste of time to try to keep clean".
"It makes you lose heart".
"Fed up trying to keep place clean".
"The dust and grit are making life unbearable".
"Impossible to cope".

The word "impossible" is mentioned no fewer than eleven times. The replies suggest that apart from the direct effect of smoke in causing or aggravating respiratory illnesses, additional ill-health is likely to be caused **(1) by lack of proper ventilation, (2) by the physical exhaustion and mental stress due to the continuous demands for effort necessary to keep the house clean.**

CONCLUSION. The replies to the questionaire suggest that in the immediate vicinity of Camden Motive Power Depot excessive smoke is giving rise to grave concern amongst the residents who fear their health is being adversely affected. **There is strong evidence to suggest that there are good grounds for this apprehension.**

October, 1954 "CONSULTANT CHEST PHYSICIAN"

From: *The Record:* Newsletter of the Chalk Farm Residents Association, 1954 *CLSAC*

Cliff Wyndham
50 years in Primrose Hill

I was born in Cardiff in 1915 and was brought up in Hampshire. My father worked for the same firm as had Charles Dickens (Day and Martins). Following the war, I moved to London. My first 11 years were spent in West Hampstead, after which time I began looking for a house to buy. The prices in Primrose Hill were low because the Rent Act prevented landlords from increasing the rent. Landlords could not sell property occupied by tenants, nor could they afford to make the necessary repairs and so the houses became very run down. Basements would be filled with earth, concrete and railway sleepers. At that time the great houses of the area reminded me of massive stranded whales.

It was also cheap to live in the area because it was so dirty from the trains that took an houror more to get up steam; the trains took on coal at the end of Fitzroy Road and this part was the smokiest of all. Even today, if you lift up the tiles on many roofs you'll find the coal dust that penetrated there from the dirty air.

In 1955 I bought my first house in Primrose Hill, and started repairing it immediately, using bricks from a derelict Kiln in Gospel Oak. During this time I worked as a clock winder in the Adelaide Pub, and fell in with a crowd of artists who showed me their paintings. After seeing some Japanese prints, I was inspired to take up painting, and some time later my paintings were shown by a friend to the head of the Slade School of Art. They subsequently offered me a place there, and later I began teaching art: this job provided me with great satisfaction for quite a time to come.

Having lived in Primrose Hill for 50 years, I've been in a place to observe many changes and in general the process of gentrification. In my early days here many architects and designers moved into the area, buying up dilapidated houses and restoring them.

One day I remember well is the opening of Sesame, and in fact I was told that I was their first customer. I think this was an important moment in the development of Primrose Hill. And I can remember the day when the laundromat closed, a pitiful day, affecting many of the older residents of the area.

Another unhappy change was the replacing of the cast iron street lamps with their modern and graceless equivalents, and I fought long and hard against that. In my view what gives Primrose Hill its charm is its peculiarity, with so many architectural details differing from each other, as we see in the variety of designs for coal hole covers. Many visitors to Primrose Hill remark that the village is so unlike the rest of London. But in fact what makes it special is the extent to which it still is London, the original London.

Ironwork in St. Mark's Crescent *Virginia Smith*

Priscilla Astrop
Primrose Hill Studios

In 1950 John Astrop and I were married. A few months later I discovered I was pregnant, and our landlady asked us to leave the bed-sit we were living in.

My husband worked for a commercial artist, and when he learnt of our predicament, he said we could be his tenants at 12, Primrose Hill Studios. He and his wife were moving across the courtyard to number 1, where there was a garden. These studios had been built for artists in the Edwardian era in Fitzroy Road. We went to see our future home the next evening; it was a huge space with skylights and an anthracite stove. There was a gallery at one end, and a bedroom, kitchen and bathroom on the ground floor. The front door was wide enough to get large pieces of sculpture through. The rent at that time was £2 a week.

We were overjoyed at our good fortune and thanked John's boss profusely.

We stayed there 10 years; in which time we had two children. It was safe to leave the front door open all day, and the babies outside in their pram, or playing in the courtyard.

Our next door neighbour, Muriel, lived in the lodge. Her mother had lived there before her, and she looked after an elderly man called Montague Smythe, whose eyesight was failing, although he still painted rather misty pictures. Frank Mason, who designed railway posters, was another of our neighbours, but Martita Hunt, the actress, was not very friendly. One day she came to my door and demanded that I take my crying baby out of earshot. 'Take him away – take him on the Hill.'

But my daughter made friends with Lord Methuen, who called her 'little red shoes', and they had long conversations in the courtyard.

Because we had no real garden, we spent a lot of time on Primrose Hill, where we met other families and the children would play on the swings.

Mary Aitken
Primrose Hill and I

I first visited the Primrose Hill area in the early sixties, when I had dinner with a colleague in a house in Chalcot Square. I remember big, elegant rooms. Then about 1964, I came house-hunting with my sister. A huge house on the corner of Chalcot Square and Chalcot Road was £8,000. A house in Chalcot Crescent was about £11,000. These seemed large sums to us, at a time when a good quality house in a good area was £3,000–£4,000. I recall the area as shabby and the houses were peeling and unpainted.

I came to live here myself in 1972, occupying a ground floor flat in Chalcot Road as a tenant at £13 a week. My landlady was Mrs Hone, who also owned a house in Fitzroy Road, just round the corner. The house had been in multi-occupation for as long as anyone could remember, but about 1971 it had been converted into four flats. I was the first tenant to occupy my flat (apart from a brief tenancy by a colleague). It had been part of a maisonette, lived in by the Attewells since the early thirties. George Attewell, the younger son, moved into the newly-converted first floor flat and lives there still.

My neighbours were, and still are, Peter and Helen Newnham. Mr Digweed, a retired bus driver lived next door. He could have bought the freehold after the war for £500. A Polish man lived on the ground floor with a wife who had been housekeeper to a doctor who had a practice in the grey house on the corner of Fitzroy Road and Regent's Park Road. Upstairs was a woman who never left her room, and eventually disappeared when the house was 'gentrified'. The Satows were, and still are, opposite, and I knew slightly an elderly couple obliquely opposite, who were said to run a steam laundry in Camden Town. They emerged regularly with a large bulldog and drove off in a very small Fiat. The last bulldog, before they both died, was their tenth.

The view from my kitchen has changed little since 1972. There was however a huge ash tree in the next door garden. It had to be cut down when its core was found to be rotten. A washing line on a pulley was fixed high up on this tree, the other end being attached to a point at first floor level at the back of one of the Fitzroy Road houses. This washing line was loaded from the top of the steps leading up from the garden to the ground floor and jerked laboriously across by the pulley. It must have been many feet above ground level.

One big change in the gardens is the nature and number of the birds. In the early years there was a deafening dawn chorus. This gradually ceased. Now there is an early morning (4.00 a.m. onwards) robin or wren only, but with impressively complex songs. A couple of blackbirds nest nearby every year. Sparrows have declined, tits have increased. A jay comes very close from time to time. The eight to nine pigeons in the nearby big tree are down to two to three. Three squirrels are daily visitors. Twice I have heard an owl in the trees nearby.

There have been changes in the little parade of shops in Chalcot Road, though a hard core of the originals remains: a newsagent, hardware store and a little supermarket. There was a butcher, Mr. Hutchings, on the corner of Manley Street who, it was said, once had his own abattoir in the yard behind the shop. There was a good restaurant, Chalcot's Bistro, and a shop, called Adeptus, that sold chunky foam furniture. I arrived too late to know the bakery.

In Regent's Park Road there were two butcher's shops, one of which I was told had been the scene of a bloody murder. The current greengrocer was then Shearns, who also had a shop in Tottenham Court Road. The baker nearby had a remarkable heating device. It was like a mini old-fashioned gasfire with flames burning up past claypipe panels and it was suspended from the ceiling well above head height. Harper's garage, where Shepherds now is, serviced or mended my car, and there was another garage, with petrol pumps, where Bibendum is now. When that garage went out of business, or was demolished, I remember going behind it to find two very old cottages – derelict I think, which were said to be the oldest in Primrose Hill. There were two supermarkets and a chemist, Mr. Alderson, about whom I'm sure others have written. Shops that have come and gone in my time have included Kirby's (greengrocer), breadshops, florists, an optician, a secondhand clothes shop, a woolshop and briefly a wax fruit shop.

John & Mary O'Donnell
Chalcot Road: its Shops and Factory

My husband John and I came to live in Chalcot Road about 1956. The shops were very different then. Where the restaurant is now there was a bakery, called Arthur Worth, and a hairdresser where Clare's Kitchen is. There was a paper shop run by Arthur Haskins, who stocked a lot of toys and other things for children. Next door to that was a fruit and veg. shop owned by Miss Hunt and beyond that a cleaner's, next to a working men's café.

On the other side of Chalcot Road at the end of Egbert Place was a factory called Westminster Laboratories, where they made Sennakot and Ex-Lax. I worked there before my eldest son John was born. With several other local women I worked in one large room, filling and packing the tins and boxes. The pills were made on another floor. Both men and women were employed in the factory, but when it moved to Hull only a few went with it, and the rest of us had to find other jobs. Now the site is occupied by Utopia Village.

Hutchings & Son: once had its own abattoir behind the shop *PHCAAC*

Anthony Stoll
Shops and Businesses

As in other parts of London, the big changes that brought the middle classes back to this area were the Clean Air Act, and the electrification of the railways. The other impetus to move back was the very favour able improvement grants available in the sixties. That said, even in the early seventies there were still many multi-occupied houses in the area, and car owners were in a decided minority.

I have known the area since the fifties when I used to visit my father's surgery. The first change I saw was the demolition of the buildings on what is now the Meadowbank complex. Little girls from the surrounding area used to come along to Miss Brooking's ballet school in St Mary's church hall where Meadowbank is now. There was also a mews with a mixture of car mechanics and the like.

As in much of inner London most of the light industry has gone now. The Ultra TV works in Erskine Road closed down in the sixties, I think, and when I moved to Regent's Park Road in 1970 their factory was occupied by the printers of Green Shield Stamps. The small engineering works opposite who had reground the crankshaft of my 1929 Morris Cowley in 1963 was then a repair shop and is now housing.

In Regent's Park Road, there was Deubelbeiss Battery Works at No 77 and Thurston's Billiard Tables off Sharpleshall Street, in what is now Primrose Mews.

In the late sixties, Souhami Veneers moved out of the former chapel of the Boys' Home fronting Regent's Park Road and the premises became an offshoot of the Hampstead Theatre and was used as rehearsal rooms for West End and TV productions. The Alla Marinella café in what is now part of Hart's Bathrooms was always full of stars at lunchtime, tucking into the wonderful home-made lasagne.

About 1971 the Hampstead Theatre stopped using this building and it was then squatted by the artist who painted the murals on the railway bridge. Squatting was taking place on quite a scale and when Simon Jenkins bought his house in Regent's Park Road he is said to have had someone to live there as soon as it became vacant, to stop it being squatted. Much of Ainger Road was squatted and parts of Gloucester Avenue and St Mark's Square. The squatter moved out of the Boys' Home chapel after about a year, and it became the Howff, Roy Guest's folk/after hours drinking club

In the mid-sixties, antique shops moved in, but during the seventies there was still a good mix of ordinary shops. On the even side they included a Polish continental butcher, Worth's, the bakers; a Greek hairdresser, Keulamann Antiques, who had started out on the opposite side; R.J.Welsh, Yeoman's, Alderson's, Langton's Builders Merchants, and an upholsterer.

On the odd side among others already mentioned by other contributors, were Blind Alley, roller blind design, Cosprop, theatre costumes, Ron Weldon's antiques, Richard Dare's kitchen equipment, Thompson's pharmacy and Post Office and the Retsina

The Stars... enjoyed home-made lasagne in Alla Marinella *PHCAAC*

restaurant. The music industry has had a presence for some time: Mayfair Studios behind the library, and Creation Records in the Boys' Home chapel.

In the sixties the pubs in the area had separate public and saloon bars. The Lansdowne featured topless dancers: the Princess of Wales, bar billiards, and the Pembroke, bare boards in the public bar.

Finally above Worth's the baker's, there was for a time a tutorial college specialising in difficult boys, one of whom is now a local *Big Issue* seller.

Ron Weldon's antique shop, 1972 *PHCAAC*

Irene Dowie
Front Door Keys

On 8 December 1959 I persuaded my husband to attend an auction in the City of London of houses in NW1. That evening we met to take our children to the ballet, and he calmly announced he had bought 36 Regent's Park Road at the auction for £6,500. I was dumbfounded. I had not even seen it.

Camden Council bought some of the other properties to prevent wholesale demolition, thereby turning Primrose Hill into another St John's Wood.

36 Regent's Park Road had 49 front door keys and many painted walls. On the stucco walls outside was scrawled 'do not touch me', because large chunks of plaster fell off. Eventually it was done up and we moved in with various music students.

Kingstown Street 'railway' cottages, two-up, two-down sold individually at £1,000 each. In 1976 we moved from St Mark's Crescent to Kingstown Street where I now live, look out and enjoy the gardens of Regent's Park Road. That corner had been bombed and my house was a plain two storey uninteresting replacement.

When we moved to Kingstown Street, Auden Place was already built, a modern housing association for teachers in Camden. It was very pleasant living until the gates were locked in Auden Place and we no longer had easy access to Princess Road. Neighbours, friends, school children no longer came past my house and my life was never the same again.

Stanley Newstead
Stan the Man

I've been working in Primrose Hill for many years, but I started in Hampstead at 14 working for a builder – a semi-relation – on bomb damage repair: there was no glass for windows: plastic was nailed over instead.

Next came National Service – two years in the Tank Corps in Catterick and with BAOR – British Army on the Rhine. I never drove a tank, but I did drive three-tonners – motors very high off the ground – you had to climb the wheel to get into the cabin. I finished as a CO driver – in and out of the officers' mess, while others were out on manoeuvres, sleeping under canvas in soaking clothes!

Back home to plumbing: I worked 14 years in Covent Garden Market, repairing lead lights and gutters, and at the weekends I began working for a builder at 26 St Mark's Crescent – Copps – three generations – himself, father and grandfather. He got on to big work in the West End and in the finish I went to work for him full time. When he died I ended up working for everyone round here. Davies the milkman at Princess Dairies recommended me to people as he went on his rounds. They used to give me their keys and I went in and did the work: whole bathrooms, leaks, burst pipes etc: And so it's gone on – you get to know everyone and everyone gets to know you!

As for old systems and conversions – I've taken many sinks off landings, and many old slate tanks out that fed the basement. Years ago no water pipes went higher than the ground floor, and there was only one loo to a house – nine times out of ten out in the back yard. When fitted baths came in, they put them in the scullery, where the copper was to heat the water. Its fire burnt wood – tar road blocks best if you could save them. Many houses round here still have the chimley going up the back. Many a time I've cut a copper out – they were cast iron – and there was brickwork round them, like a little house. Before the fitted bath you had a zinc one – you'd see them outside in the yard, hanging on a nail. Baths were shared: children would get in one after another – hot water was in short supply!

Butcher's (Plastering Specialists) Fitzroy Road: Casting Room *CLSAC*

Jenny Marriott
A Good Place to Live

We moved into the area on a strictly temporary basis in 1955 and became entranced. In 1959 we bought a house in Chamberlain Street, for £2,300 with vacant possession, but we had immediately to spend more than that to make it suitable for us. The work included taking out the old gas light fittings, rewiring (there were lights but no power points), and installing some plumbing: there was a cold supply to the basement scullery, a single loo, and a small sink on a half landing. The old couple who sold it had used it as a rooming house, and we had to remove electricity meters from several rooms. They chose us as purchasers rather than a developer who had offered more than we could, because they wanted it to return to being a family home. We kept faith with them: our two daughters, born in the two or three years after we moved in, still live there with their families.

Celia Kelly

When we moved to the area it still had a rich mix of inhabitants, among them labourers, writers, railwaymen, lorry drivers, actors, tradesmen, builders, skilled craftsmen and technicians, BBC producers, lawyers, and the first of the eventual flood of architects and designers. It was far more a local shopping centre than it is today: we had a baker, and a choice of butchers, greengrocers, and doctors, and Mr Alderson the chemist, who could advise on all our minor ailments. The then chippy also sold fresh fish, and we had something rarely seen these days – a cobbler.

There have been many changes: the library was then in a shop, where it was succeeded by Ron Weldon's antique shop and later by Ian Mankin. Where the library is now, there were dilapidated Victorian houses.

I remember two particular tragedies which hit the community. Eirwen Griffiths, who ran the Dairy, nearly died (and never fully recovered) from being knifed late one Christmas Eve when he went to challenge some youths kicking milk bottles about the street. Two neighbours who went to his aid were also wounded but less seriously: and Harry, a greengrocer, was crushed to death by a lorry early one morning in Covent Garden Market.

It must have been towards the end of the sixties when one of my daughters, somewhat startled, came down to me in the basement kitchen to say that 'a man has fallen through the roof'. Indeed he had; he had been inspecting the corrugated sheets forming the roof at the rear of Regent's Park Garage (now Shepherds) and one had given way. He must have fallen some 30 feet, but his injury was not life threatening and I believe he made a good recovery.

When we first moved in, Regent's Park Road was a major traffic route: one constantly had to dodge heavy lorries charging through. Efforts to reduce traffic included placing a barrier across the road, and many times we were woken by the sound of cars crashing into it in the small hours. Fortunately better judgement prevailed: it was removed and the closure of the bridge over the railway proved a far more satisfactory deterrent.

Erskine Mews then housed a small factory: again we were awoken one night by loud bangs and pops as it went up in flames. People on the north side of Chamberlain

Street had to leave their houses and one complained to me that though it was a frosty winter night the temperature on her outside window-sill was 70 degrees Fahrenheit (about 21 centigrade).

Another night, loud banging on our front doors about 3.00 a.m. revealed police, warning us that a broken pipe was causing the road to collapse: several Chamberlain Street residents were paddling around in dressing-gown and slippers, removing their cars to a safer place.

A more pleasing diversion was the regular arrival in each street of the Chalk Farm Salvation Army Silver Band on an evening shortly before Christmas to delight us with their renditions of carols.

There have been other changes: Chalcot Square used to be surrounded by a chicken-wire fence, as the original railings had been removed in the forties, as many were, to help the war effort (though I never discovered exactly for what purpose they were used). It was a phenomenal improvement when they were replaced and the square re-landscaped.

The area is also much cleaner: at one time engines used to sit in the sidings behind Gloucester Avenue and let off steam, not to mention dirt and filthy smoke. A residents' protest put a stop to the practice, and we all noticed how much easier it was to keep our houses clean and how much less frequently our curtains needed washing.

It has always been a good place to live, with a friendly and supportive community. We made lifelong friendships by doing all our shopping locally, by taking our children to play on the Hill: and I by sharing the same carriage commuting to work with the same group and my husband, by walking to work with countless others across Primrose Hill and the Park.

I moved out of London on retirement, but it is good to return and still be greeted in the shops and on the street.

Elizabeth Anne McGuinness

Chop chop Charlie and his Loan Club

Chop Chop Charlie Ronan dressed neatly, always in a suit. He was a big man, about six foot tall and not visibly suffering from hunger and thirst. He was not patient. 'Get it done', he would say, 'Chop Chop'. He was a Londoner, but from south of the river. What brought him north was his business ventures, some of which he kept tight-lipped about. One of these was a loan club that he operated from The Engineer pub in Gloucester Avenue in the seventies. Loan Clubs were widespread throughout the country and were usually operated from pubs and community centres.

The principle on which a loan club was based was that every member would, without fail, pay a minimum amount of £1.00 a week for 50 weeks of the year, but they were also obliged to take out a loan on which they would pay interest. The interest was comparatively lower than any bank would offer, hence the popularity of such a club. Members would borrow money for holidays, and many a wedding was funded through the auspices of the loan club, but, primarily, the club was run to provide extra money for the main holiday event of the year, Christmas.

Pay-out time was usually two weeks before Christmas. People would begin to congregate at the bar of The Engineer from 5.00 p.m. onwards; Chop Chop would start paying out after 6.00 p.m.. Charlie would arrive by car accompanied by two rather heavy and fierce looking men, his minders. In those days it was not unknown to have anything up to £40,000 in the bag so one had to guard against any attempt to steal the spondulics.

The landlord, Bill, and his wife, Maggie, would have engaged extra staff to cope with the demand for drinks, as everyone would be in a generous mood. Copious amounts of food would be on the bar: roast potatoes, sausages, bowls of chips, chicken portions, and so on, all on the house as they say. On this particular night the whole atmosphere in the pub would be one of enormous generosity and great humour. The women present would be in little groups separate from the men. Every now and then a tray of drinks would be sent over which would be repaid with lots of hugs and kisses. As the night wore on you would notice the women making their way home long before the men, most of the Christmas money tucked safely away in their handbags; otherwise, if left with the old man, it would disappear behind the bar.

Running a loan club committed Chop Chop Charlie to two hours service every Friday night, keeping the books and banking the money. I don't think he made any great profit because if any member reneged on a loan it was met from accumulated interest. This rarely happened as most members were known to each other, and again it was a community venture and nobody wants to be ostracised.

A similar club was run from the Lansdowne pub in Gloucester Avenue. Unfortunately for the members the landlord ran the club. It seems he was a bit of a gambler and heavily in debt, owing some rather nasty people large sums of money. The temptation to abscond with the loan club money proved too much, and come the Friday night of the big pay out one December there was mayhem outside the Lansdowne as angry members threatened to set fire to the pub unless the brewery compensated them. The police were called who advised the staff to close the premises. This infuriated the crowd even more as many were still hopeful that the landlord would turn up. The police searched the living quarters of the pub and established that all his belongings were gone.

For many people a blight was cast over Christmas that year. Rumour has it that some years later the ex-landlord was spotted serving in a bar in Newcastle. A small posse of men set off for Newcastle one weekend and it is said to this day that this particular landlord will never cheat or steal again in his life or for that matter father a child.

Times have changed. Banks and building societies have softened their attitude towards extending credit to a wider section of the population. They have the money to spend on advertising the merits of borrowing money, but you find that more emphasis is placed on borrowing rather than saving. Credit cards make it easier to spend and what has materialised is a society that lives on credit, people are not inclined to save anymore. I believe that this is one of the main reasons for the demise of Loan Clubs.

When the banks moved in, the community spirit that the Loan Club generated was lost. Those Friday evenings after you paid your club money in you had a drink with your neighbours, exchanged gossip, and generally it was the start of the weekend. Come Christmas the buzz and expectation of getting actual money in your hand cannot compare with a plastic card. I don't suppose clubs such as the Loan Club, also known as the Christmas Club, would ever have been established unless philanthropic characters such as Chop Chop Charlie were prepared to give their time and effort to the community. People like him still exist but they are few and far between.

The Engineer, where Chop Chop Charlie ran his Loan Club *Virginia Smith*

Ilse Gray
Princess Road in the Sixties

When we bought our Princess Road house in 1961 it cost only £5,000, but we had to borrow the money privately because the mortgage companies refused our application on the grounds that, among other things, it was an undesirable area. At that time trains out of Euston had not yet been electrified and they often stopped to let off steam behind the houses along Gloucester Avenue; we were warned that net curtains would be dirty in a week and disintegrate within a year.

Of the shops opposite us only the newsagent, hairdresser and restaurant have survived as such over the years (under different owners). During the sixties the other shops included a Post Office, a wool/sewing materials shop, a butcher, a dairy and a greengrocer. The rather genteel lady who owned the wool shop had worked for many years previously for a diamond merchant in Hatton Garden. She was always immaculately dressed (twin set and pearls), coiffed and made up, and I was careful to be on my best behaviour – but I really warmed to her when rumour alleged that the establishment had been bought for her by a 'gentleman friend'.

The butcher's was owned by an Austrian woman and her son; it later became a rather

The Primrose Dairy: run by Mr and Mrs Davies *PHCAAC*

good antique shop; we browsed there quite often and still have several interesting items we found there. Ian, the greengrocer, was a large, jolly man who in winter wore trousers in the traditional, low-cut 'building site' fashion and shorts in the summer. His dachshund was never far away. Although diabetic, Ian seemed to spend quite a lot of time in the pub and he also took bets for his customers. Later he moved the shop to Chalcot Road and his brother opened a betting shop in its place, where Ian joined him when the greengrocer's later closed.

Everyone knew the Davies family and the dairy. They delivered milk to our door and we all bought our groceries in the shop and stopped for a chat. It was how one got to know the neighbours. When Mr Davies died, Mrs Davies carried on for many years together with her son Vince. She eventually retired to her native Wales, followed more recently by Vince (who, sadly, died in October 1999).

The name of the first restaurant I recall was Froops and belonged to a red-headed actor (I've forgotten his name – anyone remember?); it got good write-ups in the press and people came a long way to eat there. It was equally well known when it changed ownership some years later and became the One-Legged Goose.

In the old days The Prince Albert (now just the Albert) had a public and a saloon bar separated by an off-licence. Like most pubs then, before the betting laws were changed, it had a regular – or irregular? – bookie, taking bets in the public bar. The landlords, Toddy Squires and Daisy, were an institution long before we arrived. They were related to the stall-holders in Inverness Street market (everyone in the market seemed to be related to each other) and years later when Toddy Squires died, the entire length of Princess Road was lined with wreaths for the cortege on the day of the funeral. Their son Freddy and Freddy's wife Rose took over the pub and I remember the many evenings and weekends when both bars were crowded with locals and you couldn't see for the smoke. And then there were the New Year's Eves when you weren't allowed in unless you wore fancy dress.

Unlike today, very few well-known faces lived round us in the sixties. But in the basement of the house next door, whose owner was known to everyone as 'the major' and who seemed to know a great many young sailors, lived the photographer, David Bailey, and the, then, top model Jean Shrimpton. Jean Shrimpton's sister was at that time going out with Mick Jagger and excited pre-teen girls used to regularly ring our bell asking if he lived there; and, straight-faced, we would ask in judge-like fashion, 'who is Mick Jagger?'.

Princess Road: Froops Restaurant, 1972 *PHCAAC*

Amanda Craig
The Seasons in Primrose Hill

We first came to Primrose Hill in 1962, and I hated it. I was three, and my parents rented a flat opposite the library in Sharpleshall Street. We had left behind the paradise of Italy and arrived in one of the coldest winters on record. My mother was pregnant with my sister, who was born a couple of days before Sylvia Plath committed suicide in Fitzroy Road. It was a grim time – so grim that I still remember the intense cold, the stand-pipes in the streets put up because the water froze in the taps. I remember looking out for Father Christmas's sleigh to appear over the roof-tops of the library, and being convinced that I saw it. I was ill a lot, and most of the children seemed to go around with a rivet of snot between their nostrils and their mouth. Even though the Clean Air Act had been passed, there were impenetrable fogs – one of my first memories of London is of walking along Regent's Park Road in the fog with my father, and the relief of finding the next lamppost

There was a whole gang of us who went to Biddy's nursery in Chalcot Square. We would play chase in and out of the bushes, and play in the streets as well. In those days, there were hardly any cars, and all through the summer we could play hopscotch, skip or football. Little girls wore halos of plastic round their heads at bath-time, in order for shampoo not to go in their eyes. Something similar protected us from the kind of knowledge children now get stung by. We knew there were bad men in the bushes on the other side of Primrose Hill, and were drilled never to accept sweets from strangers. Otherwise, most us were left to go to the park and the playground alone from about six onwards. The only real danger was the traffic, and even that lessened after the Bridge was closed. (As usual, it was a child's death that prompted this.)

I was very aware of how powerful and irritable adults were. You would get told off by complete strangers for saying 'OK' and 'Ya', yet we were much more free than modern children, too. Old women would watch us play in the street behind twitching net curtains, and even if we hated them they made us feel safe without realizing. The other really special place for me in Primrose Hill was the library. I learnt to read when about three and a half, largely because my mother was an inspired teacher. I still remember the amazement and joy of being able to read *The Cat in the Hat Came Back* – all the toys pouring in a cascade of water down the stairs because the taps were left on. I became, and still am, a compulsive reader, and so the library was a magical place. I still love the wooden floors and the big windows that make it seem light even on dull days. Years later, when I came back to Primrose Hill as an unemployed graduate and began the arduous process of turning myself into a journalist and novelist the books and newspapers of the adult section were equally crucial. But the children's section is what matters most. I remember the thrill of discovering first the Andrew Lang fairy books, then C.S. Lewis's Narnia books, then the complete works of E. Nesbit, then John Christopher and Alan Garner .... The library still smells the same, but it's very sad these are for the most part no longer in stock. I get cross, as a novelist, at the number of middle-class people who can afford to buy books borrowing them from the adult section – do you realise, most authors earn £10,000 a year at most, and that every time you borrow a book we get a miserable 2p per loan? – but for people who can't afford books, and for children especially it is as much a basic right as clean air and water.

Books became more and more important for me because when I was six we moved back to Italy. We revisited every summer, because by then my parents had bought a house in Chalcot Crescent, but from then on each summer was an intense snapshot of how London was changing. Being exiled (as it felt) was particularly painful for me, because I had had my own tiny bedroom in Chalcot Crescent for the first time – a perfect little girl's bedroom with a screen of green Boston ivy hanging down over the window, overlooking the back gardens. I would spend hours in this green room reading or just looking out at the cats crossing the gardens by means of their secret alley-ways. (The study I write in now is very like it, I have just realised!) People used to hang their washing out on long, long lines; some of the houses didn't have indoor toilets. Most back gardens were pits of sticky yellow clay with nothing growing – it's amazing, walking round now, seeing what miniature bowers so many have become. In my childhood you were more likely to see plants growing out of cracks in buildings than in the gardens.

In those days, Primrose Hill was still a place for ordinary families, though even then an increasing number of media people were moving in. We were the beneficiaries of a socialist vision of society, and the gulf between rich and poor didn't seem so deep. There was no question but that everyone went to the local state primary, or caught the 74 bus into town. We were among the first children to have polio vaccine on a lump of sugar – the terror of going into Dr Horder's surgery was intense – and we were all expected to take cod-liver oil and malt, wear vests and have our tonsils out. We would go to each other's houses to watch Dr Who from behind the sofa, and play at being Daleks in the playground later, screaming with terror.

There was *Andy Pandy, Bill and Ben* and *Lost in Space.* We watched them and tried to make sense of the adult world, which was full of mysterious quarrels and silences, of people falling out with one another or becoming terribly close friends, Later, when I read Fay Weldon's novels, I realised how many of the rows and outbursts that puzzled me as a child were the manifestations of marriages breaking up. (Fay rented my parents' house for a while, the first time she left her own husband, and teased me about being the landlady's daughter. She was the first professional woman writer I'd met, and a subject of secret fascination for years after.) Some families were marked by deep tragedy – I remember one in which the mother was crippled with polio,

Alderson's the Chemist, Regent's Park Road, 1972 *CLSAC*

dumped by her husband, and then one of the boys lost an eye (I think) from fireworks on Bonfire Night. It is my impression that people are more compassionate now than then, because children and adults alike regarded them with a sort of horrified awe. You heard of mothers who committed suicide, or became alcoholics; it was always the women who seemed to suffer, especially when they didn't have jobs. My own mother lost her job as a journalist at one point and tried to keep the family finances afloat by making raffia dolls for sale at Patchouli – another shop that has now gone – but we would come back and find that from one year to the next people had disappeared.

Children had very few sweets – there was a bakery in Princess Road that sold fairy cakes, and when we were older my sister and I would walk past the shop window salivating, because the fondant icing seemed like the most delicious thing in the world. Things like a trip to see *Bambi* or *The Sound of Music* were huge events, as was going to the Little Angel Marionette Theatre in Islington – partly because there were chocolate biscuits in the interval. I went to the primary school at the end of the road where we all had free milk. Most of us hated the milk, because it was warm. Then we discovered that putting Ribena in it made it pink and sweet. If we have good bones and teeth now, it's probably thanks to that.

It was a time when the Ladybird Book of family life was being challenged by feminism. All we knew about it was that from one year to the next ordinary-seeming men started growing their hair and women took up the guitar. I remember one astonishing sight which to me still sums up the sixties, seeing a beautiful young woman walk down Regent's Park Road, wearing a mini-skirt, boots, a cloak – and nothing on top.

It wasn't the safe, cosy little island it seems. Just as you could hear one of the lost rivers of London gurgle beneath the basements of these pretty houses, so you could feel that some families were being eaten away by dark, irresistible underground forces. But to me, Primrose Hill has always been a kind of idyll, even though it has changed almost out of all recognition. I still love Chalcot Crescent, which looks so respectable and monochrome at the Park end, then twists itself into a rainbow of colours, even if it has become infinitely less raffish and more respectable. Almost all the shops have gone, though Yeoman's Greengrocer's and R.J.Welsh remain. But I remember when the patisserie was a launderette, and before that to when it was a hardware store; when there was a cobbler's, and a butcher's where the pet-food shop is, when there were no restaurants, not even Lemonia. I miss Alderson's the chemist, partly because I loved the huge old fashioned bottles that he had in his window. I miss the nice Ugandan man who ran the corner-shop for years, and I'm not thrilled by all the boutiques and interior decorators. We all still go to the dentist above what is now Shepherd Foods, and I'm almost reconciled to the pet-food shop now we have a dog. I don't think it's necessarily better, and I don't think it's necessarily worse. I don't in fact think I'd want to live here because it no longer feels quite real, but we still enjoy visiting. We walk our dog on the Hill, have ice-creams at Cachao and buy books from the wonderful Primrose Hill Bookshop. I am thrilled to see that primroses have at last been planted on one side of the Hill. The equipment in the playground is luxurious beyond the dreams that we had then. My children are convinced, just as I was, that they'll see Pongo and Missus from *101 Dalmatians* at the top of the Hill, that every lamppost might be the entrance to Narnia, and that Mary Poppins will float down at the end of one of the kites. As long as libraries like the one in Sharpleshall Street survive, other children will, too.

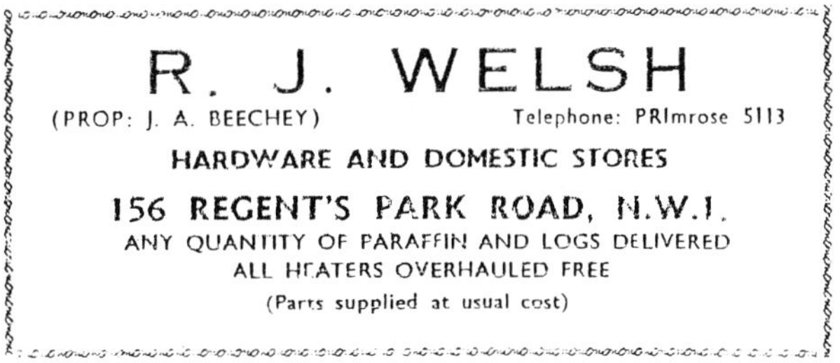
R. J. WELSH
(PROP: J. A. BEECHEY)
Telephone: PRImrose 5113
HARDWARE AND DOMESTIC STORES
156 REGENT'S PARK ROAD, N.W.1.
ANY QUANTITY OF PARAFFIN AND LOGS DELIVERED
ALL HEATERS OVERHAULED FREE
(Parts supplied at usual cost)

Advertisement from 'The Record' Vol. 6, 1960 *CLSAC*

Nora O'Donovan
Manley Street

My dad, Daniel O'Donovan came to this country in the fifties in search of work. He was the son of a farmer, and one of 15 children. In Ireland a landholding could not be divided, and went to a single heir, so members of large families were thrown on their own resources, and many emigrated.

For my father, a man with a family, the attraction of British Rail lay in the house that came with the job: a railway cottage in Manley Street, two-up, two-down, no bathroom, but a water closet. Though this was outside in the yard, it was an advance on none at all, as at home in the country. So my mother came over with three children and that is how I came to be born in Manley Street.

My dad was a train examiner, and based in Granby Terrace off the Hampstead Road. The maintenance shed was there, and when engines came in, all their systems were checked to see they were working, before they went out. The days of steam must have been over – I've no recollections of dirt, smuts or soot!

Two Commotions stand out in my childhood! First the Fire. It was 8 in the morning – I was in the charge of my 13-year-old brother, Bernard – and standing in my nightie, with my back to the kitchen fire. 'Don't stand so close to the fire' he said – and then – 'you're alight!'. I thought he was joking – but I felt the heat in my leg and put down my hand. Then, as he told the papers: 'I picked her up, put her in the sink and turned on the tap until the flames were out. Then I wrapped her in a blanket'. He put me on the bed upstairs and went out to phone – working-class people didn't have phones then any more than they had cars. The ambulance came. I asked the ambulance man if he was taking me to hospital and he said 'no' but this was not true – I went to Great Ormond Street where they bandaged me up and sent me

Railway Cottages, Manley Street *HP*

back home to mum and dad.

Bernard received an award for his bravery from the Mayor of Camden. I owed my life to his presence of mind and quick action. He himself was not to live beyond the age of 20 – he was killed in a car accident.

The second Commotion happened about the same time, when I took the initiative and went to school! I had a friend, Jessica, about a year older than me, and we played in the street every day: then one day she wasn't there – she wasn't there any more, because she had gone to school. So I went off to school myself – I made my way into a classroom full of children. They let me sit down and join in, but they did not know who I was or where I'd come from! Eventually my mother turned up and took me home, but the next day I did it again, and again, until the teachers said 'let her stay' and I went in every day. I was then about four.

One more story about times in Princess Road: Mick Jagger lived there at the start of his career. My sister who was 10 years older remembers him well, but my recollections are hazy. Dad used to drink in the Albert, and, according to him, whenever Mick Jagger went in he used to buy everyone a drink. Dad really liked him and years later, whenever he was mentioned, dad would recall this, and there would be this old Irishman going on about Mick Jagger – this real rebel into rock and roll.

In the school holidays – Easter and Summer, we children went off to Ireland, where there were loads of different aunts and uncles to stay with. My mother stayed at home because of her job.

Then, when I was about eight, came the news that Manley Street was to be demolished and we would all be moved. Camden's reason was the outside toilets and the lack of bathrooms, but young as I was I realised Manley Street was a good place to be – it was safe – it was friendly – we all had the railway background. People were upset and anxious about having to move. No promises were made about keeping us all together. We were all dispersed to whatever place was available.

We moved to a flat in a block in Islington: its large bathroom was in its favour – an end to the tin bath in front of the kitchen fire. But the upheaval amounted to severe culture shock. Manley Street was quiet: the people were friendly: I could play safely in the street: we knew every one: we were a long established group: I was happy at school.

Next thing we were in a block on a big council estate, among aggressive people, and I was at a really rough school (a primary!) where I was picked on, and my life made a misery by bullying. After a year my mum got me into Blessed Sacrament in Copenhagen Fields, where I was happier. We could see too some of the reasons for trouble on the estate: you get a few big families who dominate: they write graffiti everywhere: they hang about: they bring the place down and ruin it for everyone.

We just longed to get back to Primrose Hill – and when we'd been there about a year – my parents realised and asked for a transfer back to our original borough, Camden. Eventually we got a move to Somers Town, which has quite a hard reputation but is not that bad. The people in our street were friendly: it was fairly quiet and by the time we got there –in the seventies – bathrooms were more common!

I got a place at La Sainte Union. Things were different there. The nuns really had control: they didn't take any backchat or nonsense. There was the Saturday Morning Detention – you had to get up at week-day time, put on your uniform, travel to school and work on an assignment till 1.00 p.m. They were good at stamping out bullying too – they talked to you and made you really think about what you were doing. There was the religious aspect as well – they would ask you whether you were going to turn your back on God. Every school should have a few nuns!

Recently I've made two friends who live in Primrose Hill, and gone back to visit. It's the place I came from – I have these memories – but there is no one who knows me. The school is still there, the pubs are still there but the people are strangers. The old community has gone without trace.

Alison Langan
Dora Wilner

Many Primrose Hill residents will remember Dora who lived at 5 Chalcot Road.

I will never forget her. Dressed in black, with wonderful white hair, she would wander around Chalcot Road. Making her way to St Mark's Square, she would occasionally manage to board a 74 bus, and to the amazement of the conductor and passengers, she would urge the driver to take her to Vienna!

I first met Dora when she was attempting another of her poignant searches for her mother. She was then over 80, obviously vulnerable, as she suffered from Alzeimer's Disease. As I walked her back home, she insisted on singing to the customers sitting outside the lower Queen's Pub. Tony, the publican, and Mickilova had always been kind to her, and indeed had sometimes invited her in to play the piano. This venue was somewhat different to those where Dora had performed in her former career as an opera singer.

With her beloved husband, Gerhart Wilner, a brilliant pianist, she fled from the Nazis in the Second World War, and settled in Egypt immediately after leaving Vienna. Later they made their way to Australia, eventually settling in this country, where they much enjoyed life in Primrose Hill.

They had performed and taught in several countries before the war, and continued to do so. Among their shared interests was a love of animals. Gerhart became a Fellow of the Zoological Society, and many happy hours were spent in the Zoo.

One of Dora's former students was Dr Clare Anderson, who had lived in Princess Road. She had become a friend, and as Dora became increasingly frail, she made contact with Mrs Isabel Friedman and other friends of the Primrose Hill Neighbourhood Advice Centre (at that time based on the corner of Manley Street and Chalcot Road).

They brought Dora's plight to the attention of the Medical and Social Services, and she was assessed and placed in a residential Care Home. However, attempts to introduce Dora to a 'safer' way of life in care were doomed.

Dora Wilner and friends at a Summer Festival, 1980s *Alison Langan*

Dora ran away from two homes that the Social Worker had worked so hard to find for her, and returned to her flat and the local community. There her friends came up with a solution to support her. In spite of the acknowledged risks, it was decided she should continue to live in her own home, and would have 'hands on carers', with Social Service input.

I was invited to be one of the carers, and in this way Dora was enabled to live for several more years in her own home and to die there. That this was possible was due largely to the enormous understanding and goodwill of her two downstairs neighbours, Duncan and Fiona Mil, who would often hear her singing or indeed calling out during the night: many other friends and neighbours also contributed to her care.

Towards the end of her life Dora would sit on a chair outside her home and sing or call out to passers-by. She would be thrilled when neighbours, particularly children, stopped to chat.

Speaking personally, the experience of caring for Dora allowed me the confidence to train and qualify as a social worker. I have been able to call on this practical experience, as well as theoretical knowledge, when training and advising professional carers: for I have learned that efforts of individuals to understand people with dementia can succeed at a profound level.

Dora, this once gifted and proud woman, was aware that she was loved and valued by her carers, and I am proud that Primrose Hill as a neighbourhood has this concern for those who are frail and vulnerable.

Diana Gurney
Living by the Canal

I had been interested in the canal from the moment I saw my house and it was one of the reasons I bought it. In 1965 an engineer, Lewis Braithwaite, wrote an article in *The Times* called *Across St Pancras by Punt* and it was the story of how he had gone with a friend from a mooring near the Zoo at the Cumberland Basin and had crossed the whole of the Borough, through the locks, in their punt right down to King's Cross. They said how neglected the canal was and that everybody turned their back on it. I was then living by the canal and I'd ridden my bicycle on the towpath as far as Limehouse. It wasn't open to the public then but nobody stopped me and I loved it.

We discussed this article at a Civic Society meeting and we agreed to respond to it, for we were interested in the canal. That was how the Canal Group was set up. We got in touch with the people fronting the canal and with all the amenity societies covering the areas that it went through – The Paddington Waterways Association, The St Pancras Civic Society, The Islington Society, later The Hackney Society; later still The Tower Hamlets Society. Fairly quickly the GLC had its own Canal Committee and then the Greater London Archaeological Society came into it. We called ourselves the Regent's Canal Group. We didn't have a constitution since all these organisations had their own. John Hulton got the maps from the Town Hall and we marked up on them the land uses adjoining the canal as it flowed through our patch.

It was then pretty derelict in places and in 1967 we produced a booklet called *The Regent's Canal – A Policy for its Future* and the Civic Trust gave us money towards its production. We campaigned for the opening of the towpath and eventually British Waterways agreed to open it up to the public. It was a marvellous asset for the area and it was lovely to walk along it, no matter what the season was. Now, however so many people moor along it and there is so much litter and graffiti that I sometimes wish we'd never succeeded.

Christine Porter
Communal Living in the Sixties

Back in the early sixties, some friends and I (myself and two females) bought a house in Primrose Hill. How did we manage to do this with no money? One of the friends managed to persuade her family bank to lend us the money – as long as we paid the interest and eventually the borrowed sum! Of course we failed dismally to pay more than the interest and so we only owned the house for about four years in all. However it was a very interesting four years and many interesting things came of it.

The house was number 174 Regent's Park Road, on the corner with Berkley Road. We bought the house from a Cypriot gentleman who had been running it as a shirt factory or sweatshop – the whole house was full of sewing machines including a converted garage in the garden. The house was in a fairly bad state of repair.

My contribution to our project was going to be a practical one. I had recently been an art student: my main skills had been applying paint and making stained glass. I felt at that stage that I knew a great deal more than I actually did (I now realise)! Everything had to be done on a shoestring, we could not afford luxuriance in the form of central heating for example. The house was basically stripped out, cleaned up, repainted mostly white, new floor boards where rotten, and polished up. We then went to auction sales to buy nice old furniture and old oriental rugs to furnish the rooms we intended to let hopefully to 'interesting' people. I suppose this was an early version of a sixties 'commune' we thought we were inventing! One of us had recently studied at the Cordon Bleu cookery school and wanted to set up a Cooking – then Home Delivery Service from our basement, and a Cookery School, so lots of second-hand gas stoves were installed, and large wooden real kitchen tables etc. There were already there some ancient wine cellars ready to be filled!

The ground floor rooms were quite grandly arranged and decorated (there were a pair of rather nice black slate fireplaces – after we had stripped off all the paint layers, and very little else). Our plan was to let out this room for people to hire for parties or wedding receptions. We did this for a while until we realised that it was very hard work (very messy cleaning up stamped in wedding cake and spilled drinks, etc.) for very little reward. We decided to divide the L shaped room and let it, as the rest of the house was already filling up with students. Meanwhile the Cookery School and Food Delivery was chugging on quite nicely.

There were four student rooms upstairs and now two on the ground floor, one basement room and the converted garage 'studio' and another studio at the side which had flying buttresses and a glass roof, long and narrow, and a cement floor – perfect for a sculptor we thought. I used this space to make two stained glass windows for WCs and a bathroom at the house – two of which are still there.

The house has a nice courtyard, which had a boring cement surface. One of our sculptors suggested we should make a large tiled mosaic to cover the cement area. I could not wait to begin: – following his instructions we began this mammoth task. It was rather a wet summer that year, so I think it was not quite all finished by winter, and continued next summer. The design was quite influenced by the artist, Fernand Léger, I seem to remember. Now 30 years on, some of the mosaic is gone as the new owners have added a conservatory, thus reducing the courtyard ground, but I have been back to replace the new edges which rejoin the new building and create some new sections. Happily, they still like the old mosaic. By now the courtyard is very beautiful, as all the plants and trees have matured, and the little studio house has a beautiful tiled roof.

Our third partner in the project was Flora, a Rumanian writer who had been married to Stavros Papastavrou and lived in Cambridge for many years, as a don's wife. Flora was a wonderful hostess, and was used to being surrounded by students. She was a very good cook, and besides working at her writing and translating, was also running the guest house side of things. The house was always buzzing and interesting people were coming and going.

One of the sculptors who worked afterward in the studio was Norman Mommins from Hampstead, where he lived with Patience Gray, the writer. Norman was Flemish originally and was mainly a stone-carver, but he also produced prints and wrote and illustrated children's books. Patience wrote for many years for the *Observer*, and also made silver and gold jewellery. After some years they became very involved with Italy, going to work near the marble quarries, they decided to settle in Calabria, where I believe they still are.

João Cutileiro was a young Portuguese sculptor who had worked at the Slade and used to come for six months each year, living at the house and working in the studio. I know that now many hotels and public buildings in Portugal have work by Cutileiro, besides many private collectors.

Elizabeth Fritzch the potter lived in Ormonde Terrace and was studying music at this time. She was just beginning to get interested in working with clay. She hired the garden studio and would appear from time to time and work for a while quietly on building mysterious things in clay. She brought with her medieval Welsh stools to sit on and always wore a black cloak. She was from Wales, I think. She is now very well known in the pottery world and makes very beautiful hand-built sculptural pots.

There were several musicians at the house for a time. Oliver Broom, who sang opera, rented the garden room which he liked because his music would not annoy anyone. There was an elderly Bechstein piano there too (we later had to move it into the house as it appeared to be suffering from damp). When Oliver had a party, my offering to liven things up was the new and latest 45 rpm recording by a little known group called The Beatles – *Let it Be*.

The photographer, Edwin Smith, came to take photographs of the interior of the house – as he had heard it was interesting! There were many interesting people whose names I can't remember who passed through – it seems there were many interesting people about!

Opposite, the first shop was opened as a furniture/junk shop by Ron Weldon, and we bought many things from him for the house, and for a later project after we had moved.

Many of the 'ordinary' shops were being replaced by boutiques and shops selling trendy pine furniture. There were new eating places – I remember making a 'stained glass window' for a new restaurant near to Ron's shop. Manna, another new 'hippy' restaurant, was then just a place of plank tables, rice and beans! Sesame, likewise vegetarian, was the earliest Health shop in London, I believe.

After we had sold the house (to someone called Clutterbuck) we moved on, but I have always kept in touch with Primrose Hill and never really feel that I have left!

Edward Mustoe

Mustoe's Bistro

After military service in the Horse Guards, and some experience in management and accountancy, I knew I must follow my own way and I became self-employed as I had always wished.

In London at that time – the early sixties – a large number of new restaurants were opening. I had seen some of them, and I managed to find this property in Regent's Park Road. I already knew the area because my family had a flat in St John's Wood. Its character was changing at the time: property was cheap: young people were moving in, as well as many from more expensive areas like Chelsea. Those who sold up there could buy a house here and have a great deal of money to spare, so the outlook seemed promising.

It took me some three or four months to put the place together, and in that time I had got to know a great number of people, who were interested because there had been no restaurant here before. I served a mixture of English and continental food, but followed no national or ethnic style. There are fashions in food and people today have no interest in some of the dishes we served then. We used to make quantities of borsch, five or six gallons at a time – Russian soup of beetroot and cabbage: and what I call 'container dishes' – stuffed peppers and vol au vent. In those days that kind of thing went very well. Then a large number of fairly simple dishes were prepared in advance, whereas now they are fewer in number, but more elaborate, and mostly individually prepared. Not that people are prepared to wait an unreasonable time – that will lose you your customers – in fact a much higher standard of service is required. At that time I was the only restaurant between

Camden Town and St John's Wood: now 16 or 17 are in competition in Primrose Hill alone.

When a restaurant fails, as some do after a brief time, I would put this down to a misunderstanding of the local clientele. Property prices may be high, but it does not follow that its occupants have a large disposable income. If local residents do wish to eat expensively, they may prefer another neighbourhood, just as Odette's looks beyond the immediate area. More than one restaurant has had a shot at the top end of the market here but has failed to get it right.

At one time it was easy to fill the restaurant with your friends: when we were the only restaurant, I could look down a sizeable booking list and know exactly who everyone was, but this is no longer the case, though we have some regulars of more than 20 years standing. Gossip is the lifeblood of a small restaurant but the restaurateur must be the soul of discretion. On one occasion a regular customer brought two different ladies in succession to dine on the same night. He ate two meals, but less the second time round! We have entertained a number of celebrities on the way up, but once they 'arrive' we see them no more, nor on the way down! It is no secret however that we feature as 'The Shepherd's Crook' in Kingsley Amis's *The Folks That Live On The Hill.*

As for my own tastes in food – nothing insubstantial for me – beef complete with its fat – oxtail – pork chops cooked in the oven with onions, garlic and beans – treacle tart – apple crumble. Sometimes I'll make six treacle tarts – proper food. And I'll ring up various people who share my tastes and tell them in advance what I'm cooking and they'll come round and we'll eat together.

At one time I did all the cooking, but now I only cook on the chef's day off. Fortunately I can turn my hand to anything – repairs – plumbing – electrics – not gas, which is much too dangerous. I also have the great advantage of living over the 'shop'. No commuting!

It used to be possible to buy proper food in Regent's Park Road. There were two butchers here – a Belgian pork butcher and Mansons: another halfway down Chalcot Road and one in Princess Road: there were two greengrocers, Shearns and Phillips further along. On each side of me were shops that sold papers, sweets and tobacco: one was run by Ruby Sparkes, a retired cat burglar, who fell off a roof one day and could not pursue his trade any more: he sold his story to the *Sunday Dispatch.* There was also a car showroom here, whose repair business was conducted on the street!

The area has always been noted for the number of its pubs, and these have changed. The Queens once had a Saloon Bar and a Public Bar where beer was 3d a pint cheaper than in the Saloon: you could not buy mild ale in the Saloon, so it was the Public Bar for mild or mild and bitter. Such distinctions would not now be feasible in any pub that I know.

The Chalk Farm Tavern, now the restaurant Lemonia, was an old fashioned pub with a long history, but of no distinction. Behind the bar stood the landlord's aged mother, perpetually confused over orders and change. It later suffered a make-over, becoming Pub Lotus – named after a brand of sports car. The décor featured leather bucket seats, steering wheels and so forth, but the clientele was not the smart car crowd as hoped, and the racing car on display attracted thieves, who stole its parts.

The Pembroke was a solidly working-man's pub, as was the Engineer while the Lansdowne was Irish. It sometimes provided lunchtime entertainment in the form of strippers, or go-go dancers in a cage.

In those days there were many more people to a house: in Sharpleshall Street perhaps a family to a floor. When I came here, as far as possible you didn't attempt to shop in Regent's Park Road on Friday or Saturday: there were queues 10 or 12 long out of all the food shops.

The Express Dairy had a shop here, and their depot was at the back of the library, where John Hudson's recording studio is. During the war that was a torpedo factory, and there were enormous gantries and rails to move them out. Later stars like the Bay City Rollers recorded there, and ate at the Bistro: as did Primal Scream, much later.

Today life has become so respectable and bland …

Alan Bennett
Thank God for the Odd

One of the inevitable regrets one has when anyone dies is that he or she is no longer available to be questioned. It was only after my parents died that I realised how little I knew of their early lives and that it was now too late to ask. I didn't expect this to be the case, though, with John Leather. To me he was just a member … a colourful member of the cast of Camden Town eccentrics, a band to which in bleaker moments sometimes I think I myself belong – eccentrics like the late William Roberts, the Vorticist painter, a round, seemingly jolly, apple-cheeked man who lived in St Mark's Crescent who, if you dared to cross his path, gave you a volley of abuse. You might also get abused by Miss Shepherd, the old lady who lived in a van in my garden. As society gets more homogeneous, it's a dwindling band, though lately I noticed there was a new addition in the woman who collected cardboard boxes and camped out in the old Plaza cinema doorway. Now the Plaza has gone and she with it.

Unlike William Roberts or Miss Shepherd, John Leather was, in the time I knew him, a gentle and benevolent presence. Sitting at my window working I would see him … or hear him since he was often singing … coming down the street in a variety of indeterminate loose-fitting garments and, if he was coming back from the market, with a sack over his shoulder. If he had been the mediaeval saint he sometimes looked like, the sack might almost have been his attribute. Sometimes, passing my house he would stop and lift the amulet he wore on a chain round his neck and lift it in the direction of the sun. I've no idea what he was doing or saying but I took it that he was calling down some sort of blessing upon me and my house and felt obscurely comforted by this.

I was encouraged too by his postcards … the most recent ones from Cairo where he seemed to go in the winter. They consisted, as most of his writings did of the words Mummy mummy mummy endlessly repeated, the space for any more informative message severely circumscribed. But there was generally a message there and it was thoughtful and encouraging.

The postcards would be signed Nancy and John Leather. Knowing nothing of his life

John Leather, early 90s *Peter Haxton*

I took Nancy to be his wife to the extent that when he died I wrote to Nancy saying I was sorry to hear of his death and that I would miss him. It was only when I read Anthony Symondson's obituary in *The Independent* that I realised I had been addressing my condolences to someone who herself was long dead and not John Leather's wife but his mother. But insofar as this testified to a sense of her continuing presence in the world I think John would have been pleased by that.

I said at the start how the dead leave no end of questions unanswered and it was Father Symondson's obituary that made me realise how many questions there were, or topics at any rate which we could have talked about. I never knew, for instance, that John came from Ilkley a place I know well, that he had acted with Gielgud, been taught by Gertler and Meninsky, painters I admire, and that John Minton had designed for the touring theatrical company John ran in the years after the war … a time which still seems quite vivid to me but which is now history and with fewer and fewer survivors.

In some ways John reminds me of another figure, more exotic … and certainly more kempt … but whose background was very similar and that is the writer Ronald Firbank. Like John he came of well-to-do parents, with the money one generation made in business the next generation squandering on art. Both came from the north but hardly belonged there; both of them were determined to live life according to defiant aesthetic principles and were enabled to so because of parents who were probably more understanding than they were given credit for. Firbank's legacy was a clutch of exotic novels, John Leather's is less permanent but that's how I would like to think of him, as he holds up his medallion to the sun and calls down blessings upon us … the Firbank of Primrose Hill.

A measure of how civilised a society is lies in the way we treat our eccentrics and it's sad that as people grow more conscious of appearances so eccentrics grow fewer. So we should celebrate John Leather, singing and dancing on Primrose Hill, for a kind of courage. I'm tempted to say I hope there will be more like him but I can't imagine that will ever be the case.

Eulogy first given on the occasion of John Leather's death in 1997 – and revised by the author for this book.

Marjorie, Viscountess St Davids *The Pirate Club*

The club was started as a boating club for boys and girls by my late husband, Jestyn, Viscount St Davids. We bought our house in St Mark's Crescent in the early sixties because it was on the canal, and we had often been past in our boats. At that time the canal was closed to the public, and the towpath was rough and stony (to be paved later when an electric cable was installed along the path). We kept our boats (a Thames camping punt and two dinghies) at the bottom of the garden. But closure means nothing to small boys and we regularly had requests 'Can I row your boat, Mister?'. We had a succession of boys and girls in our garden enjoying our boats and my husband taught them to row properly. Numbers grew and he decided to make a club of it. He acquired a huge Thames barge and brought her up from Brentford with the aid of child power: those who were not inside cleaning her out were towing with ropes on the towpath – an all day job.

The club, at that time called the Regent's Boat Club, was roofed (free) by the local dustmen with clear corrugated heavy plastic. We had a large wood-burning stove to keep everyone warm and dry, fuelled by wood collected by the children from the canal – in itself a warming task. The club ran happily from the barge *The Rosedale* for some years, but obviously something better had to be acquired. My husband ran it personally with minimal help, in between his daily duties at the House of Lords. Although not an architect, he spent many months designing a castle to replace the barge – doing the job properly on squared paper. Seiferts used his design and built the castle to his plans (free of charge) although we raised funds for the materials. It had to be secure and strong and was a proper castle with battlements etc. A free site on the edge of the canal (at what were then Chalk Farm Locks but are now known as Camden Lock) was secured by my husband's negotiation with a Jewish charity, which owned the strip of land. The castle was opened by Robin Knox Johnson (the round the world yachtsman), and the site agreed by

Camden Council for a peppercorn rent. The peppercorn was handed over in a velvet box to the Council representative, who said he would have it audited.

Later, the Lord Mayor of London, in full regalia, came to the castle, accompanied by the Sheriffs and their ladies. It was my job to look after the latter, and we rowed them to the castle in a flat-bottomed pontoon, with musicians playing away. By prior arrangement the Lord Mayor was thrown into the dungeon, and peered through the bars until ransomed by Shell for a tidy sum.

Later again, when we had acquired a narrow boat, *Pirate Princess*, to take children for holidays up country on the canals, Prince Charles came to launch her and, to his alarm, was asked to take the helm. He spoke to lots of children and everyone had a very good day. We now have a second narrow boat and the club asked me if they might name it *Pirate Viscount* after my late husband, which I took as a great compliment.

One nice touch – we were walking up Parkway years later when we ran into a couple of huge young men who greeted us with bear hugs. One, half Polish, said 'you were always telling us about your plans for a castle, and I was walking along the towpath recently with my mate and, forgive my language, I said to him "The sod done it"!' A happy phrase which entered into our family language.

The Pirate Castle opened by Robin Knox Johnson, 1977 *HP*

Jean Rossiter
A Sense of Community

In 1960, having lived all my life in Tottenham, I began to look for a flat closer to my work near Oxford Circus. One day a colleague suggested Primrose Hill. 'Where's that?' I asked, to be told 'It's a small area north of Regent's Park that's pulling itself up by its boot-straps'. A friend of his had bought a five-storey Victorian house and was busily converting the top floor into a self-contained flat. I saw it, we negotiated a rent and, in the summer of 1961, I moved into 4 Princess Road, where I lived very happily for seven years.

Opposite the house, on one corner of Kingstown Street was the Post Office, with letterbox outside. Years later I took part in the campaign to keep the Post Office open – collecting signatures on a petition and monitoring hourly the number of its customers. Unfortunately the campaign failed, and all the business moved to the Post Office in Regent's Park Road.

To the left was the entrance to the Nurses' Home, which occupied four or five large houses in Regent's Park Road. Here a coach would draw up morning and night, taking nurses to and from their shifts in the London Clinic. My flat looked down on the lawn that stretched behind these houses to the canal, beyond which I could see the gardens of the houses in St Mark's Crescent, including one bestrewn with statues, occupied by Clive Jenkins, the Union leader. The Nurses' Home has since mainly been converted back to individual dwellings.

I loved my walk to work each morning through Regent's Park, where from the Broad Walk the day was brightened by the sight of the flame-pink flamingos clustered round their pool. There must be few places in the world where one can wake to the song of the blackbird and the squawk of seagulls, and later in the day, hear the roar of lions at feeding time or, sometimes, echoing round the Hill, the clip-clop of horses from St John's Wood Barracks.

I used the shops in Princess Road, but most frequently I would cut through the network of little streets, Egbert Place, Manley Street, Kingstown Street and Calvert Street, on my way to the library. These four little streets criss-crossed the terraces of small two-up, two-down houses, originally called Railway Cottages, built for nineteenth century railway workers in the 1860s.

While living in Princess Road, I bought my first car and was able to park it easily outside the house. Petrol I could get at the garage on the corner of St George's Mews in Regent's Park Road, and my car was serviced in a little garage in the mews in Fitzroy Road. Now called Fitzroy Yard, this area was also occupied by tumble-down workshops and storage sheds.

Although very happy in Princess Road, in 1967 I decided it was time to buy a house of my own. I was determined to stay in Primrose Hill, though small houses were few. I was lucky: one of the seven remaining in Manley Street came on the market. It was built in 1868, as the initials and date on my back room window testify. With a mortgage and generous improvement grants from Camden Council, I was able to buy it.

When I moved into Manley Street, I did not know that planning permission had been given some years before to clear the workshops, storage and garages that lay beside Primrose Hill Studios, between Manley Street and Fitzroy Road. Developers had already moved in and, by the time I was there a modern and ugly office building had been erected. I disliked it, and still do. However, from my roof patio I could watch artists at their desks busily designing Christmas and birthday cards – for the first occupant of this building was Gordon Fraser – of greeting card fame. Industry yes – but not smelly or noisy. This site is now occupied by a large architectural partnership.

Before I left Princess Road, I had become a member of the St Pancras Civic Society, whose aims were to maintain and improve the environment in which we lived. Thanks to its activities the unity and attractive quality of Primrose Hill has been maintained. One of the Society's initiatives was to urge that particular areas be designated as conservation areas, each with its own 'watch dog' committee. This led to the establishment of individual committees for Primrose Hill and Regent's Park Conservation Areas.

Through the St Pancras Civic Society (later to become the Camden Civic Society) I became aware of the GLC's proposal to demolish the terrace houses in the enclave formed by Manley, Calvert, and Kingstown Streets, together with the terrace of larger houses in Chalcot Road between Calvert and Manley Streets. This whole site was to be covered by a square of four, five and six storey blocks of flats in traditional GLC design. Jonathan Sofer, Labour Councillor for the Ward, prompted by many local residents protested to such an extent that the GLC sold the site to Camden for about £1 million. Here we were on home ground and the lobbying continued. Local residents were anxious above all to save the houses in Chalcot Road, most of which were already multi-occupied, while Camden's main concern was to keep costs down, and to maintain a high density of living units for the site.

Local architects, drew up a completely new design, which kept the Chalcot Road houses, and intermingled terrace houses and flats in an attractive maze behind them. This led, after some amendment and much negotiation, to the present Auden Place. The design of this estate brought architectural acclaim and many visitors to the area – vindication for the commitment of local people.

The Environmental Scheme was another cause that brought us all together: the Council proposed to pedestrianize Regent's Park Road from Primrose Hill Road to Gloucester Avenue together with the horseshoe formed by Berkley Road, Sharpleshall Street and Chalcot Square. The Scheme roused all who lived in the vicinity but it pitted commercial interests against those of the residents; and Gloucester Avenue residents, where traffic was to be diverted, against those in Regent's Park Road, who vainly sought relief from increasing traffic.

The tussle lasted for months with several noisy public meetings but a compromise was eventually reached. An area at the top of Chalcot Square was cobbled and 'landscaped' with a few shrubs and seats, and cars were prevented from going from Chalcot Road to Regent's Park Road, via Chalcot Crescent and Sharpleshall Street or Berkley Road; the Railway Bridge was closed and traffic was prevented from continuing along Gloucester Avenue at Cecil Sharp House.

Fitzroy Yard: Architecture in the 1970s *Virginia Smith*

Since coming here I have seen many changes – especially in the shops in Chalcot Road. In the sixties the Manley Street corner shop was owned by Mr Hutchings, a butcher, who with his partner trained at Harrods. They had lovely cuts of meat, and would willingly bone, stuff and roll a shoulder of lamb on request. They were open very early in the morning, so that if you had forgotten to buy enough bacon for breakfast, it was possible to buy some there. I was so sad when I heard that the very day after Mr Hutchings retired he had a heart attack and died.

Almost next door to the butchers was a café – a good 'pull-up-for-car-men' where from early morning there would be a queue of telephone repair vans outside, waiting while their occupants stopped off for 'a cup of tea and a wad'. Sometime later this became a small restaurant run by a former architect who much preferred cooking. And good cooking it was, too – even if one did enjoy it on rough wooden tables and sat on old church pews. He did very well and, after a few years, left to set up a bigger restaurant in the country. The French restaurant that followed it was equally good until it decided to go 'up-market' and introduced linen napery – and higher prices. By that time the Greek restaurant Fanari's had established itself on the corner of Fitzroy Road, since when this spot has always been a restaurant. Fanari's was a great success, full each night mostly with people from the immediate locality who enjoyed the Greek food at reasonable prices. When Fanari's closed down it was followed in quick succession by Café Rouge, the Gourmet Coffee Shop, Basilica and, currently, The Black Truffle.

Chalcot Road shops have changed hands repeatedly, notably to ones with less local appeal that depend largely on advertising in a wider market – a couture milliner and dressmaker, a specialist cheese shop and a cabinet maker, for example. Only Clare's Kitchen, Nisha's General Store, Christine Hairdresser, Dominic's Hardware Store and the Newsagent meet the needs of local people.

Towards the end of the sixties when, with the redevelopment of the piano factory in Fitzroy Road, the opportunity arose to obtain what was sorely needed in the area – a hall for meetings and other community activities, a public meeting was held, and Primrose Hill Community Association was formed. Early activities were mainly concerned with raising interest in the community and with deciding how the Community Centre – if we got it – could be used. In those early days we had some lovely parties by courtesy of Auden Place residents who gave us a home until the Hopkinsons' Place building was finished.

Once we had our own building in 1981, the activities of the Association expanded. There were twice-weekly youth clubs for all ages from seven to 16; an over sixties club; a members evening with a variety of entertainments; a drama group which put on some superb pantomimes and every excuse was taken to have a party – Hallowe'en, New Year and St Patrick's night.

Each year there was a Summer Festival and sports day on the Hill, and then the Bonfire and Fireworks Display five months later, all organised by local people. The first really notable Summer Festival was devoted to the Victorian period when we had Queen Victoria arriving in a yellow vintage Rolls Royce and rides around the area in an old open-top bus. This was followed by 'When North West One Was Won' devoted to Cowboys and Indians with horses performing and a real sheriff with his whip and lasso. Then there was the theme of 'Primrose Hill on Sea'. They were splendid affairs and everyone dressed up appropriately. The stalls and side-shows extended from the top of Chalcot Road, over the whole of the Square and as far as Fitzroy Road. There was music and dancing and side shows for all ages. Hundreds of people came.

For several years, on the Sunday following the Summer Festival, there was a Sports Day on the Hill with parents and children taking part in many sporting activities. The highlight of the day was the inter-pub tug-of-war when almost all of the pubs in Primrose Hill mustered a team of big, brawny men.

The other annual event was Bonfire Night on the Hill. We dreaded the possibility of rain; for insurance premiums were far too high and meaningless for us to consider - yet we'd paid thousands for the fireworks – in advance. Despite the potential for accidents only one, that I know of, ever took place. That was to Keith Bird the then organiser who tripped and fell back into the bonfire. There was another near-disaster however when the tapers to light the fireworks failed to ignite and Keith and his team had to light each one with a pocket lighter – certainly a case of 'light the blue paper and retire immediately' for all concerned. For an amateur production those early days were a great success – and tremendous fun.

The Primrose Hill Community Association was a wonderful force fusing the community together. All its activities; parties, festivals, bonfire and fireworks were organised and run by local people, and we loved it. I made lots of friends through it: friendships that have long outlasted our participation in its activities.

Finally, a word about the Hill itself. For many, dashing to work by bus or tube, it provides a quiet, pleasant start to the day. At weekends it offers a wonderful place for those who live in bed-sitters or studio flats in the locality to stretch their legs, while in the summer the grass is almost entirely covered by a colourful pot-pourri of reclining bodies intent on sunbathing or picnicking: to say nothing of the many tourists who climb the Hill to see the wonderful changing skyline, from St Paul's to the 'Eye'.

I became even more familiar with it in all its changing glories, when in 1985 my father and his dog came to live with me. Barney had his walk on the Hill at least twice a day. My father would spend many more hours there. Like so many elderly residents he had his favourite seat. When he died in 1991, I too spent more time there with Barney, and soon became a regular member of the dog-walking community. We all knew each other by sight, but more than that we knew each other's dogs - Freddie, Primrose, Chloe, Zara, Nipper, Beau, and Tom – to name but a few who seemed to be there at the same time. Vary your arrival by only 15 minutes and you were part of a different dog population.

Some time after 1987's destructive storm, which had decimated the number of trees there, the Park Managers invited people to buy and plant a tree on the Hill for £100; there was no shortage of takers. My family all contributed to the cost, and in 1997 we planted an oak tree in memory of my father and the many happy hours he had spent there. I know of several other local residents who have commemorated a loved one or special event in this way - and long may it continue.

Victorian Summer Festival, 1980s

Virginia Edwards
Let us Spray

When the one-way traffic system was introduced in Camden High Street (late sixties?) it naturally enough caused great unrest in the residential streets surrounding the business area, as they foresaw that these hitherto quiet streets would have to bear the burden of a great deal of the displaced traffic. Regent's Park Road Residents' Association was started, to express residents' views and try to ensure that the new traffic flow was not too excessive. A protest demonstration was organised, and got off to a fine start with a trumpet solo from a young musician.

Virginia Smith

The parade along Regent's Park Road was very jolly, and enlivened by one resident who roared along the road in his car encouraging the protesters – then raced home, changed clothes and car and raced back up the road the opposite way, protesting against the protesters.

The then vicar, Michael Dean, suffered, as many did, from the increased lack of parking space and was often inconvenienced by people parking across the entrance to his driveway. I asked him once why he didn't ask for help from the police and he said that they were unable to help in that situation, and I suggested that he ask for a 'No Parking' white line to be painted on the road outside his house, but he said again that the traffic police wouldn't arrange it. I suggested that he paint the line himself, and he said he'd thought of it, and even bought the white spray paint to do it, but thought it would be illegal and therefore not fitting for a vicar. I suggested that a grateful parishioner might do it for him, and he looked the other way and handed over the spray can.

As an artist I would not have chosen spray paint for the job but was reluctant to waste it. As a conscientious craftsman I went out at midnight that night to wash the strips of road I intended to paint, and then went home again to wait until they dried. About 2.00 a.m. armed with a newspaper to mask off the area each side of the strips, stones to hold the newspaper down and the spray can I went out to do the job. No cars, no people, no sound. I placed my newspaper and my stones. Then from far off I heard a car engine coming my way. I discreetly merged with the bushes to wait for it to pass. It ambled slowly along, closer and closer and drew near to the kerb at the house next to the vicar's, very nearly touching my newspaper. Three inebriated young men got out. I emerged from the bushes and asked if they would mind moving the car back as I wanted that bit of road. They asked what I wanted it for and I said I wanted to paint white lines on it. And the reply was a phrase I had never expected to hear in real life.

They said 'Crazy, man!'

Elizabeth de Kerbrech & Christine Kay
Needles and Pinz

Both came to live in the area – King Henry's Road (Liz) – Regent's Park Road (Christine) in the sixties.

Liz on her marriage lived in St Edmunds Terrace, Primrose Hill, for 14 years, and moved in 1963, to King Henry's Road – still her home. 'I fell in love with a lovely great tree that grew in the garden, but sadly it had to be felled later because its roots were thought to be undermining walls…'.

On the opposite side (the railway side) a number of houses belonged to British Rail and railway men lived there until Dr Beeching had them sold as part of his programme of railway cuts and closures in the sixties. He had been seconded from the Coal Board to make British Rail pay.

Liz's son, François, went to school at Quinton Grammar, and his tolerant, if sometimes amazed parents had first-hand experience of the sixties teenage revolution.

'Our lovely son, without warning – overnight it seemed to us – became a rock and roll raver – the leader of a gang, and a follower of fashion: if anyone was dirty, he would be the dirtiest: ragged jeans in fashion – as ragged as possible – and when it came to bouffant hair!

'I'd said to my husband "whatever he does, don't be surprised – just ignore it" – so when we returned after two days away, we opened the door and there he was with this big bouffant hair: I merely asked "nice weekend, darling?".

'However, unfortunately, it could be neither ignored nor combed. His girl friend had back-combed it so much, and used such quantities of lacquer that it had become impenetrable. It began to itch – but he could do nothing: he had to admit defeat and appeal for help. I tried my best – but it was solid – impossible. In desperation we had to cut the whole thing off: it was really dreadful.

'Then one day he said to me "Can I have a white T-shirt and a black leather jacket?": and I thought "how wonderful". Before he could change his mind I took him off to Great Portland Street and we came away with three nice white T-shirts and the black leather jacket. I was happy, but not for long. Three days later as I turned his mattress. I saw this black soggy mass beneath. It was the expensive jacket: now being pressed, after a soaking in the bath to achieve the proper scruffy look!

'The whole phase ended as suddenly as it began. He acquired a girl friend and everything changed almost overnight. Hours were now spent in the bathroom: it was virtually monopolised. But everyone was happy!'

Christine too was at school in the sixties, and walked daily to Parliament Hill School and back, but she was not one for teenage rebellion!

'I arrived here in the fifties from Cyprus as a baby. My parents lived in Camden Town for a while, and mum took a job at Cecil Sharp House in a tiny canteen, making snacks and sandwiches. ITV used the big hall for rehearsals so mum met all sorts of celebrities of the time – including the Beatles, the Tiller Girls (a glamorous troupe of dancers), Sid James (the comedian) Bruce Forsythe, and many others.

'It was dad who picked on the empty shop at 55 Regent's Park Road. It was all black inside, and empty, except for a pair of scales and a big ledger, with one surviving page, headed SUGAR, followed by a long list of names and local addresses, many in Chalcot Crescent. He guessed that this must refer to wartime rationing, and that the shop had been a grocer's. It was here that mum opened her famous haberdashery shop in 1963.'

Haberdashery covers everything needed for sewing, dress-making, knitting, darning, mending etc. For example, buttons, hooks & eyes, bias binding, cotton, thread, needles, elastic, tape and much much more – as well as baby clothes. It remained open for some 20 years, and when it closed everyone felt its loss and the loss of Mrs Kay.

Liz and Christine agree 'sixties Regent's Park Road was very different – no expensive shops or restaurants – instead greengrocers, grocers, butchers, Mr Griffiths' Welsh Dairy, a baker that baked marvellous bread, several sweetshops cum tobacconists and newsagents' all mixed in with small industries – an upholsterer, motor engineers – all kinds of things.' Eating out took place in Coffee Rooms or Dining Rooms – not restaurants of today's kind, 'Mustoe was the first of these.'

Stripped pine furniture was then the fashion: Liz remembers 'Keulamann of Keulamann's

Antiques, working out on the pavement, stripping away paint and varnish with steel wool – she was one of the first. My first dining room was all pine.'

Both Liz and Christine have fond memories of sweets and sweetshops: 'you chose your own mixture – quarters of whatever you fancied – not ready packaged.'

As Liz said 'each shop had an atmosphere of its own – and you went in for the atmosphere – not just to buy.'

Kay's Haberdashery decorated for the Queen's Jubilee, 1977 *Christine Kay*

Julia
Mid-Sixties
Primrose Hill

My parents married in 1955 and I arrived a year later. My father was from Pakistan, my mother English. They had difficulties finding somewhere to live. I don't know if it was because of the mixed marriage or because they did not have much money. My uncle found them three rooms in Ainger Road in a house, where five other families lived, all sharing one bathroom and one toilet. Upstairs lived two women, one of whom was always complaining at the noise I made. My mother was always telling me to be quiet so as not to upset her. There were two other families where the husbands had just come out of the 'nick'. The gas meter was constantly being broken into, and one of the men was strongly suspected of doing this, so we were always owing on the gas. He later went back to prison, I don't know what for. There was an old lady living in the basement, whom my mother would visit, but I don't recall ever seeing her. I suppose we were all families who might have had difficulty due to prejudice finding accommodation elsewhere.

The street was full of working-class families. I remember one family moving in who actually owned and lived in the whole house: this was considered quite an unusual thing.

Us children would play in the street. We liked to collect empty beer bottles and take them to the off-licence in Regent's Park Road to get money back on them. We would also go over Primrose Hill on our own. My best friend was Mary who lived across the road with her mother. One day we were in the park and a man approached us wanting to take our photographs, so we duly obliged. I remember my mother questioning me when I got home, telling me to stay away from strangers. But all us kids would play out in the street every day and went to the park on our own.

I remember getting our first fridge: before this my mother would keep the milk on the window sill. It was such a delight to have a fridge: my mother made ice lollies with squash and water. I thought this was wonderful. I also remember getting a telephone for the first time, this was another cause for great excitement. My mother and father would sleep in the living room on a sofa bed: this was bought on the HP as was our new carpet. My mother told my friends and me that the carpet cost 'a hundred pounds' and we were no way to drop anything on it. A hundred pounds was about the most money we could imagine, so we were very careful with the carpet.

My mother would take me round to shops in Regent's Park Road. I remember going into the dairy where a lady called Doris would always say to me 'Daddy gone to bed'. I used to get into a fury and state that daddy was at work and not in bed. There were loads of dairies then, mainly run by the Welsh, as I recall: they later changed to mini-markets, where you helped yourself.

I went to Primrose Hill Primary School: my mother would walk me down every morning and collect me afterwards. We would always get a doughnut or something from the baker's in Chalcot Road. Primrose Hill was a pretty multi-racial school, as was the whole area at that time. Lots of my friends were Greek Cypriots, and there were a lot of Irish families in the area as well. I remember we would have a Commonwealth day at school and in assembly they would have a child at the front representing each country. I would always want to be out there, but was never picked. There was one boy, Barry, whose parents were both British, so he always represented Britain. I never got to represent Pakistan either, because there was always at least one child from Pakistan.

Peter N. Clare
Thurston's of Sharpleshall Street

John Thurston, who had worked for Gillows (of Lancaster) established his business in 1799 in Catherine Street in the Strand, making them the oldest billiard business in the world. In 1814 the Company was incorporated and set up their factory at The Waterloo Works, Cheyne Walk, Chelsea.

In 1964 this site was earmarked for redevelopment and it was then the Company moved to Primrose Hill – 1/1a Sharpleshall Street. At that time it was a slightly run down area. At first it was both a shop and a factory, but in 1979 a shop was acquired at 220 Camden High Street.

The premises at Sharpleshall Street included the end house of the terrace and the workshop mews running to the rear of the houses. It had a narrow entrance leading down to a cobbled, yard which ran the length of the buildings.

On entering the passage the first part of the building housed the small shop and showroom on the ground floor, with the office situated above. Entering the shop was 'stepping back in time', with rolls of billiard cloth stored on the wall, and cues in racks on display: dart boards, bingo machines and lawn bowls equipment were also on offer. The rest of the building was the workshop. The ground floor was the factory, where Billiard and Snooker tables were made and renovated. It was mainly woodworking, handling the timber used in the construction of billiard and snooker tables. There was also work on the slates used in the tables. It housed the usual wood-working machines, circular saws and bandsaws, as well as a small polishing department for both hand and spray polishing. The first floor was a store, where the 36ft long lawn bowls test table was also kept. In the yard were garaged the three service vans driven by the Billiard fitters who installed and serviced tables at clubs and private houses all over the South-East and South-West of England. The three service fitters made up the total factory workforce of eight persons with a further four staff in the office and shop.

In 1983 the Sharpleshall Street house and mews were sold to purchase a larger factory site in Brecknock Road. By this time the Primrose Hill area was recognised as a fashionable district and probably not the right place for a woodworking factory to be.

Philip Gundry
Iron Bridge House

Towards the end of 1969 I bought and slowly moved into No.1 Bridge Approach. Bridge Approach by the rights of logic should be a continuation of Regent's Park Road but in fact it continues at right angles towards the Round House. At the end of my garden there was a grim mid-to-late Victorian orange brick building which seemed entirely deserted but in a good state of repair. I found a little later that in reality it had an elderly caretaker and an elderly cat. As a cat-lover I soon made contact and was given a guided tour of the building. The caretaker told me that it had once been a hostel for train-drivers on the route into Euston but for a number of years modern drivers had found the accommodation unacceptable. On the tour this became very understandable. Four floors of wooden cubicles stretching in every direction gave me a concrete image of what I had always imagined an old-fashioned Borstal to look like. Ablutions took place in a separate building located midway and to the front. Pretty chilly in winter!

Summer 1970, caretaker and cat disappeared. His flat at the south-east corner of the building became the playground of a group of pleasant youngsters. Unfortunately the numbers and the delinquency increased. It wasn't long before they had broken through into the main building and there was the occasional fire. (I put three out myself.) So I phoned British Rail to find out their intentions. It didn't seem they had any, so I proposed that it would make a convenient hostel for London University. (I myself am a UL academic though I teach at Imperial College, Kensington.) Two stops on the tube to University College, the Slade, Birkbeck .... I even thought I might add to my income by becoming warden. It was not to be. British Rail wanted more money than the University had at its disposal, but at least it was now clear that the old hostel was on the market and that we were entering a property boom! No

Iron Bridge House, Bridge Approach *Philip Gundry*

problem. Alas, the next fire occurred while I was abroad, and it was a big one. No more floors of cubicles, no roof or windows. But the boom was getting bigger too.

The next decade: I seem to have been endlessly courted by property development companies. In order to get permission for anything except a hostel, the developers needed more parking space. The first applicants were a pair of Lebanese doctors who wanted to turn the hostel into an abortion clinic. Then it was to be an hotel, a block of flats, an hotel again.... Some were even more ambitious and wanted No.1 as well. I was offered many times the purchase price, plus a mews house in Hampstead with more fully mirrored bathrooms (ceiling too) than any other kind of room. When escort services were mooted as well, I got scared. Then a more ordinary developer offered to take a 65-year lease on the back 20 ft of my garden. He planned flats and I agreed, and we became leaseholders.

After five years, rent on the garden ceased and I made the slightly alarming discovery that the only asset the company had was the 20 ft of garden. I lost interest. The other downside was that the now derelict hostel was occupied by alcoholics, drug addicts and other undesirables. I had 17 burglaries and two muggings during the time. Interest returned when suddenly I noticed activity was going on. Architects, plans, builders. The next I knew was that (with permission) a wooden wall was going up round my garden and I had learnt that there was a railway tunnel underneath running between No.1 and No.2 along the party wall. So Iron Bridge House was born. I think it had its problems too because the conversion was to 13 flats, complete with kitchens and bathrooms, and then Planning required that they be non-residential. We now have Carling Music and a string of Information Technology firms.

It is a pity that it is so hidden that few people know of its existence and contribution to the area's architectural beauties.

Diana Gurney
William Roberts: an Artist and his Family

I met them first in 1959 when collecting signatures for a petition concerning the location of the proposed new central library. They lived in St Mark's Crescent. I got to know Sarah first; she was a forthcoming person. She and her husband walked on Primrose Hill every evening, when she practised the Bates method of eye control. This meant focusing on objects alternately near and far and after a lifetime of this exercise she was told, at the age of ninety, that her eyes were good enough for an airline pilot. She was a marvellous woman and I enjoyed her company tremendously, as did everyone who knew her. She would ring up and say 'I'm dyeing today, is there anything you want done?'. She did dye several things for me. She always used natural colours, greens, browns and yellows. She used to take clothes to pieces, dye them, remake them and always looked wonderful. She had exquisite visual taste and everything in her house was beautiful.

I didn't know John their son very well until after Sarah died, because he didn't talk much when Sarah was there, but after her death I got to know him well. He was a poet and guitarist and had different areas of interest each in its own compartment. People he knew in one compartment rarely knew the others. He belonged to a poetry reading group in Kentish Town, and read his own poems there. As a guitarist he wrote for a guitar magazine and was writing a history of the guitar for which he learned Arabic, but sadly, it was unfinished when he died. He had begun life by taking a degree in Physics at London University and had done some job on merchant ships during the war, but didn't continue with such things. I asked him why he had studied physics and he replied 'because I thought I might learn the secrets of the universe'...'And did you?'...'No.'. He was very well read and had thousands of books. He collected editions of particular writers and was very knowledgeable. He was also a book dealer and knew that world very well.

William Roberts used to go out every day

The Artist at his easel with a painting of John and Sarah, c.1950-5 *The William Roberts Society*

with a sketch book and draw people in their various occupations. He had a dry wit and his drawings are very amusing. I once took Margery Cooper to a William Roberts' private view in Bond Street and she said 'I had no idea how funny he could be'. Sarah used to dress up for these occasions and look lovely in her self-designed clothes.

Before the war they lived in a house on Haverstock Hill which was later replaced by flats, but during the war they lived in Oxford and when they returned they rented a couple of rooms in St Mark's Crescent which was at that time a rather neglected street of houses multi-occupied by working people. Sarah said the house was a brothel when they went there but I don't know if that is true. Gradually they extended their occupancy as people moved out and finally acquired the whole house.

William's father was a carpenter and his son had obviously inherited his skills. He made the cupboards and arranged the shelves. All the rooms he and Sarah occupied – their living room with bedroom above and his studio at the front are as they left them, because it was the desire of Sarah and John that the house should become a William Roberts museum. A lot of his work was there when John died, but the Tate kindly took them into safe keeping. He was a Royal Academician and we hope the Academy will back the idea of a museum.

The Roberts were always hard up because William believed that good work would find its own market, but it doesn't. It has to be promoted. He became a recluse, though polite and amiable on occasions of contact. I once asked him if I could have some bricks which were piled outside his house and he urged me to take the better ones. Sarah was his intermediary and arranged his sales because he spent all his time working. He was working on the day he died, aged 84. He did wonderful portraits and every year did paintings of Sarah and himself. There are 60 portraits of each of them and some years ago the National Portrait Gallery held an exhibition called 'An Artist and his Family', showing paintings of himself, Sarah and John.

There is now a William Roberts Society dedicated to the greater knowledge of an important twentieth century English artist and to promote the museum project which would be an asset to the neighbourhood.

Vicky Lee
Just Extracts

I arrived in Primrose Hill in spring 1968, an eager new graduate of Leeds Dental School. My school friend Bridie had rented a flat at 43 King Henry's Road, and I was the seventh girl in a two bedroom flat. Since then I have always lived or worked in Primrose Hill.

I had been working in a practice in the City, and travelled from Primrose Hill Railway Station to Broad Street every day. My friends had been patients of the dentist above the garage, so when it came up for sale I decided it would be perfect for me. My intention was to study painting and work part time. Soon Angela Baldock who had been my assistant in the City came to join me and is now practice manager. We have worked together for over 30 years.

The patients of those days were fascinating:

- Mrs T used to arrive with a gift of the most wonderful butter ring cake that she had lovingly baked.
- William the dancer arrived with flowers picked from the gardens roundabout and had time to run errands for us.
- Miss Plum was growing her own dentures or so it appeared. Our beautiful teeth made down at Mornington Crescent by Austin Johns definitely didn't pad out her face like the stars she had worked for, so week by week she glued more pink 'snug' to her teeth and wrapped them round with black cotton. My dentures were never a patch on her art works.
- 'I have a lucky eyelash in my false teeth' said Mrs K (it was a bristle from a polishing brush embedded in the pink plastic), we of course never removed it.
- Mr A hated his teeth so much that he extracted them himself with electrical pliers and stuck a grubby elastoplast over his top lip to hide his efforts. The result was extraordinary.

Dentistry has changed we rarely see full dentures nor those colourful characters who were born before the First World War and for whom I could provide a full set of teeth for five pounds.

The mid-seventies brought the three day week and perpetual power cuts. Halfway through a filling, off went the lights, and the poor patients had to go home with teeth half filled. In those days our compressed air came included in the rent: we used the air that the garage used for the tyres!

Suddenly everything changed and the modern world arrived with lots of new equipment and techniques. The past was evoked for me the other day when a young man impatiently asked if I had finished checking his teeth. 'Yes', I replied 'they are fine'. He then thrust his hand towards me and asked me to read his palm and strangely enough I was able to oblige.

Veronica Brinton
The Advent of the Glitterati

I moved (up from Chelsea and Kensington) to Primrose Hill in 1964, to Albert Terrace. I remember the scheme to block Regent's Park Road to traffic. This was thwarted by a protest – from the shops. I also remember the proposal to lock the gates of Primrose Hill at night, and sat in to prevent this.

From 1967, until Primrose Hill Community Centre took over, I and my friends held the biggest firework party on the Hill each year – back to us for sausages and potatoes!

In 1973 I moved to Chamberlain Street, and subsequently (1976 or '77) wrote for *Vogue* magazine what I think was one of the first pieces, if not the first, about 'Primrose Hill Village'. The sixties and seventies were an extraordinary time – I worked for the magazine and my flat mate was photographer David Bailey's assistant at 177 Gloucester Avenue for years. The literati and glitterati were in and out of his house/studio and many shoots were done on Primrose Hill. For some of us, the recent new arrivals and attendant publicity make us smile.

The sixties and seventies were most enjoyably and appreciatively spent on and around Primrose Hill, and there's not much chance of improving on those times!

The Rocking Horse House, Regent's Park Road *Virginia Smith*

François Portier
The View from Versailles

My parents and I first came to Chalcot Square in the early seventies – we were looking for a holiday-let rather urgently, as the hosts we had relied on previously were suddenly unable to invite us and warned us at the last minute. We knew nothing about the Primrose Hill area of London then and were rather apprehensive – I immediately fell in love with Chalcot Square, though it took my mother a bit longer (now she more than shares my enthusiasm). It was so different from France and particularly the Paris area. The idea of having rows of family houses arranged around a square is so uniquely British – Continentals live either in flats when they reside in cities, or detached houses in the country.

The houses around Chalcot Square were still a bit neglected, but their gaily painted fronts and elegant architecture, the air of seclusion and tranquillity made them very attractive to me – this impression of aloofness from the bustle and noise of urban life has, if anything, been amplified over the years. The area has been closed off to traffic, Primrose Hill Railway Station is no longer in use, and of course 'gentrification' has quite perceptibly changed the atmosphere – the houses are all clean now, everything has been spruced up. Parts of Chalcot Road were still a bit rough in the seventies, it is certainly not the case now. And the trees have grown.

While the square and the crescent seem so peaceful, they are in fact extremely close to the centre of London and shopping has never been difficult. Parks are so close that it is always possible to take a relaxing walk or sit down on a bench and enjoy the scene. When I was a student and a researcher I often walked across Regent's Park to the British Museum and back after a day's work: walking was so restful after long spells

Chalcot Square in the snow, 1980s *Jean Rossiter*

sitting behind a desk and scribbling away.

It was in the nineties that change became most visible. Many of the familiar shops in the 'village' were replaced by trendy boutiques, galleries, restaurants and cafés. The metamorphosis must in retrospect have been less sudden than it appeared to us, but it cannot have taken more than two or three years.

It is a fact that prices have gone up quite abruptly in the area, and not just the price of houses. The opening of new supermarkets like Safeways and Sainsbury's within walking distance has compensated for this in some ways.

Some local 'institutions' like Primrose Hill Bookshop and the hardware shop, and of course the newsagents and Post Office remain, and may they endure for many years yet.

One of the most attractive features of the Primrose Hill area is its sense of community combined with a quite extraordinary, easy-going tolerance of eccentrics, and 'characters' – people respect each others' privacy, and are not intrusive, but never grudge a helping hand if it is called for. We miss George very much, his extrovert lifestyle and 'panache', combined with a good sense of humour never failed to impress us.

I wonder what our best memory of the area will be. One moment which I personally treasure is the good-natured celebration of the wedding of the Prince and Princess of Wales: the locals raising a pint at the pub near Primrose Hill and later, on that long, balmy evening, watching the fireworks from the top of the Hill. Nobody then could guess it would all end in bitterness and acrimony, and even the grouches joined in the fun. Perhaps we have lost some of that innocent good-will, or maybe this writer has grown older.

Whatever, we love Primrose Hill and the Chalcots and hope to return for many years to come.

Ramona Darvas
The Runaway Horse

Back in the mid-seventies, I recall an incident which was the talking point of the whole village for days. I was sitting by the front window of our house in Rothwell Street one afternoon when I heard the clattering of a horse's hooves and the sound of shouts. On looking up I saw a very small pony galloping past the window pulling a totter's cart piled high with all sorts of odds and ends – furniture, junk, pots, pans and rolled up bits of carpet – on top of which was precariously balanced an old bath rocking from side to side.

The pony and cart were followed by a man running as fast as he could and shouting loudly. At first I thought he must be the owner, but on reflection I realised he was far too well dressed to be a 'totter' or rag-and-bone man. I didn't take much notice of the scene until I heard a colossal crash coming from the direction of Chalcot Crescent. People started running past the window and, out of curiosity, I joined in. Near the junction of Rothwell Street and the Crescent, the Council had recently installed a metal barrier in a pilot scheme to stop the through traffic (a scheme which was very soon after abandoned). It had certainly stopped the pony in its tracks. Sweating and shaking, the poor animal was standing looking over the barrier having come to a very abrupt halt. The contents of the cart were strewn about and the bath had finally toppled off on top of a nearby parked car – doing neither the car nor the bath much good.

By this time a small crowd had collected at the scene. Someone produced an old blanket with which they covered the pony, another neighbour gave it an apple to eat: the man who had been doing the chasing caught his breath again and explained that he had seen the pony and cart going at full speed down Primrose Hill Road and had done his best to catch the animal. He said he had originally seen a man standing on the cart with a whip in his hand, lashing the pony to go faster and faster until he fell off. The horse and cart continued at great speed, crossing Fellows Road and dashing through the lights at Adelaide, miraculously avoiding the traffic.

While all this was going on, someone called the police, and in due course a fresh-faced young policeman appeared. Keeping his distance from the horse (of which he was obviously very scared) and taking out his notebook and pencil, he asked who was the owner. We all looked blankly at each other. I do remember suggesting that, by now, someone might have contacted the police station about the missing pony and cart, and this, indeed, is what had happened. A totter had left his horse and cart outside a pub in Hampstead while he nipped in for a bit of lunch and while he was inside, some drunk or lunatic had taken it into his head to have a free ride down the hill into Englands Lane and from there down Primrose Hill Road, where he eventually fell off.

Finally the concerned owner arrived at the scene in a police car, and was very relieved to find his horse alive and reasonably well after the adventure. He carefully inspected the horse's legs, thanked the donors of the blanket and the apple, and went on his way.

Glen Macdonald
Strippers at the Lansdowne

My cousins came from Kentish Town – I lived in Malden Road. One day in the seventies sometime my cousin Malcolm said to me: 'Let's go and watch some strippers'. I was about 15, – just about sneaking into pubs – to watch strippers was a fantastic idea! And the Lansdowne was a perfect pub for a fight – big velvet curtains – absolutely perfect! And there was a family of boys half way down Gloucester Avenue – an Irish family – a bit of a crew – a good outfit – and this was their turf!

A lot of boys from Queens' Crescent were going down there – it was a regular thing – this was Punk Rock days! And we'd have to run home – dodging the people from the Pembroke – across the Bridge – past the

Dumpton Place, Railwaymen's access to Camden Motive Power Depot - the Engine Sheds. The Lansdowne, next door opened for men coming off the early shift, and did a roaring trade. N.B. ASLEF slogan chalked on wall. *Derek Sprange*

Adelaide (now no more) to the Fiddler's Elbow in Malden Road, and there we felt safe.

So we went: the Lansdowne was nowhere like it is now. It was all heavy curtains, the girls would come round with pint jugs (you don't get them now) – it was metric though – 50p in the glass. There was hardly a stage – a few tables put together – heavy trestles – basically you'd watch the girls – and then they'd come among you with the jug – scantily clad.

The audience were mostly men working on the railway I guess in the sheds behind: there were still a lot of rooming houses in King Henry's Road, Gloucester Road, Edis Street where they lived.

There were also large families of boys patrolling the streets. It was never enjoyable coming here – I was always frightened – I found it more frightening coming here than I did going down to Somers Town – yeah – I was a proper punk with safety pins – I got three holes in my ears still there – but that was in the days when men didn't have earrings – nowadays everyone's got them but in those days it was hard work! Three of my friends got gammy ears – mine only swelled.

Another thing – to be part of the gang you had to run along the wall where King Henry's Road began – that was frightening – one side the pavement – the other a 30 foot drop to the track – you shouted and yelled all the way. Lindsay de Paul had a flat opposite and she opened her window and shouted 'Clear off!' or words to that effect. We'd only just seen her on 'Top of the Pops' – something to tell them back in Kentish Town.

Jan
25 Years in Ainger Road

When my wife and I first came to this house 25 years ago, we had the ground floor and one room in the basement. We then bought the basement flat, but couldn't afford to live in it all so we let off a bedsit. During the housing slump, the top floors came on the market, so we took a deep breath, borrowed the money and bought the rest. Now we live on three floors and there is one self-contained flat.

This process has gone on all down this road. When we came here first many houses were owned by housing associations, and others were let off in rooms. Now more people own a complete house here than ever before. Our children were born here and went to Primrose Hill School – everything we need, or most of it, has been within walking distance.

There used to be a barrier across the road outside this house – part of a one way traffic system. One night we were all wakened by a terrible crash and awful screaming. Windows flew up – heads came out. A woman, driving up the hill simply had not seen this barrier, which was bedded in concrete. We thought she was terribly injured or dying – but there was nothing the matter at all – just a hysterical fit. After that the barrier was taken away.

There were a number of characters here in those days – Molly for one was well-known. She would ask you to do her shopping for her which we did from time to time. She used to lower a basket from her first floor window, and put the money in an envelope and her list which would often include half a bottle of whisky. She suffered from appalling arthritis. Once her ceiling fell down and we cleared it up and sent for the builders.

Alf and Edie lived next door but one. He had been a fair-ground booth fighter – that's how he earned his living. He was small in height, but built like an ox and incredibly strong. He was related to the internationally renowned sculptor Eduardo Paolozzi, who is also built like an ox!

At the back here there are splendid trees, creating an almost park-like area, where our gardens back on to those of King Henry's

Road. One day, back in 1976, to our dismay we heard the sound of chain saws, and saw a man up a tree. He was intending to cut the trees down. In no time seven or eight neighbours had collected and in true Primrose Hill fashion telephoned the Council to protest. When the official from Camden arrived, he took one look and agreed to put a preservation order on them: and – what was so wonderful, he came back shortly afterwards and like Orlando in *As You Like It* literally did what he said – affixed a little notice to each and every tree, and so they were saved.

People here are prepared to make direct protests, when they feel things should be changed or prevented, and I don't regard this as NIMBYism. The protesters are trying to protect things for everybody, not for their own selfish purposes, and many, many people benefit from their actions.

Finally one regret – that snow seems to be a thing of the past. I shall never forget the Hill under snow – the complete and wonderful mayhem up there. We have a thirties Canadian toboggan that goes like a bullet – but most people were on trays, tyres, bits of lino, milk crates, old bedsteads, madly going down on anything they could lay their hands on. Nice memory!

Mary Wylie
The Siege and the Oldfield Plot

When I first arrived in London, I stayed in the West End and thought, when my brother began a course in Merton Rise, that he was going to another world as he described Primrose Hill, and the wonderful ice-cream (Marine Ices) from a tiny shop in Chalk Farm. To me Regent's Park seemed quite an excursion, though St James's Park was almost my back garden, soon to be replaced and pale into insignificance, when Primrose Hill became my front garden, shared by the people who lived around it.

They, the local people, fought to keep the Hill accessible day and night in 1976, when the gates were to be locked at dusk in keeping with Regent's Park. The strategy was to have people at each of the nine gates every night, and at first there were lots of people at every gate, champagne flowing at one on the first night, but it was a cold wet June and on the last night there were scarcely enough people to man each gate, with one man driving round to relieve, in case of dire need. At about 3.30 a.m., however, the Parks' Police came to me, said they were going home, and that the gates would not be shut if we left.

That day a small group of us went to the House of Lords to meet Baroness Birk, Minister for the Environment: which should have been exciting, but I, for one was asleep on my feet, and could only marvel at the reasoned speech our spokesman made on our behalf!

Perhaps we had already won when the Parks Police said we could go home, but we were euphoric when the Minister said the gates would not be locked. The celebration party took place a few days later, when we'd caught up with our sleep, and were sure that the siege of Primrose Hill was over. Today, however, there is a sneaking feeling of pride, when late at night, people are able to walk to the top to enjoy the view.

In 1963 an elegant, if somewhat run-down terrace of houses, called Regent's Park Gardens and Regent's Park Garden Mews were demolished to make way for three ugly blocks of flats for the elderly, called collectively

'Oldfield', not in anticipation of the tenants, but after the Mr Oldfield who originally bought the plot of land in 1840.

Prior to that Regent's Park Gardens, set behind a narrow garden of mainly trees, with its own little road, always seemed rather dark and mysterious, and there were rumours of squatters and drug addicts even then, which may have contributed in some way to its destruction, a fate I doubt would be permitted now in our Conservation Area. It seems strange today we did not join the squatters in their protest against the demolition.

I doubt, however, if the many people, who have welcomed a home in Oldfield, would agree with that sentiment, and I would not like to have deprived Judy Fogarty, for instance, of her great enjoyment of Primrose Hill. Before she became a well-known figure in the area, I'd admired her posture and grace as she walked in Hampstead. In fact she came to Oldfield on a temporary basis, but fell in love with the Hill, and stayed to hearten us all at the sight of such a beautiful old age. Summer and winter, her shoulders bare, head held high, she glided up and down the road to the shops, very often shopping for others in Oldfield who were not so fleet of foot. It was on just such an errand that poor Judy, crossing the foot of St George's Terrace, was knocked over by a taxi reversing into it, an accident from which she never recovered.

There was Alice too, a great gardener who worked tirelessly, planting and tending flowers, making a beautiful garden for all to share. Claire Bennett who lived for a long time at 116 Regent's Park Road, and to whom as a moving spirit we owe the boules park on Primrose Hill, ended her days, happy to be in Oldfield, happy to be still in the district.

Another resident, still living there, has given much pleasure to so many with all her artwork on the railway bridge, and her animals, painted recently to raise £100 towards the library.

Some residents in the Primrose Hill area, whom I have known, have never moved from the house where they were born. Jessie Suchwell for example was born in 40, Chalcot Crescent in 1915, and lived there all her life. Jessie and her mother were haute couture dressmakers, and Jessie made at least one dress for Princess Margaret. Her love of opera and ballet led her to work for a time in the wardrobe at Covent Garden: but she was interested in all the arts – music, exhibitions and the theatre, and her capacity to recall past productions and performances was phenomenal. Tall and elegant, she was well known to the dog fraternity on Primrose Hill, where she exercised the succession of Cocker Spaniels she owned throughout her life. She is commemorated there by three trees, a mark of the esteem in which she was held by her many friends.

Another well-known character, a neighbour of Jessie's in Chalcot Crescent, was John Leather, who died some years ago. He too spent much time on Primrose Hill, where he seemed to find some comfort.

Dora and Rita also, sisters, who did not leave the house in Rothwell Street where they were born, were inveterate walkers, even in old age.

Primrose Hill has been a focal point for many like Jessie and her friends, and a solace to those who frequent it.

Jessie Suchwell enjoyed all the arts *Celia Kelly*

Keith & Betty Bird
Fireworks on the Hill

Over the century, firework displays have taken place in Primrose Hill, but apart from the big display to mark the end of the Crimean War in 1856, held on Primrose Hill before an enormous crowd, they were mostly private ones in the many gardens that lie hidden behind the large Victorian family houses. In the late seventies, Auden Place organised its own firework display on the estate and then when the Primrose Hill Community Centre came into being, the same people who arranged these displays instigated a much larger event on the Hill itself. This took endless negotiations with the Royal Parks Agency and the Manager of Regent's Park, but eventually permission was granted for the PHCA to have a firework display and bonfire on Primrose Hill – the only people other than the Queen who could legally do so!

From about 1981 to 1996 the annual Primrose Hill Firework Display was wholly organised by the PHCA and for the first eight or nine years of these the local residents were totally responsible for the preparations and the display itself. Each year about 200 people were involved in collecting wood for the bonfire (and then protecting it once it was built and before it was lit); baking potatoes in their own ovens and then taking them hot and wrapped in silver foil to be sold with hot dogs and soup, cooked on the spot on camping equipment, to the crowds who came to watch the display of fireworks, painstakingly staked out throughout the day. Each of the nine gates to the Hill was manned by two volunteer collectors, for there was no entrance fee (precluded for a Royal Park), and this money not only provided the 'float' for the following year's display but greatly assisted the financing of the Community Association and its activities. Then, when everything was over – the Guy Fawkes competition, the official opening and the splendid firework display itself, watched by thousands of local residents with their families and friends – there was soup and sandwiches in the Community Centre for the many helpers who had taken part, before the task of counting and bagging up the buckets of coins and notes began. Everyone enjoyed this break – all but the one or two volunteers who stayed by the

dying embers of the bonfire until it was all quite dead and safe to leave. And then on Sunday morning while counting continued, others were out on the Hill gathering up empty fireworks and the rubbish left by the spectators.

Initially the whole event was organised and carried out entirely by local people and its success owes a lot to the co-operation and support of Mr Legge, the then Park Manager. Thanks to him, equipment was lent to stake out the areas for the bonfire and display and Parks Police were available to keep an eye on what went on. Equally, a blind eye was turned to the fact that food was actually being sold on the Hill other than by the Parks' Agency itself. Over the years, however, the crowds grew, the display became bigger and the whole event attracted spectators from wider afield: the firework manufacturers, professional people, took over the display and the Regent's Park Restaurant franchise took over the catering. Many of those who had basked in the camaraderie of the earlier years were now content merely to be spectators and those that took their place restricted themselves to collecting money at the gates.

Then in 1996, when the crowds became so large, important issues of safety were raised and took a long time to resolve to the satisfaction of the local Council. The display for 1997 was cancelled. By 1998 the Council had agreed to take responsibility for the event, ensuring that it was safe and properly policed. The money is now shared with a chosen charity and Primrose Hill Community Association who still man the gates. It is an event to be proud of and one that has helped to make Primrose Hill more widely known, but, to some residents' regret, it is no longer the local affair that provided so much fun and community spirit for those that lived there.

Anne & Jonathan Sofer

On the Buses

During the seventies and early eighties we were both Councillors (Jonathan on Camden Council and Anne on the Greater London Council) and as such we were involved in local issues: Jonathan in the cross-party campaign that led to the re-design of Auden Place (named from a random choice of famous poets by the Housing Association when told they couldn't use the Manley name), and in the creation of Hopkinsons' Place and the Community Centre.

We both went to the packed meetings on the Environmental Scheme and took up the campaign for a pedestrian crossing over Regent's Park Road by the Oldfield Estate. There was a meeting of the GLC and Camden Officers in our kitchen, when we were solemnly advised that a crossing would cause more deaths! However, in the end they agreed to it.

At that time Primrose Hill residents were far better served by public transport than they are now. The 74 bus ran to well beyond South Kensington and the museums there, while the 3 and 53 would take us from the top of Delancey Street to Trafalgar Square and way beyond. All these routes ran through the best scenic routes in tourist London to popular and useful destinations in the West End and Westminster.

Then about 1987, under the guise of improvements, the 3 bus ended its journey at Oxford Circus. It wasn't long before these formerly useful routes were 'improved', and we were left with the present-day C2 Hoppa. A similar fate befell the 74 route – first a shortening to Marble Arch, and subsequently translation to the 274 single-decker Hoppa.

I admit that even in their halcyon days, the double-deckers rarely kept to their stated frequency – but at least when they arrived they could take on board all those who were waiting.

Traffic in Central London continues to create delays and difficulties, and has become for many hours of the day all but impenetrable. I well remember the occasion when we were a good half mile from Oxford Circus and the Hoppa driver shouted back; 'Seems very slow today – anybody in a hurry better get out and walk!' And all but the halt and the lame did.

Jim Garner
Campaign Memories

We purchased number 12 Rothwell Street in October 1970 at a price of £17,950 from a limited company. Receipt of the title deeds showed that it had already changed hands that year for £4,000. It was a time when the term 'gazumping' was entering the language.

Outwardly, number 12's brickwork was blackened by the railway soot and the stucco was in its original unpainted style. The interior was in a state of disrepair and chaotically split into four flats with the, probably original, gas light fittings and Olympic sanitary ware still in place. Our surveyor had judged it structurally sound, apart from dry rot, but suffering from countless years of neglect. Research in *Kelly's Street Directories* suggested that it had become a lodging house in the late 1870s, and it possibly remained so until our own purchase.

Our initial impressions of the street and neighbourhood were of the general friendliness and village atmosphere: there were a great many young couples with children who had recently moved into the area.

When we arrived there was still a threat that the Greater London Development Plan would be adopted. Its proposed 'motorway box' of three rings of fast roads meant that one ring would pass and form a junction to the south of Haverstock Hill School with all its implications for the area. Fortunately Sir Frank Layfield's report scotched our ring road.

It was immediately apparent how vital Primrose Hill Park is to the neighbourhood: it is by far the area's most important resource and amenity, and many of the key events that I recall have concerned its use and condition. The formation of the Friends of Regent's Park and Primrose Hill in the eighties emphasised this aspect, and in my personal view any lapse in vigilance could jeopardise these precious assets.

In the mid-seventies, a TV documentary sounded alarms about the sometimes fatal Toxocariasis disease contracted from dog droppings. Concern about the Hill, which is

Boys' Home Chapel interior *CLSAC*

ideal for walking one's dog, and adjacent streets, was countered by Camden's appointment of an officer to deal with this street pollution problem: notices of penalties were posted for owners, who failed to comply with the requirements of hygiene. Further, special refuse bins were established in the park. Now only the bins remain, and the street area, within a 75-metre radius of each entrance gate, is made unpleasant for pedestrians by dog droppings: multi-dog walkers too, a recent feature, must be taken into account.

The early Ordnance Survey marks a Shakespeare Oak in the park. In 1964 on the quater-centenary of his birth, another oak was planted by the noted actress, Edith Evans. This was vandalised, together with its plaque, in the mid-seventies. A substitute, planted shortly afterwards, still survives, though the replacement plaque soon disappeared.

The playground and gymnasium stood with their stark utilitarian metalwork when we arrived, but they have been imaginatively redesigned, with a much higher safety margin. A boules area was introduced and provides an oasis on a crowded day.

Since our arrival there have been many other campaigns for local causes. The first was against the destruction of the piano factory on Fitzroy Road. In this the Civic Society played a key role.

Another prolonged campaign, which failed, was fought to prevent the closure of Primrose Hill Station, and of the Watford/Broad Street branch of the North London Line. This amenity was lost in the eighties.

In 1995 a developer proposed to demolish the Boys' Home Chapel, at one time a theatre – the Howff – later a club, and then offices: and made an application to build flats on the site. This would have compromised the appearance of the Conservation Area, but an energetic campaign prevented any encroachment.

Chalk Farm Library's opening hours were reduced from six to three days a week, but threats of closure have so far been defeated by a series of determined campaigns on the part of local residents.

Since we arrived the village street has evolved gradually and haphazardly with many short-lived enterprises. Today, Primrose Hill still remains a village alongside acres of parkland, through a blend of vigilance and community spirit: long may the inhabitants and visitors enjoy it.

Gael O'Farrell
Home

For me, as for so many others, Primrose Hill is 'home'. My son John and I moved into Edis Street in 1984 having previously lived in Belsize Park for eight years.

It was a year later that the Primrose Patisserie opened, affording villagers a place to begin to congregate in that public, yet still somehow intimate place, the street. Today there are no fewer than eight cafés in Primrose Hill and we all have our favourites.

I think one of the things that makes Primrose Hill so special is its curvaceous quality. Crowning all is our mother, Primrose Hill, said to lie on the same energetic line as that other pregnant mound, Silbury Hill at Avebury. The Hill's spiritual significance has been acknowledged for a very long time and as early as the first century, in the days of Boadicea, it was called the 'Temple of Heads' because legendary leaders had prescribed that their heads be buried there after death.

We see this circular quality reflected in the layout of the streets of Primrose Hill. Imagine the loss of mystery and charm if Regent's Park Road were a dead straight road.

For myself I feel held, embraced by this little community, contained as it is by the long sweep of the railway lines and the gently curving waterway of the Regent's Canal. For this reason Primrose Hill has been referred to as 'the Island' because one must cross a small bridge to come into it.

It would appear that in the main we are a hardy band of vociferous individualists, innovative, questioning, sometimes cross, always concerned.

It was in 1987, following three years of entreating the Council to plant trees that the residents of Edis Street got together and collectively decided to break the law and plant trees themselves. After much discussion, the *Robinia pseudacacia frisia* was selected for its beautiful lime green leaf and on a Sunday afternoon after considerable horticultural debate, wine and laughter, the trees were planted. The Council immediately sprang into action, rounding up the ringleaders and threatening to remove the little saplings, and then, gratefully, disappeared, and today they use Edis Street as an example of what residents can do to improve their neighbourhoods.

A grass roots environmental campaign was initiated by local residents in 1991 and within six months we were recycling the second largest quantity of bottles in the country (being the responsible wine drinkers that we are!). Unfortunately, when the Council realised their potential loss of income (half of the revenue for the glass was to be returned to the community for further environmental improvement), they removed the majority of the community funded bins. Aghast! we took to the street, picketing the Council, but to no avail. Still, we continue to recycle today, now in a Council-run scheme.

Over the years we have banded together, first against, then for the parking scheme, and first, last and always for the support of our cherished library.

A very successful campaign was enjoined by residents when our high street was threatened by a major development, and residents raised funds for legal expenses with the help of local writers such as Alan Bennett who read from his diaries one winters evening in St Mark's Church. After two years of persistent campaigning, the case was finally taken to the High Court where we won the day and the developers went elsewhere.

In these days when so much of life seems caught in the net of commercially driven homogeneity, let us celebrate our unique and original little village, Primrose Hill, and its residents.

Driving home down Primrose Hill Road late one evening, I saw a film crew setting up a scene on the Hill. I rushed indoors, grabbed a camera, bolted on a fast lens and caught the shadow-play of the floodlit figures and trees silhouetted against the brow of the Hill. *Ronald Hooberman*

Simon M. Roland
Down Regent's Park Road

I worked in Vicki Lee's dental practice as an associate for three happy years. The practice was in Regent's Park Road above a Citroën garage in a courtyard and I have memories of car engines revving to drown out the sounds of the dental drills!

In the same building on the first floor was an animated film production company that had invented a movable manikin cartoon technique that I believe was a precursor to the animation of Nick Park of Wallace and Gromit fame.

Along the road from the practice was the Queens' pub of Lillie Langtry fame and this had red plush velvet upholstery with Victorian and Edwardian fittings. It was a delightful place to have a drink and a bite in the restaurant upstairs after work.

The other hostelry was the Chalk Farm Tavern towards the other end of Regent's Park Road. This changed its face a number of times in my stay, at one point becoming Pub Lotus. This was named after the famous sports car company that was doing very well in Grand Prix racing at the time. All the fittings in the pub were designed to resemble parts of Lotus sports cars with racing car seats and tables made from steering wheels and the like. Photos and posters of the cars adorned the walls.

Restaurants were always in profusion in Primrose Hill and some from my time still remain. Mustoe's Bistro was, and still is a wonderful place for sensible inexpensive and enjoyable eating with no frills or major sophistication. Edward and Sharon Mustoe still run it in the same style and fashion. Lemonia has expanded across the road in the building previously occupied by the Chalk Farm Tavern, but it remains in place with a new name in much its original if somewhat extruded form. Aux Gargouilles de Notre Dame has become Odettes, and Retsina across the road still remains.

In Chalcot Road there was a wonderful restaurant, Chalcots, run by David and Sylvia Rosen, who later move to Hampshire and opened a country house restaurant of great repute.

In those days there were so many useful shops that now seem from a bygone era, when a shop was somewhere you went to get something you actually needed rather than a frock or a pair of shoes you just had to have.

Welsh's hardware store was an Aladdin's cave of wooden boxes and drawers full of gadgets and nuts and bolts and Mr Beechey was always there to actually tell you how to use them.

Alderson's the Chemist was an old fashioned pharmacy where Mr Alderson could diagnose better than most GPs and dispense accordingly. Having said that, I should add that Dr John Barlow is still diagnosing and practising, with great skill, along Regent's Park Road.

Adams Antiques was next door to the practice and I still have a huge Edwardian mantelpiece mirror purchased from his store.

One of the first importers of Scandinavian glass, Mr Haase, had a wonderful shop selling all manner of gifts, soft-furnishings and kitchen gear. He could also arrange any kind of building, plumbing or electrical work if you needed to build a kitchen around the glassware purchased from his store. Regretfully services such as these are less common these days.

Primrose Hill will always have a very fond place in my memories.

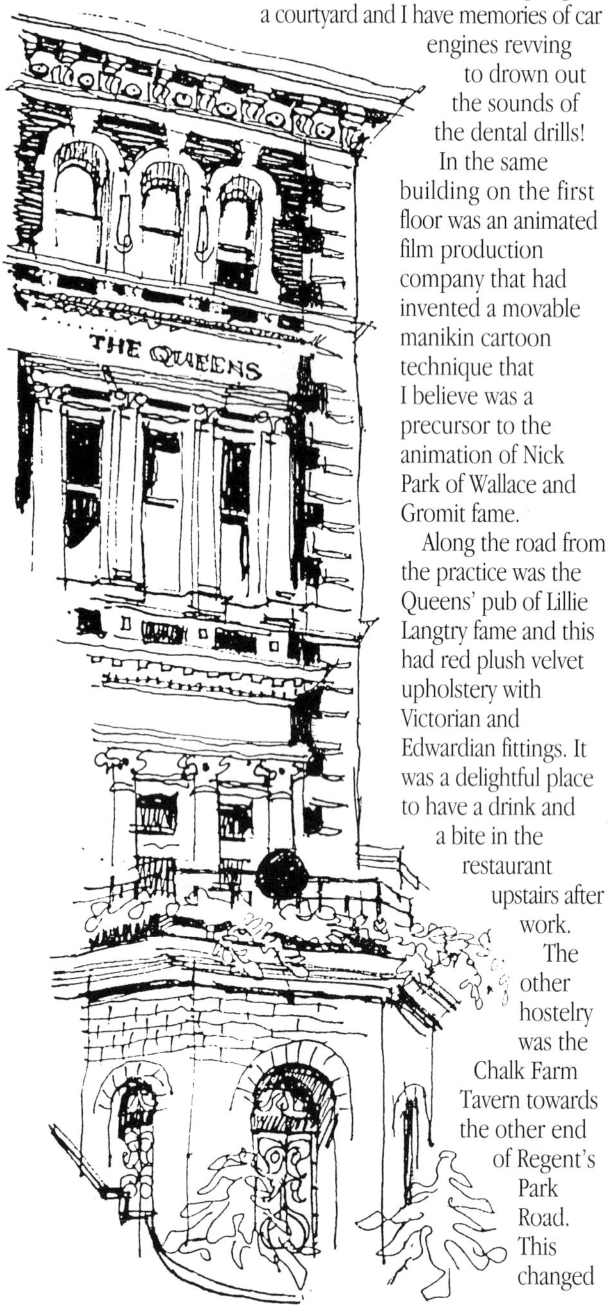

The Queens, Regent's Park Road *Virginia Smith*

Celia Kelly
The Other side of the Tracks

I have lived in Bridge House since 1977, but I still feel part of Primrose Hill. Not long after I came, the Lansdowne in Gloucester Avenue was gutted by fire, and given a designer interior. This upset me as I had just discovered this pub and been entranced by its nooks, snugs and steps in lovely old wood.

Another pub I loved was the Queens' on the corner of Regent's Park Road. In 1977 this had an Edwardian interior: red velvet curtains, red walls, a nook approached by carpeted steps, and stairs leading to a lovely room. Old prints adorned the walls and photographs of locals such as Robert Stephens. All this was swept away. It was redone in pale blue, with further alterations, and is now a pub with pop muzak, so I mind very much the loss of a cosy, quiet pub.

The shops in Regent's Park Road have changed too many times for me to recall exactly what used to be there. Various shops have disappeared, Francesca's painted furniture being one. Now the street has a variety of restaurants and gift shops, which seem to be popular, and in summer, people eating outside give the road a Parisian atmosphere.

Sadly, Primrose Hill Station closed in the early eighties. My son used to catch the train to school in Highbury from that station, so I was able to wave to him from my flat. I loved the view of the station, prettily painted in red, white and blue, and I loved watching the freight trains go past. When the station was open, one could see them at night. Since the station closed there are no lights, so the trains go through in the dark. The booking hall has become a florist shop.

This reminds me that there was a newsagent on Bridge Approach, where the present florist has pots and plants and bits and bobs, opposite the shop. I, along with others refused to believe that there was a shop in this cubby-hole, which was mostly shuttered, but there was. A lady who said she was related to the Bowes Lyons then took over. The shop was totally chaotic with a wealth of silks, ribbons, and other luxurious goods; possibly even second-hand clothes. She once paid me to help sort this paraphernalia out.

Primrose Hill Bridge: the cubby-hole *Virginia Smith*

Hervey F. Blake

Primrose Hill Sit-in

I was rehoused in the area by the Council in 1975 and I think it was a couple of years later that the great night of the sit-in on the Hill took place. Rumour got around one day that the Royal Parks' Authority wanted to bring Primrose Hill into line with Regent's Park, and close the gates between sundown and sunrise.

Word about this quickly spread around and the folk who lived near the Hill were outraged. Everyone loved the freedom to come and go on Primrose Hill as they wished anytime night or day. Surely it was a lawful right of way too, with its old fashioned lampposts, along the paths, which were never extinguished.

Well, this was in the days when we were more literati than glitterati, and so letters flew swiftly to and fro between official departments, the Council and the local paper.

PRIMROSE HILL IS OURS.

They shall not lock us out.

PROTEST

Write to The Department of the Environment, 2 Marsham Street, SW1. Write to your MP: Kenneth Baker (St Marylebone), Geoffrey Finsberg (Hampstead), Jock Stallard (St Pancras North), House of Commons, SW1.

Designed: Tony Coghan *photo: Adam Wolfit*

You could not go to the chemist, the greengrocer or the little paper and sweetshop in Erskine Road without hearing fierce debate as impassioned hearts spoke out.

Within a week or two at the most, the most stunning poster sprang up all around urging everyone to support a campaign to hang on to our Hill's freedom and join in by spending a night on the Hill to show our solidarity with the organisers. The poster was a copy of a black and white photograph and pictured the top of the Hill with a lamp-post in outline. It was stark and moving. I cannot for the life of me remember the words on the poster, but it was something like: *We shall not be moved*! or *Leave the Hill alone!*

The great night arrived, surely it must have been summertime? And me and some girl friends were determined to sit the night out, with the other brave souls, to show our support. As most of us were single mums, the kids would have to come along with us as well. I still remember the thrill of packing our provisions and containing the wide-eyed, excited children until we joined the silent throng up the hill with our cushions and candles.

The sit-in was all very civilised and mild mannered with the lights of the candles flickering quietly in the darkness. A few people spoke and we sang some songs as we shared what we had, and said 'cheek' to even think of closing the gates to this wonderful place of ours!

As the night drew on the children stopped running around and sleepily asked when we could go home. We shivered and, though stalwarts of protest of other years in other places, felt perhaps we should be more responsible now and tuck our little angels up in their warm beds.

We trooped back to our own flats and heard the next day that many had braved out the whole night! I think more sit-ins were planned but it was over sooner than we thought. The Parks people caved in and the Hill was to remain open day and night,

A week or so later I nicked one of those splendid posters off a tree in Chalcot Road and stuck it up on my kitchen wall where it remained for a few years until it finally fell apart. I have always loved that picture and have racked my brains to think of the emotive words that were printed on it. Please if anyone can tell me, let me know!

Normski (Norman Anderson)
I am a Camera

My memories of Primrose Hill start in 1975. I was at the tender age of nine, and my mother had the good fortune of finding out about a new housing scheme called CHA. She was offered a two-bedroom flat. Up until then she'd been offered plenty of homes for her position which at the time was a single parent family with two young boys.

I was always in the North of London, but as if by fate I was destined to spend my most formative years in the North West of London. I didn't start going to school in the area until the Third Year. My mum worked as a conductor on the buses and was soon transferred from Willesden Garage to Chalk Farm. My baby brother was born in 1976 and he was soon a member of the Impala day nursery on Chalcot Road, whilst I was one of the many gifted and privileged children to start life off as a pupil at one of London's finest state schools, Primrose Hill Infants and Primary.

We were living in Auden Place, Manley Street NW1. The people around this housing estate were like a family. I couldn't believe how nice, friendly and different we all were. Yet everyone seemed glad to help anyone. I remember the old lady who lived halfway up Chalcot Road, who would stand on her doorstep and talk to everyone that walked past, and she would sing opera and nobody complained. Then again I'm talking of a time when all of us kids would spend hours playing on the streets or over on Primrose Hill. Or we'd go to the Pirate Club and row and canoe until we were shivering: and I can't remember a single occasion when any of us had any trouble, or went missing long enough for any adult to start to worry – long long are the days of the late-seventies when we would go to Primrose Hill for hours to play on the old witch's hat for hours on end, building stronger and stronger relationships with kids of all cultures and classes. These were the times when wise old men that didn't quite fit into the system would talk to us about all sorts of intriguing subjects, or they would tell us about the world when it was better for them, convincing us that we should study and learn about the things we were interested in.

Back in the late seventies I can remember all my friends seemed to be connected to someone or something very special, and there was this great feeling of creative support coming from every angle. My first ever best friend was Paul Nickson. His was also one of the first families to live in Auden Place with his mum Jasmine. Now Jasmine happened to be a wonderful angel who happened to be a teacher at Primrose Hill School. I remember meeting one of her friends who played bass guitar in a group. That group was 'The

Wombles' – they were a great fun thing at that time. Then there were Keith and Betty Bird: they would do so much for everyone – especially the initiation of various projects for the community. Auden Place had a real mix of friendly, community minded people and they would all be looking out for everyone.

My group of friends consisted of Teo Bailey, Mark Wild, Marc Doran, Derek Bourne from Jamaica, Tim, who turned out to be a Kung-fu expert from Japan, Gareth Jenkins, the son of the Union leader, Clive Jenkins, Colin Darlington, who was one of four brothers, Ollie, Kenneth and Anthony; Jonathan Hawk, whose dad was my woodwork teacher once I got to Haverstock School, Alison and Stuart Daglish. Emma and Jessica Seal lived with their mother Jane on Ainger Road, and I can honestly say this family liked me a lot and took me in as one of their own. We all knew each other, but didn't spend all our time together. I just seemed to be friends with all these groups of random ages, generally a few years apart. This was a very special time for me, as I developed social skills that would benefit me in the future. Some of us put a group together because we all loved music: even though we didn't have any instruments, we still listened to all types of music and saved what pocket or work money we had and started to invest in what would turn out to be one of the most influential pastimes – our Group called 'Nice Ice' then 'Night People'. Then there were the Cromptons: they lived on Regent's Park Road. Their daughter, Catherine, was my first girlfriend, and her brother, Dan, was the trombone player in the group. Now Dan's dad was Dennis Crompton, and he was a serious architect in the sixties and seventies, and a top lecturer at the Architectural Association. I remember when I first went to their house, I thought I was on the set for Space 1999 which was a well watched series in the early eighties. So between 1975 and 1984 we all had the most socially aware and creative forces encouraging us to express ourselves as much as possible.

Some of the best memories I have of this time are things like having the first ever community fireworks display in the car park of the estate. I can't remember what year it was but I do remember Keith Bird collecting money from as many tenants as possible to pay for what was then about two or three boxes of fireworks. We were all encouraged to help build the bonfire, and enjoy ourselves. Then very quickly this location had to be changed because the fire had melted a huge hole in the tarmac. The following year the display had spread to the rest of the Primrose Hill community. Donations came from all the tenants and residents all around, and the first display on Primrose Hill was born.

At around age 11, some of us got into coarse fishing, and we would spend hours sitting on the far bank of the Cumberland Basin, catching sticklebacks and the odd tiny roach. I always loved these days, especially when the *Jenny Wren*, the tourist barge, would come past us – because we felt really proud to live here: it must have been special if people would pay to see us fishing and throwing maggots at them.

Then there was animal awareness that we gained from our local Zoo 'London Zoo'. Once again one of my best friends at Primrose Hill School was David Bramble, and of course his dad was a zookeeper, and he lived with his family by the canal on the Outer Circle in one of the keeper homes. I must admit climbing

Firework Display: Boys with Guy, 1980s *Jean Rossiter*

over the fence to get in for free was a great idea, until we were caught! We were still only young and we learnt our lesson quickly. It just wasn't a Primrose Hill thing to do.

The school Summer Fair was another great event that felt like our own as we nearly all went to the school, and our budding dub, reggae, and jazz funk band even got to play there a couple of times, as well as playing live at the Chalcot Square street party. It was such a good feeling to be appreciated and to show all the locals that we were talented and good kids really. We became so popular at one point, I can remember a rich lady buying a bass guitar and small amp for the group, and buying me, the youngest member, a full drum kit. She didn't really take her ideas of getting us on tour in Nigeria too far, I think, because we were very young. But she did get us started, and we'll never forget her for that.

If someone could do something to help our projects, they would. Even when I turned my career ambitions from music to photography, I had maximum support from my family, friends and adults that I didn't even know. There was the time when I was walking down by the canal behind Primrose Hill School and I saw the legendary photographer who lived on Gloucester Avenue, David Bailey. He was walking towards me with his assistant who was carrying a huge plate camera on an even bigger tripod over his shoulder. Mr Bailey had a couple of small cameras round his neck and his pet dog on a lead. I think I asked him why he needed all that equipment to take a picture that I had previously shot on my little Mamiya 35mm. He didn't really respond too well and so I just watched him for a bit until I got bored. Though it was incredible that I was able to watch one of the great masters of photography of our time, I was more excited with finishing my roll of film and rushing to process it in the cupboard at home. By my twelfth birthday I was a member of the Beehive Photography Centre, nearly opposite Mr Bailey's house. After a four-week course in basic photography, my friend Teo decided I was the better photographer out of the pair of us, and he gave me his Olympus OM10 to use. This is what I meant about support. The Beehive would be a regular place for me to go and practice my hobby that very quickly become my first professional career.

Living in this area has had a massive impact on my appreciation of the surrounding areas, such as Chalk Farm, Belsize Park and Camden Town. For instance, until I was in my teenage years, the furthest we would venture away from Chalcot Road was to Parkway, and we would only go to Palmers' Pets, the model shop, Harvey John's Toyshop, and the cinema for those Saturday morning matinees. More than everything we needed was right there between Princess Road and Regent's Park Road, NW1. It was safe to walk to the laundry, dragging my mum's wicker basket behind me and there was always some kind lady in the laundry helping make sure that I did the washing correctly. This was all good source material for producing some of the finest characters the country has to offer. I mean when your area is mentioned in a Dickens novel, and you witness the filming of a classic Ovaltine commercial, you know that where you live is special.

When it snowed, we had the Hill, and our home-made tintray sledges, unless you were a slightly wild and very graphic adult, like my friend Buzby's dad, David. He decided on a sledging mission, to go down the hill in a canoe. The ride was destined to a disastrous end with Buzby's dad, slamming his back into a milestone halfway down the Hill. His accident resulted in a broken back, and the closing of the Hill until the snow was all gone. I mean, life wasn't always just plain sailing. But whenever we as a community were faced with an issue, some sort of change, or even a good idea, it would be information for all, and we would all have the opportunity to affect that decision, and so we would all benefit.

I cherish the many fond memories I have of my childhood years in Primrose Hill, good and bad, because I am now in my 34th year, and when I look back I see myself as a lucky young black boy, who with the help of my brother Kevin and my mum Cynthia sprouted into an excellent articulate professional musician and pioneering photographer, and went on to become a household name: the leading youth television presenter on BBC Television, and was then deemed a perfect representative for the Nation's urban minded youth of the nineties. I can really only say thank-you to everyone that knows or knew me well in the area. You know we are all responsible for making me what I am, but I cannot deny that the community spirit of Primrose Hill NW1 is the best in the world. I will always love its magic. Well done for sharing it.

Alexander Faris
Upstairs, Downstairs

The time: Spring 1982. The place: Shepperton Studios, Middlesex, where I was conducting for videos of Gilbert and Sullivan.

A telephone rings. The message: 'Don't alarm Sandy Faris, but there is a van in his kitchen.' I would not have believed this, (was the ghost of W.S. Gilbert playing a practical joke) had it not come from 'a usually reliable source' namely my neighbour Teddy Darvas, not a practical joker; but it was true. In the presence of a score of people enjoying a drink in the warm evening outside the 'Queens' pub, a scruffy little van had come hurtling out of control down Primrose Hill Road. The driver, unable to go on into no-entry Rothwell Street, evidently decided (inasmuch as he was able to decide anything) to veer left, crashing through the railings of no. 118, thence onward into my kitchen. Before the police arrived the man had wisely disappeared, abandoning his uninsured truck.

My own insurance company paid up. I claimed for damage to a door, a window, much kitchen crockery and five free-range eggs, size two.

Regent's Park Road: Slight Accident, 1986 *Normski*

David Birkett
Metamorphosis

Today's perception of Primrose Hill is perhaps one of a fashionable and expensive urban 'village', where celebrities congregate, shoots are done, and films are made. Sam Mendes even mentioned it when accepting his Oscar! Yet beneath this glittering surface there still survives a community with memories of a very different Primrose Hill – of grime, polluted air and tenemented houses.

The big move to suburbia of the twenties and thirties saw the area's darkest period. The railway was in its heyday belching forth smoke and blackening the surrounding houses with soot. The idea of moving out to the green suburbs, as depicted in the posters on the underground can never have been more enticing, particularly to those with young children. Commuting was far easier then: the tube network was rapidly expanding and trains and buses reliable.

By the end of the Second World War, houses in this area were shabby and dilapidated – let off in floors or rooms. Their value was low and so were rents. New groups of people began to arrive: the Irish had long been a strong presence here, and they were joined by Greek Cypriots after the Turkish invasion of Cyprus and Asians from Uganda following their expulsion by Idi Amin.

The seventies saw the arrival of pioneering – less conventional and less affluent – members of the 'middle classes' and with them the start of 'gentrification' – a process well on its way by 1987, when I moved in. It was still too 'bohemian' however for those from society's 'top drawer'. I had even been warned, as a newcomer to London, that to live anywhere NOTP (north of the Park – Hyde Park that is) would invite sneers, though Hampstead or St John's Wood might escape utter contempt!

Then one day by pure chance I found myself in Primrose Hill and loved it at once. I had discovered a little enclave, isolated from the mainstream, whose residents formed a close community, quick to defend their unique environment against unwelcome changes. It might be a second choice after the heights of Hampstead or St John's Wood, but it had a vital quality of its own, and valued the individuality of its many 'characters'.

One of the first people I bumped into here on my arrival was Trolley Molly, in what is now the bathroom accessory shop, H2O. Then it was the Primrose Village Store, run by 'The Boys', Mush and Moon, two young Asian brothers from Uganda. Molly was trying to negotiate her way out with her trolley whilst I was trying to get in. Molly was very short and walked with difficulty and pain. She had her shopping trolley in front of her, which I soon learned was employed for several different purposes. Firstly it gave her support, like a zimmer frame on wheels, and secondly it held shopping and anything she needed to carry.

Over time I often saw her about, and learned a little more about her. She lived on the second floor of a house at the bottom of Ainger Road. Because of her arthritic hips, she did not always go out, but if she needed something, she had devised a method of delivery. A shopping basket on a rope would descend from the front window, and a passer-by would be prevailed upon to 'just pop' to the shop for, bread, milk, the *Sun* or whatever was needed. The 'Good Samaritan' would dash to the shop and back, and the purchases would be hauled back up to the flat. She did have a couple of journeys, which only she could make – the bookies and the pub! Being of Irish origin, her tipple was stout and her language would deteriorate after a few as she sat on a stool at the Queens. Eventually she had to move to Oldfield, and died fairly soon thereafter.

Elizabeth Bordass
Princess Road Robberies

One sunny Friday in 1984, I was returning from the park, pushing my two-year-old in her buggy along Princess Road and holding my three-year-old son by the hand in readiness for crossing Kingstown Road.

We were just passing the Post Office at the corner (now Videodrome), when an alarm bell sounded, making us all jump. The door of the Post Office flew open and out shot two young men in balaclavas. One had a gun in his hand, which he was waving. As they passed us they peeled off their helmets and I clearly saw their startled faces as they jumped into the waiting car.

I looked down at the children. Ellie in her buggy gazing after the car, her thumb in her mouth. Peter looking up at me with saucer

Post Office, Princess Road, 1972 *PHCAAC*

eyes. 'Was that a real gun Mummy?' All I could think about was whether I would be able to identify them in a police line up. I had seen them so clearly; and yet couldn't remember any details. I was lucky because the postmistress had managed to press the alarm bell so promptly that the police were there almost immediately and the young would-be thieves were cornered by the painted bridge at Chalk Farm.

The robbery had gone badly wrong when the lads rushed in, expecting to force the postmistress to hand over the pension money which had just been delivered. They had expected to hold her husband at gunpoint in the shop and threaten to shoot him. However, when they entered he had just gone out into the store area; and she – safe behind the security screen – was able to crouch down and press the emergency button.

This bungled job was a contrast to the slick operation one Sunday a year or two later when a removal van parked outside Caroline Bosly's Persian carpet shop. In full view of unsuspecting neighbours, they packed it with all the beautiful rugs in the shop and drove off. These thieves were so confident and matter-of-fact that no one suspected it wasn't a legitimate removal. We were amazed when Caroline Bosly knocked on our door next day and asked if we had seen anything. As it happens we were away that day, but I fear that if we had been in we might well have been duped too! I don't know if the robbers were ever caught or any of the carpets recovered.

Tom Selwyn

Places that Matter

All the buildings, streets and open spaces of Primrose Hill are full of stories about those who have lived and worked here in the past. Memories and places go together. But the stories we, who live in the present, tell about the past involve selecting what seems today to be worth remembering. In that sense our memories are as much about the present as they are about the past. Moreover, since there is always a tendency to think about both past and present with an eye to how we would like the future to look, our reminiscences necessarily (if paradoxically) involve looking forwards as well as backwards.

Our son Ben went to Primrose Hill School in the late seventies and early eighties. Now half way through his Ph.D. at London University, he says that what he liked about the school was that he made friends and had fun there. There was, he recalls, little pressure (not a great deal of homework in those days), and the staff supported children growing up at their own pace. His experience was that the school nurtured self-confidence and friendliness. As parents, Ruth and I remember such events as the Summer Fair which was, as it remains, not just enjoyable but a moment when the school became one of the centres of the community. Indeed, at a time when 'the community' is invoked with increasing insistence by politicians of all kinds, the values which the school stood for and stands for now, seem more and more relevant every day.

Naomi, our daughter, remembers Chalcot Square and the surrounding streets as safe and protective spaces, where she spent time playing and growing up with her friends. She recalls the streets of Primrose Hill having an almost Mediterranean flavour (socially, not climatically of course) with plenty of people out and about, often in summer sitting on their doorsteps or narrow balconies to catch the sun. On the way to her friend Lucy's house in Egbert Street for example, she would see Mrs Wilner in the doorway of her house in Chalcot Road: a former opera singer and refugee from German-occupied Austria, she was much given to singing to the street and always pleased to see Naomi pass by. The house of another friend, Naomi Engler, in

Regent's Park Road, is still the same, surrounded by small shops with people as knowledgeable, friendly and caring as ever. As parents, we felt fortunate to bring our children up in what was, thanks partly to the road system, effectively an island in the midst of a city.

It was perhaps this particular sense of place, described in all its varieties so carefully and lovingly throughout this book, which people came to feel the library in Sharpleshall Street embodied and personified when Camden Council attempted to close it in 1998. Plans to sell the building were drawn up on the Council's instructions by a management consultancy firm. But Primrose Hill residents reacted simply, clearly and directly. The plans were to be resisted absolutely. Whatever needed doing (and there were some extremely exotic plans waiting to be put into action) would be done to prevent the library closing. The campaign, which was inspiring and exciting to be part of, will one day be written up – perhaps by a student of English literature, local government, sociology or social anthropology.

This is not the time or place to do that. But, we can ask, why did the library matter?

Judging from the enormous quantity of letters, talk, petitions, speeches and other texts produced about it at the time, Chalk Farm Library came to stand for certain fundamental ideas and values. These may well have been grounded in memories of what was good in the past, but they were also, and crucially, about imagining a good future. The library came to represent a number of positive ideas: freedom (wander in and select whatever book takes your fancy), creativity (facts and fantasies at your fingertips), social solidarity (lots of news, gossip, information and friends), fun (look in at the Under Fives on a Friday), democracy (meetings and discussions), help and care (for the elderly amongst others) – and perhaps above all, a sense of a small and manageable local space and place, where anyone dropping in could feel at home (thanks to the familiar, friendly, knowledgeable staff). The library reminds us what a community can be, how precious it is, and how we have to fight for it every inch of the way. That's why the library matters.

Harriet Garland
On the Council

I was a Councillor for Chalk Farm Ward, which really means Primrose Hill, for eight years, from 1990 until May 1998. I wanted to find out how Camden Council worked and then make it work for people living in the Ward, as well as elsewhere in the Borough.

During the first summer after the May elections I remember walking through Chalcot Square, on a hot sunny morning, watching the children playing there and worrying about the state of the play equipment. I knew it was dangerous and had to be replaced. That was my first experience of getting stuck in the treacle that was Camden Council at that time. In those days the streets were filthy and hardly ever swept. Parking was impossible and the Primrose Hill Action Group had taken Camden to Court in order to prevent them from introducing a residents' parking scheme. I used to be so scared of the litigants that walking down Regent's Park Road was something I really only dared to do on Sundays. (How mistaken I was: much, much later, I learned that they were really all very nice individuals who had just had enough of Camden not listening to their point of view).

Gradually things began to get better: I found two people in the Leisure Department, for instance, who agreed that it was high time that the fragile wire fence surrounding St George's Terrace should be replaced. The iron railings had been taken away for the war effort nearly 40 years before. I remember watching in amazement as people, on Bonfire Night, rushed towards the pub, knocking the wire down, and then trampling all over the carefully tended gardens. The restoration of railings has made all the difference.

I learned that everything you want to achieve takes ages. Years in some cases. People had been constantly complaining about the difficulties they faced trying to cross into Regent's Park from Prince Albert Road: yet the Pelican crossing has been installed only recently – the whole process having taken four or five years.

I was soon to learn that the views of the people living in Primrose Hill were something you ignored at your peril! No sooner had the opponents of the parking scheme won their case than a new issue arose – the proposed redevelopment of the former Boys' Home Chapel. Once again the residents had to resort to law, and it was a bitter sweet moment to sit in the Law Courts, and listen to the Government Solicitor ripping Camden to shreds for their failure to consult. I had not succeeded in making the powers that be understand the inevitable consequences of this omission, and I hated the fact that Camden could still get things so wrong – particularly after the parking fiasco and their much-publicised failure to consult then. It was a victory for public concern and the developers retreated.

When the proposals to close the library in Sharpleshall Street first surfaced, I again urged caution, but it was clear that no lesson had been learnt. I can only repeat my conviction that the people of Primrose Hill are a group whose way of life you ignore at your peril!

I believe I did learn a lot about how Camden Council works and I enjoyed the challenge of trying to make it 'listen', rather than 'impose'.

Avis Hutt

A Perfect Place

Since 1960 I have lived within easy reach of Primrose Hill, but I did not move to the 'village' until 1982, when I retired from the National Health Service. I moved from a 15 room house in Regent's Park Terrace, built in 1840, to a maisonette in another terrace, built in 1860, in Berkley Road. Houses in Regent's Park Terrace now go for £2,000,000, but when Allen Hutt, my husband, moved there in 1940, they were shabby, disreputable rooming houses. By the time I left, they were occupied by a selection of the great and the good: everybody was Somebody there, I can tell you! A similar process has taken place in Primrose Hill. Of all the changes in this area since the war, gentrification is by far the biggest.

Here I found the perfect place to live: nowhere could be more convenient for me at my time of life! Everything's to hand – better than sheltered accommodation and in Camden too, where facilities are so good! For instance I have a special bath-lift from the Occupational Therapy Services, and during a recent incapacitating illness, an NHS Community Physiotherapist visited me at home. These are examples of services I have campaigned for since I started training as a nurse in 1935, and saw every kind of health and social problem in the slums round Mile End Hospital.

Allen Hutt unveiling the Engels plaque, 122 Regent's Park Road *Morning Star*

In fact I feel I'm being repaid for my 60 years of work in the health service and I'm very happy here!

My connections with Camden are professional too, not only residential. I worked as a Health Visitor in part of Kilburn (now part of Camden), at the invitation of Willesden Medical Officer of Health, Dr Sam Leff. Like Allen, he was an old friend from the Communist Party, of which I'd too become a member, politicised by treating casualties from the Mosley marches in Stepney.

Allen's daughter, Jenny (named after Jenny Marx) was living at 62 Regent's Park Road during our time in Regent's Park Terrace, and thanks to her initiative the Greater London Council placed a blue plaque on Engels' house, 122 Regent's Park Road. Allen, a Marxist historian and author of *The Condition of the Working Class in Britain* unveiled this in 1971, making an eloquent speech before a fair-sized crowd. The event was reported, with photographs, in the Communist press of Europe and in the USSR.

Later I worked with Age Concern in Camden – I was Camden vice-chair at one time and gave many talks about positive ageing. I also made visits to local schools, Haverstock and Primrose Hill, to talk about ageism, as part of a series on prejudice. My grandchildren went to both these schools, and on another occasion, for a talk on the Peace Movement, I got them to record the songs we used to sing on the Aldermaston Marches, and played them to the students.

I have also given talks in Chalk Farm library on more than one occasion – for example the anniversary of the NHS – on Positive Ageing and Health. I'm seen now as a Consultant on Age!

On my retirement I joined Primrose Hill Neighbours' Advice Centre but that is another story.

I have often tried to analyse the charm of Primrose Hill and why it draws us all. You have the walks, the Hill, the Canal, Regent's Park, the Zoo: good transport: the canal again, buses, tube, railway – the oldest in the country: the trees, the buildings, the quality of light, the wide views: the community feeling of a village.

Perhaps it is to do with contour, height, a sense of elevation, of climbing and descending: a feeling that the environment is bigger than the people and that we can mould ourselves into its contours as into a nest!

Jean Wallis
Hallowe'en at the Library

At the beginning of the nineties I was posted for three years to Chalk Farm Library. I had been a librarian in Camden for 23 years, mostly working with the housebound and disabled readers in the Borough. This was a new experience – this was a revelation!

Never will I forget that library and its small customers. Such undiluted enthusiasm! Such knowledge of exactly what was wanted! Such a lot of questions! The library was full of colour, of captivating books, toys, illustrations; of fun mixed with concentration.

Homework was tackled there, computer word searches made, acting explored, stories listened to attentively. Those readers were a determined lot – they knew their Dahl, and (whisper it) Blyton: they painted with abandon, cut out and pasted with zeal.

I loved every minute of my job, and left with great regret.

One horrid memory remains – the Hallowe'en Party! I cannot banish the sight of them all arriving – pleasant children suddenly turned into devils and witches, many of the wrong age, slipping in under cover of terrible masks. Food was trodden into the parquet, competitions wrecked, stories abandoned. I was truly amazed when they finally left for home, flushed and bright-eyed, full of thanks, still bursting with energy.

Now retired, I again work with children; bolster up the backward readers, assist at an After-School Club: so my chief memories are good, and have led on to more happy days.

Jasper, Lucy & Zoe: the Dalmatian Dogs
Dogs' Delight (as told to Gail Levy)

Disembarking from the motor in Elsworthy Terrace, we bound out, suppressing our vocal glee, pulling on our leads towards the wonders of 'the Hill'. Into the park and down on to the field on the right, release and freedom running full pelt towards the bottom of the field and the delights of the muddy puddle. Avoiding the joggers, whose pounding feet have made the unofficial path under the trees, the occasional horse being exercised and the sound of the bugle from the King's Troop in the distance. The echo of the barking which can resound over the buildings. We dogs have arrived. Summer shade under the trees and no muddy puddle for a few short months. Back over the field and a steady climb to the summit of the Hill, to the remains of picnics and treats and balls thrown to be caught and chased. Full steam downwards towards the playground and the precious bucket of water, to the gates in Regent's Park Road where remains of bread scattered for the birds, and onwards past the benches with readers, talkers, walkers, children in prams, those who while away the time in the green oasis in the centre of London. Around the Hill and return to Elsworthy Terrace having met with canines of all varieties and home to sleep and dream about tomorrow's promise of excitement on Primrose Hill.

And Mongrel, Puppy, Whelp
and Hound - and Curs of Low degree
Go scampering on Primrose Hill
For EVERYONE to see!
ASL.

Dogs delight (with apologies to Oliver Goldsmith) *Andolie Luck*

Philippa Huins
When Snow Came

In the winter of 1981–82 there was heavy snow in London. It started to fall on New Year's Eve, in the evening, and continued through the night.

By the next day, the whole of north London was muffled in a thick white blanket, up to a metre deep in places. And then the fun started. Down the slope of Primrose Hill they came, screaming patches of colour, on every conceivable sort of conveyance. There were the proper wooden sledges, with runners, kept in the basement or the attic no doubt, for just such a once-in-a-lifetime occasion; the plastic bakers' trays, bright red or bright green, intended for loaves of bread; cement bags, fertiliser bags, planks of wood, improvised with rope handles; and scariest of all, the dustbin lids, turned upside down to create a carriage of sorts.

The slope quickly turned into an ice run, as the brave or foolhardy slipped and slithered down it again and again. The colours of the different sledges merged with the bright winter scarves and hats, creating a dazzling kaleidoscope against the snowy background. The shouts and screams were piercing in the icy air. The sense of shared excitement was palpable.

No doubt the ice soon turned grey, and the snow became slush. But that's not what I remember.

Fun in the snow *Ronald Hooberman*

Siobhan Cartwright
I will always have the Memory

Growing up in Primrose Hill was a great place. Life was very quiet and very friendly – everyone knew everyone and children were perfectly safe to roam around the park – alone – until 9.00 p.m. in the summer months anyway. The park keeper was always on duty if there were any problems. The shops were very small and run by families that took the time to know the people – unlike today where money seems to be the main objective, understandably, but taking time out for people seems to be low on the list.

The rash of coffee bars etc. in the area now is just a joke – mobile phones on every ear and cars that make the area look like a huge car park instead of an island – in my opinion they are taking away the beauty of Primrose Hill – there are just too many of them.

Original shops are very few today – the hardware store is possibly the only one with the original owner still working behind the counter – it's great to still go in there – very warm greeting and a chat – like it used to be.

The only bad memory of the fifties/sixties was the murder outside the Baptist Church. Gate crashers had crashed a party on Regent's Park Road: when thrown out, they went to the dairy opposite and picked up all the empty milk bottles and threw them at the house – party goers came outside and a huge fight broke out – knives were drawn and the owner of the dairy, Mr Griffiths, was hurt very badly indeed, left on the pavement for dead. Meanwhile drinkers from the pub came to help and chase the mob away – the mob jumped into a minivan realising just how out of control the night had become – drove like loonies and knocked the young guy from the pub over, dragging him 100 yards or so to his death.

The men responsible came from Queen's Crescent and one from Primrose Hill – they were all brought to justice as one was

Chalk Farm Tavern, now Lemonia *CLSAC*

recognised – he lived and worked opposite the dairy and had crashed his own neighbour's party – Mr Griffiths had been stabbed by a man he served daily as a customer. The guilty man's family gave up their shop – a butchers – and moved away soon after the trial.

It wasn't all tragedy – the local area had its share of great night clubs – The Howff – Odettes – The Roundhouse – The Railway Club – the area has always been a great social magnet – just much friendlier. The Roundhouse was a great place to hang out for the afternoon or evening – very cheap – more than one band in any one session – big name bands – ten bob went a long way!

Celebrities have always been in abundance around Primrose Hill – the nice thing was they just blended in with the other locals. Now though, some of the younger celebs make themselves far more obvious – which is a shame. . . .

Housing is very different now in Primrose Hill – the big houses have mostly been restored back to single occupancy – so a lot of the family dwellings have gone. Three to four families would at one time live in the large houses – very happily in my experience – it made for an extended family right on your own doorstep – fantastic place to grow up in – it's a shame it has changed but I will always have the memory.

Bookselling in Primrose Hill
Jessica Graham

Unlike some of my fellow students, I left university with my love of books still intact and a vague hope that I could make a career for myself somewhere in the book world. At first I thought I might become an academic, but after finishing my MA I decided to take a break from the world of study and took a job as a general assistant at an antiquarian bookshop in Bloomsbury. My employers, Robert Frew and Julian MacKenzie, also owned a small shop selling new and second-hand books in Regent's Park Road. For the first year of my working life I spent part of my time in the rarefied atmosphere of scarce first editions and handsome leather-bound sets of great works of world literature, and a couple of days a week selling contemporary hardbacks and paperbacks at Primrose Hill Books.

The contrast between the two shops was extreme and I soon found out which I preferred. The antiquarian books were sold mostly through catalogues to private collectors or to libraries and institutions, particularly in the United States and Japan. This was book as artefact – more akin to dealing in fine art than bookselling as I had imagined it – security was paramount and contact with customers minimal. By contrast, working at a neighbourhood bookshop open seven long days a week and thronging with the chattering classes of NW1 was infinitely more appealing. When Robert and Julian

Chalcot Crescent *Virginia Smith*

decided to focus exclusively on antiquarian books and to sell Primrose Hill Books I had no hesitation in offering to buy it. Thus my fate as a bookseller was sealed and in August 1987 ownership passed to me and I began to learn about running a bookshop in earnest.

The most important task facing me was to learn about the area and about local people's interests and one of the more enjoyable aspects of having a shop in Primrose Hill is that, to a very large extent, those tastes overlap with my own. As a consequence there is a heavy bias in the stock towards fiction and the arts since the books reflect a customer base involved with the media, theatre, film, travel and music. There is also a particularly rich body of local authors' works to represent. Very few small bookshops enjoy the privilege of stocking such a large number of high quality works of both fiction and non-fiction by genuinely local writers.

Reading as many of the new books as possible is, of course, an essential, albeit unseen, part of the job. Stock is purchased between 4 and 6 months in advance of publication, long before the text resembles a finished book, and I read huge numbers of advance copies of books in the hope that I can find titles to recommend and to include in our Summer and Christmas catalogues. Now that I have been here for some years people generally trust my recommendations and there are customers who read only what is suggested to them. Almost 2,000 new titles are published every week in the UK so there is a great deal of ground to cover, but my husband Marek, too, reads voraciously (he was, after all, once one of my best customers – that was how we met here at the shop 12 years ago) and so do our colleagues, each of us trying to cover different areas. Many of our customers have limited time in which to browse and what appeals to them about the shop is that it carries a manageable range of carefully chosen, pre-selected titles. Sometimes too much choice can be overwhelming and it is hard for the untrained eye to spot interesting titles amongst so many in a large store. What I can offer is the cream, skimmed from the top of the huge vat of publishers' outputs.

An additional reason for staying abreast of current titles is to keep our weekly column on the UK book trade topical. Since April 2000, Marek and I have contributed a regular piece for Contentville, an American website set up to examine and discuss all aspects of the media. Some 40 US booksellers write about their own specialities and interests and we were invited to cover the field of British books. The aim is to provide the reader with an antidote to the more commercially orientated book sites where reviews are often no more than sales pitches penned by interested parties or publishers. We have a completely free rein and it is a wonderful opportunity not simply to enthuse about genuinely exciting new books, but also to draw attention to neglected, or over-hyped, titles and to share trade gossip.

I am often asked whether we feel the pressure of competition from large chains and corporate booksellers, but in fact we don't see ourselves as offering the same type of bookshop as they do. In essence we are a community orientated shop and we don't have to spread ourselves too thinly trying to be everything to every booklover. It has always been the case that the large conglomerates have a competitive advantage over us in that they can buy stock more cheaply and on more favourable terms, but it quickly became clear after the demise of the Net Book Agreement that deep discounting was only going to affect the bottom end of the market and here, at Primrose Hill, we are in the fortunate position of being near the top of the market. Customers are less interested in how much a book costs than in whether it is worth reading. On the whole they do not want the latest blockbuster at the cheapest price and when their tastes do run to popular paperback fiction we can often supply inexpensive second-hand copies. The real advantage the chains have is more floorspace, but now that ordering books has become so fast and efficient we can supply most requests overnight and the majority of our customers are satisfied with that level of service. There is a tremendous amount of loyalty towards local businesses in Primrose Hill and this is one example of how it manifests itself. Staff at bookshop chains are poorly paid and not very highly motivated which means there is a high turnover of staff with the consequence that they have limited knowledge and experience. We have extremely committed and informed colleagues and our customers appreciate seeing the same faces when they come in, confident that they will be speaking to efficient, genuine book-lovers and not simply to indifferent cashiers.

Where bookselling has changed most dramatically in my time here is in relation to the internet. Contrary to many expectations, far from damaging business for a shop like ours, it has, on balance, proved beneficial. In the first instance the internet has enabled us to extend our reach. We have a growing number of customers in Europe and North America, many of whom are former Primrose Hill residents and like to keep in touch and to regularly order books. Others are simply away from home temporarily, working abroad or on vacation, and request parcels for themselves or as gifts. The second and more dramatic transformation in relation to the internet is the way it has revolutionised second-hand book sales. Formerly, these titles were sold on a modest scale from our basement either to locals or to anyone who happened to be in the area with time to browse. Now, the majority of our more interesting titles are catalogued on the internet, accessible at any time day or night and to anyone, anywhere in the world. This part of the business is largely unseen and is chiefly Marek's domain, as is the running of the website. Visual rather than too text-heavy, the primary aim of the site is to promote the bookshop itself. By emphasising the attractiveness of the building and of the location we are exploiting the romance attached to the idea of the small local bookshop – what I call the 84 Charing Cross Road factor. This appeals particularly to Americans, who have lost most of their independent shops, and we get a lot of correspondence from customers who then visit us in person when they are in the UK. Invariably, of course, they fall completely in love with Primrose Hill.

One of the chief advantages of the internet is that we can now sell more expensive academic books and first editions without having to put them on the shelves in the shop with the attendant worries of security. Theft is an enormous problem for all retailers and people are often shocked that this should also be the case in Regent's Park Road but, sadly,it is. Nor is it just the books that get stolen – in my time here I have lost handbags, purses, items of clothing and even electrical equipment. Tiresome as it is, however, we are all now very skilled at spotting potential thieves and quite happy to use our video recordings to provide identification for the police.

Fortunately, bookshops attract interesting, eccentric characters more often than undesirables and there has always been a stream of bizarre book buyers to keep me entertained over the years. We used to have a customer we called the 'Ticket Man' who bought second-hand books and only those which had used bus, train or even tram tickets tucked inside them. He collected old tickets and because people often use them as bookmarks he sought them out and felt honour bound to buy the books in which he found them. Such encounters, of course, are part of the fun of having a bookshop and we are constantly meeting people with unusual preoccupations and passions. For them, as for us, books and a life of the mind are of paramount importance and they are keen to share their thoughts and to meet other like-minded individuals.

Over the years, I have had the opportunity to meet some of the world's greatest writers here and it is difficult to convey the thrill of meeting authors whose work I studied or admired and whom I never thought I would come across in person – particularly those such as Paul Theroux, Margaret Atwood, Jane Smiley and Howard Norman who are not resident in Britain. Most writers lead such solitary working lives that they are delighted to meet their readers and I have witnessed some very moving encounters between well-known novelists and customers, both equally pleased to be seeing one another!

I hope that we can continue to hold our readings – both our bookshop events and those we have organised in support of the church and the library – so that there are further opportunities to hear writers speaking about their work. I am encouraged by the growing support we have had from local customers; our once modest audiences of between 30 and 50 people have swelled to between 200 and 400 on recent occasions and we are now courted by publishers as one of the best London venues for events, particular emphasis being given to the enthusiasm of our local supporters and to the range and calibre of their questions to the authors.

We all feel very strongly that in a tight-knit and friendly area such as Primrose Hill the bookshop and the library are interdependent and need to be focal points for the community, places of discovery where interests can be nurtured and maintained. Since only a small percentage of the population buys books (around 10%) the library has an additional role to play in enabling people to have constant access to books. Far from being a dwindling pastime, I have witnessed a surge in interest in books and reading in my years here. I am certain that there are as many adults as children, for example, who have acquired or re-acquired the habit of reading as a consequence of following the antics of Harry Potter. As I watch the tastes of local children develop and mature I sometimes speculate that we may be harbouring a few more local authors for the future.

Pessimists love to predict the 'death' of the book but I completely disagree, particularly in an area like Primrose Hill where every day I see the significance of books in people's lives and know that they are among their most treasured possessions. Of course there is room for technological improvement and recent developments have meant that access to reference material in particular is much quicker and easier than formerly. Yet it is not every book that is destined to be read on a tiring and inflexible screen. As long as people still want to read for pleasure and need their texts to be portable then there seems to be no adequate substitute for the traditional book and in particular for its tactile qualities. Customers love to handle books, let the pages fall open, admire the typography or the cover design as well as the content. There is something precious and very personal about a special or favourite book which is unique to that copy so that taking it down from the shelf and re-examining it can transport the reader back in time to the original experience of reading it.... rather like listening to a piece of music and recalling something about the occasion on which it was first heard. Chips and silicon are too soulless for that sort of emotional experience. In years to come I know that I shall be constantly handling volumes I have acquired in my time as a bookseller here and that many of them will be rich with memories of friends and acquaintances I have made in Primrose Hill. I will always think of it as a community of dedicated booklovers.

Jacques Portier

A Piece of Chalcoterie

Thank God it has been possible to spend six weeks again in Chalcot Square this summer. For weeks we look forward to being there again. After the confusion and hassle at Orly-Sud, the frustrating search for a trolley, circumnavigating islands of bovine people blocking the way, we are, at last in a BA airliner, greeted by charming and smiling hostesses as though we were already in Blighty. Then Heathrow, into the taxi, eagerly looking out of the windows. The driver leaves the Westway near Warwick Avenue, into Bloomfield Road and my wife points at barges and pleasure boats moored along the tree-shaded banks of the canal 'Little Venice'. After St John's Wood Road, Prince Albert Road, the graceful sweep of Regent's Park Road along Primrose Hill (how good it is to see it again), Fitzroy Road and at last Chalcot Square. We've arrived.... Our dear friends are there to greet us and it is an unalloyed happiness to see them again. It doesn't take us long to resume the routine of the previous holidays. As soon as we set foot in the house we are at home once again, ready to savour the bliss of the six coming weeks. The interminable boring 46 weeks we've just spent in Versailles are, at long last, over. We carry on as if we had not left the Chalcots last year! Oh! the happiness to be back in this peaceful haven, where we've spent 28 unforgettable summers. When we first came, François, my son was 14 and still wearing short trousers, and I was 46. Francois is now 42 and I am an old geezer of 74 ready to kick the bucket and push up the daisies. How time flies.

We go off to Safeways to get some food. My wife and I admire once again the familiar landmarks, the exquisite harmony of the daintily painted facades of the terraces of Chalcot Square, which have no equivalent in Paris or elsewhere. In 1972, when we first came here, the façade of the house was painted white; many of the houses in the square are now painted with bright colours. The noble vista of Chalcot Road with the uniform houses remind one of a drawing by Canaletto, all proportions kept, orderly and Cartesian. I stop a moment to drink in the graceful curve of Chalcot Crescent, before catching up with my wife already walking under the rose buds of the bushy hedge at the end of Berkley Road. We feel once again the villagey atmosphere around us, then we cross Chalk Farm Bridge to Chalk Farm Road.

As we walk back to the Chalcots with the groceries, Françoise says suddenly that she hopes nothing untoward has happened to George – George Cernoch. He always used to be on the pavement the very day of our arrival in Chalcot Square with César his huge Great Dane dog to welcome us to England. He wasn't there to greet us. Françoise has some misgivings. I try to reassure her: 'maybe he's gone on holiday, yachting, to the Far East as he used to do, you know...'. Françoise isn't convinced and glances sadly at the closed shutters and at the unkempt shrubs in the front garden. Then we learned the sad news: while out driving George had a massive heart attack and died all at once. We remain speechless for a while. Chalcot Square will never be the same without George. He was part of the picture, such a genial person, a bon vivant! I don't believe he ever lost his temper. He was a nonconformist – like me, but also a flamboyant character. In my mind's eye I can still conjure him up, ambling towards his huge spotless convertible – a vintage cadillac – noblesse oblige, sporting a wide brimmed white hat. He would wave at us before boarding his car. César would jump on the back seat, and sit hieratic (like an Egyptian dog on a scarf by Michaela Frey). George would put on a record of bel canto or classical music, start the engine and sail away like a majestic yacht. My wife, who was very fond of him, had nicknamed him 'The Great Gatsby'. We never told him, but as he had a keen sense of humour, I'm sure he wouldn't have minded our teasing and he would have chuckled it away. We won't see him again and we will miss him. I have been told that people die twice: first, when they die; then when those who have known them, hated them or loved them, die in their turn. Since we have known and been fond of George, he is still alive. He will

Chalcot Square *Philip Sanderson*

only die when we die in our turn.

As soon as the chores are done, I sneak out into Sharpleshall Street to see if Chalk Farm library is still open. It is still there, good. I utter a sigh of relief. We did fight to keep it open last year, didn't we? François and I wrote in the book of protest. I was told that there were several demos after our departure. Never underestimate grey power! As I wrote in the Book of Protest, the library is of paramount importance for the Chalcots. London is made up of an aggregate of self-contained villages connected to each other by a grid of trunk roads, tube lines and trains. That is what makes the charm of the capital, and all the amenities which are necessary for a pleasant life, as well as parks and greens where children can play. It is a delicate balance; close the library, which is the focal point of the village and where people get a chance to meet, get acquainted with each other, form friendships and simply have a chinwag at slack hours, and you destroy the soul of the community by upsetting this delicate balance.

Before going to bed, I open up the bedroom window and gaze upon the charming little gardens at the back that have so many trees and shrubs that they seem to merge into a sort of mini park, punctuated in the background by the slender steeple of St Mark's. Early in the morning, in the stillness of the night, I listen to the chimes of the church clock. At 5.00 a.m. I get up, tip-toe out of the bedroom into the living room already suffused with the light of the rising sun. How I love that light green room with its two well proportioned high sash windows. A room lit by two windows is so harmonious! Seen through them, Chalcot Square evokes a theatre set. It is so perfect. I LISTEN TO THE SILENCE.

One has to adapt to change constantly – well I can't and what I value particularly is that the Chalcots DO NOT CHANGE when all else is changing. Every year we see the miracle, of the same dear old houses. How soothing it is! How comforting it is. I am under the impression I am stepping into the past, and for a historian what a treat! If only they could remain as they are for ever! It was clever of the Camden Councillors to transform Chalcot Road into a cul-de-sac and prevent traffic from killing the area. It makes a huge difference. Once these houses were begrimed with black soot by the steam engine; there were notorious pea soup fogs and the rumble caused by the wheels of carriages pulled by horses on the cobblestones; they must have been taxing for the inhabitants. All that is gone, gone with the wind of modernity. I keep on worrying about how long we will be able to come again and spend our summers in this little paradise.

On top of Primrose Hill I glue my eyes on the cityscape of London. The skyscrapers of the City, the Post Office tower, Centre Point and down below beyond the immense sward, the familiar and elegant curve of Regent's Park Road. I won't see this perfect and beloved landscape tomorrow and my heart is sinking. Will we be able to see it again next year? So many things can happen in the fickle world where there is no security. And yet, as I look at this part of London for the last time, a prayer I used to think of during the bombing raids of the last war comes to my mind. Only the end changes: –

Oh Lord! I who am only an insignificant and ephemeral grain of dust, without any power, lost in the immensity and eternity of thy Universe; thou who is Eternal, to whom all power belongs; who giveth life and ends it, I beseech thee: preserve the Chalcots, protect our dear friends and if it is thy will may we come back again next summer.

Histories

Crimean War Celebration *Illustrated Times, 7 June 1856*

The Railway and Primrose Hill

Derek Sprange

In 1837, when Queen Victoria came to the throne, Primrose Hill was a tiny hamlet in open country. Soon it was to become a grimy working town – so why is it now one of the most sought-after residential areas in all London? To find the answer we must look at changes brought by the Industrial Revolution, and above all at the history of the railway.

That year the first main line railway from London to Birmingham began to operate. Its track climbed the steep gradient from Euston Square to pass over the Regent's Canal, and then levelled off, to curve past the engine sheds and plunge into Primrose Hill Tunnel. Its route formed a northern boundary and with the Canal to the south made the Primrose Hill area a self-contained enclave or 'island'. In this 'isolation' from the rest of London lies its special charm.

Soon after this railway opened in 1837, large engine sheds were built at Chalk Farm, the famous Round House on Chalk Farm Road, and a second one opposite, behind Gloucester Road (now Avenue). As well as loading bays for goods of every kind, the railway company built a maze of sidings, where hundreds of carriages and wagons were parked.

Then another railway, the Birmingham East & West Docks Junction Railway, (later called the North London Line) was opened. This carried thousands of tons of manufactured goods from Birmingham and the industrial north directly to the London Docks. It also brought coal for the new steamers, plying the oceans of the world with Britain's exports.

All this needed many workers: not only men to service the steam engines, but signalmen, lamp men, porters, shunters, cleaners, and so on – all needed to control and keep the trains running. Whole streets of houses were needed to accommodate these men and their families, and Primrose Hill, the little country hamlet, began to turn into a grimy town.

Chalk Farm Road and Gloucester Road, on either side of the railway tracks, were the first building sites for these houses, which had to be close to the work place – the engine sheds and sidings. These sheds were extensive, stretching the whole length of Gloucester Road, from the Lansdowne Public House, in Dumpton Place at the end of Fitzroy Road, right up to the Pembroke Castle by Regent's Park Road Bridge, which connected with Chalk Farm Road. All along the back yards of these new houses lay the complicated tracks of the railway, a hive of intense activity, 24 hours a day.

Most of these houses were occupied by skilled men – engine drivers, firemen, who kept the engine fires stoked, guards, signal men, as well as the unskilled, who did all the dirty work – loading the engines with coal and water, to make the steam, cleaning out the ash pans, and loading and unloading hundreds of goods wagons.

A whole house was often shared by several families, let floor by floor, with one or two rooms for each family. There would be a single privy or earth closet in the back yard. Proper drains for water closets were not put in until about 1848. Cast iron stoves with ovens were installed in some rooms, but much of the cooking was done on open landings, and pails of water had to be carried up from the communal tap in the basement. As proper plumbing was gradually introduced, sinks for washing were provided on the landings of the better equipped houses. There was no electricity in those days: lighting was by candles and oil lamps.

More senior and better paid workers, like the shed foremen, or junior managers, might sometimes rent a more imposing house, perhaps double-fronted, or a larger semi-detached house: numbers 1 and 3 Fitzroy Road for example.

Some houses were run by a landlady, who let off rooms to single male workers, providing her lodgers with meals – board residence in fact. These might be bachelors, perhaps working on the more skilled tasks – engine drivers, inspectors, foremen overseers, and clerks.

Many years later in the early post World War II years, Prison Welfare Officers would get to know these ladies, as, if they had a compassionate heart, they could make a room or even part of a room available for men coming out of prison. There was always a demand for unskilled labour at the sheds. So for a man who wanted to go straight, the hope of a job on release was what was most needed. Work in the sheds was hard, unhealthy, grimy and exhausting, so there were almost always vacancies for an ex-prisoner to make a new start under these lousy conditions.

It was no wonder the 'island' had eight pubs. Heavy work in choking dust and dirt made people thirsty and the pubs alongside the line did a roaring trade as the men came off shift. Most had a private bar with a discreet side entrance. Here the ladies could sip their gin or port and lemon in privacy, hidden by shutters and screens of frosted glass.

Regent's Park Road, once a country lane, wound its way round the foot of Primrose Hill to join Haverstock Hill, the main route up to Hampstead.

It was here that the Chalk Farm Tavern stood, and as more houses were built, shops opened to sell everything people needed. Camden Town too was a busy shopping area with street markets, as well as chain grocery stores later on.

My own first memories of Primrose Hill go back to 1918, the last year of World War I. My younger sister and I used to stay with our Aunt Margie at 51 Gloucester Road (renamed Gloucester Avenue in the 1930s), while our parents went off on their travels. Auntie maintained a strict routine, and although our stay was often in the height of summer, my younger sister and I had always been bathed, been read a story, and tucked up in bed by six o-clock, such was our very ordered life in those far-off days. My two-year-old sister used to sleep in a high-sided cot by the side of Auntie's bed. I slept in the dressing room that led directly off the main bedroom on the first floor.

It was at this point that my life-long love of railways was born. This interest made me understand the how the railway influenced the lives of everyone here, and how it made Primrose Hill the place it is.

There I was on those hot summer evenings, tucked up in bed, in bright daylight and not the least bit sleepy. But as soon as the coast was clear, I would hop out of bed, duck under the drawn curtains and look out of the window. I was just tall enough to see over the sill, and there, between a gap in the tall mansions on the opposite side of the road, I would see the trains – running along beyond the garden walls; an unceasing procession of trains up and down the busy tracks to Euston.

With many a blast on their whistles, they drifted down the bank into Euston Station, wisps of steam fluttering round them, their journey from the north nearly done. Much more exciting were the heavy night expresses, puffing loudly as they climbed the bank, running over the joints in the rails with heavy, sonorous beats of their wheels. I later learned they were on their way to the far north, even

Camden Engine Sheds: Locomotives, 1923

to the remote Highlands of Scotland. These loud blasts of steam were needed to power the train up the steep incline and over the Regent's Canal bridge. They had to be banked (pushed from behind) by another steam engine known as a 'banker'. The regular chuff chuff of these engines sent a thrill of excitement through me, and I would stay by the window until it became too dark to see any more, only leaping back into bed if I heard my Aunt coming up, as she did every now and again to see if we were asleep. I would then be snuggled under the bedclothes, pretending to be fast asleep.

Watching trains go by became a life-long passion – like fishing. The intervals between the trains were restful– a time for reflection – full of anticipation – most enjoyable! Sometimes during the day I would watch from the canal bridge – a better vantage point. My lifelong love of steam engines began in those early days, and flourished through my adolescence until the days of steam finally faded away in the 1960s.

Steam engines were replaced by stages – first by diesel locomotives – and then by clean, all-but silent electric trains: their speed of 90 miles an hour soon to be increased to 140 mph. No longer can the beat of their wheels on rail joints be heard: rail is now welded into one smooth track, free from join.

Looking back on my childhood I see my interest centred on the trains running out of Euston, and on the engine sheds that ran behind the houses between the Lansdowne and the Pembroke public houses. I knew every bit of track between the end of the platform at Euston and the entrance to Primrose Hill Tunnel and I understood how the railway affected the houses nearby, and the people who lived in them. I saw the daily drizzle of black soot and fine dust, year in year out and knew that washing could rarely – if ever – be hung out to dry!

The better off, who faced Primrose Hill in their beautiful houses in Regent's Park Road and St George's Terrace not only enjoyed a wonderful view: they also – fortunately for them – escaped the murky results of railway activities, thanks to the prevailing wind, which blew all the smoke, dust and soot away eastwards over the Chalk Farm Road and Camden Town. They were only affected – rarely – when a strong easterly wind blew.

Not so for the houses in Gloucester Road: no one could keep them spotlessly clean. Flakes of soot, often an inch across, like black gossamer lace, constantly floated about, settling everywhere.

These streets of soot grimed houses, and those nearby, were occupied by hundreds of workers, whose numbers increased as railway services improved. Laundries, for example, were established to wash all the railway linen – pillow-slips and sheets for the sleeping cars and table cloths and napkins for dining cars, as well as all the bed and table linen from the Euston Hotel. This work was done in substantial buildings at the back of Gloucester Road, near the railway line. It was then packed in huge hampers for transport back to Euston. This provided much employment for the wives and sweethearts of railway men.

In the 1930s there was modernisation in the engine sheds, but conditions were no cleaner. Huge modern steam engines had to be turned round, filled with 3,000 gallons of water, and five to seven tons of coal. They were then oiled and polished before running down to Euston to haul their next train. Nearly 600 trains daily ran in and out of Euston, and their engines had to work flat out to climb the bank. It is estimated that they blew more than half a hundredweight of soot from their chimneys before they roared into Primrose Hill Tunnel. It was not yet possible to hang washing out to dry!

World War II was a time of hardship for all. The railways were stretched to the limit, transporting troops and war materials, in addition to their regular work. The North London Line carried heavy war traffic, moving troops and connecting the factories of the north with ports in southern England. Raiding aircraft, undeterred by defences, took their toll.

The 1960s saw Dr Beeching's work, and as an indirect result, the end of steam. The decision to scrap steam locomotives in favour of diesel and later electric engines meant that the air round track and sheds became slowly but surely much purer. This improvement brought the biggest change to Primrose Hill since the original developments of the nineteenth century.

Towards the end of the steam era and the closure of Camden engine sheds, a concentrated clamour by Camden Council and local residents hastened the demise of the steam train. As an interim goodwill gesture,

British Rail put large numbers of powerful 'main line' diesel engines to work the trains out of Euston. Diesel fumes, though unpleasant, were an advance on soot and smuts. It was not until the full electrification programme was complete that really and truly clean air settled over the north-eastern part of the neighbourhood.

The Camden sheds were pulled down to make room for clean, smokeless carriage sidings and washing plants. Railway workers, who were made redundant, moved out of properties near their former work-place: and the overcrowded rooming houses, with their inadequate sanitation and primitive cooking facilities, began to fall vacant, despite their controlled rents. Those workers who found new work locally were happy to be rehoused in new purpose- built flats. Many families moved into the four tower blocks of council flats on Adelaide Road, and other blocks in the neighbourhood.

As these families gladly transferred to modern self-contained flats, numbers of dilapidated houses, in streets adjoining the tracks, came on the market, sometimes with a sitting tenant at controlled rent. Astute seekers of a run-down home at rock-bottom price snapped up the vacant houses, which were given a thorough transformation. Bathrooms and fully-equipped kitchens were created, attractive patios and roof terraces constructed – all in the lovely soot-free air. Estate agents had a new lease of life, as houses freed from rent controls came on the market.

The clearer light, the cleaner air, the Hill, the nearby shops, the easy access to City or West End all combined to make it the ideal place to live: and the balance swung from London working class to young intelligentsia and established professionals.

Past decades have seen the trend accelerate. Massive rises in the price of houses are matched by increased rents for shops, and this with the coming of the Camden supermarkets has been the downfall of the small shops that once supplied our local daily needs. With few exceptions all are gone as are familiar workers – the élite who drove *The Royal Scot* and *Irish Mail* and the close community that once existed.

In this Millennium year – Primrose Hill is still a perfect place to live. I am so fortunate to have seen it all.

Auden Place

Keith & Betty Bird

Auden Place initially offered a variety of flats and terraced houses and six studios at the top of each entrance. These studios were intended for artists to live in but because one or two of the first tenants used them merely for their work, and lived elsewhere, they later lost their special distinction and became part of the normal residential accommodation. Twenty per cent of the accommodation was to be reserved for key workers, e.g. nurses, teachers, social workers. At first the Manley Housing Trust owned the new properties forming Auden Place but nominations for accommodation came through the Council. This, after a short period was replaced by the Omnium Housing Association who put the rents so high that many of the flats and houses remained empty. The Council then took a two-year lease of the whole

The view from my window, 1925 *Derek Sprange*

development and applied council rents: the accommodation all filled up but the special reservation for key workers gradually withered away. At the end of this period the managing agents changed again to Community Housing Association which still manages the estate.

A Housing Act in 1981 removed the limit on rent increases and market rents were introduced. The Residents' Association took the CHA to court over this but lost the case. Up to about 1992 the Council subsidised the rents but now council rents have risen and there is little difference between council and CHA charges. Residents do not have the right to buy and CHA has a policy of not selling the properties.

From the beginning there has been a Residents' Association, which in addition to expressing their strong concern over rents, services and maintenance, at least initially promoted a strong community atmosphere on the estate. The building which had been initially designed as a centre for older people (hence the provision of a lift that has never been used) became a nursery: the only one in the locality providing care for the whole working day and taking children from outside the estate. The Tenants' Association, started by Keith Bird and Claire Daglish instigated a range of social activities including a football team for the under-elevens, which played regularly on Primrose Hill, and a Youth Club. They also formed a team of gardeners who looked after the trees, shrubs and plants that made Auden Place so attractive. For two years the Tenants' Association organised a firework display for the families who lived in or near to Auden Place: this was the forerunner of the present London-wide annual event on Primrose Hill.

For several years, Auden Place was almost the sole provider of social activities in Primrose Hill and even when the Primrose Hill Community Association was established about 1980, it held its early meetings and social activities in the Auden Place Nursery, and was strongly supported by Auden Place residents. The Nursery was initially set up and managed by the Auden Place Tenants' Association and has been of great benefit to the community for over 25 years. The estate was fully integrated in the local community, whose members walked freely through its attractive centre. In 1998, however, the clamour from some residents for greater security led to lockable gates being placed on the terraced houses open to the outside and on all but one of the entrances to the estate. Many people had mixed feelings about this move with many residents and members of the wider community expressing concern about the loss of community interaction. Nevertheless, Auden Place continues to be regarded by those who visit it or live near it, as a fine example of urban domestic architecture and an estate they are proud to have in their midst.

The residents of Auden Place were also instrumental in promoting sports activities for youngsters in the area. Starting with their own football team and sports day, this was translated, once the Community Centre was established, to an annual day on the Hill, attached to the summer festival. The usual races and games were organised and small prizes were offered but for several years in the early and mid -eighties the event of the day was a tug-of-war competition between the eight or nine local pubs. This was fiercely fought and the shield that was awarded to the winning team still stands in one of the local public houses, which was the last one to win it.

Initiated by a resident of the Oldfield estate of sheltered housing, Claire Bennett who had her own set of boules, the PHCA persuaded the Manager of Regent's Park to lay out a boules pitch by the side of the gymnastic equipment near to the Zoo entrance. It is little publicised, but is still used by local residents.

The Hill, and more recently, the sports track on the outer circle of the park, is also the venue for some of the sports activities for the children of Primrose Hill Primary School. Organised by the school, but with extensive parent help a sports day takes place each summer. While each week, and especially on Sunday mornings, teams of young amateur footballers, cheered on by their parents, are to be found kicking a ball about on the flatter areas at the foot of the Hill. They were at one time supplemented by baseball played by pupils and parents from the nearby American School.

The Boys' Home Chapel Campaign

Adrian Richardson

Incensed by the planning application in 1995 to develop the chapel site in Regent's Park Road, local people set up a campaign to oppose it. Nothing unexpected or remarkable about that, but as the years passed by, the stamina and extraordinary commitment of the campaigners proved this planning showdown to be a landmark of its kind. It is not easy to take on the Council, the Department of the Environment and a developer.

Local people wanted the chapel building, together with the original Boys' Home Industrial School buildings on the site, to stay. They argued that the buildings functioned satisfactorily as commercial units, their history

Save The Chapel

Save this...

- Historic building
- Local landmark
- Architectural diversity
- Traditional Materials

- Clear sky
- Green Trees
- Variation in roof line
- Open for sunlight

..From this!

- Unsympathetic block
- "Bronze alloy detail... throughout"
- Loss of sunlight in the street
- Increased noise

- Increased traffic congestion
- Increased pollution
- Demolition approval in the Primrose Hill conservation area
- Enclosure

Don't let this set a precedent!

Update

Court appeal

The judgement by the High court found that residents had indeed been severely disadvantaged by the public inquiry process. It also found that the evidence we would have submitted was material to the public enquiry.

We were therefore disappointed that the judge did not find in our favour and order another public enquiry. Knowing our case is strong, we are seeking a review of the Judgement by the Court of Appeal.

Further demolition

The demolition of the chapel would set a precedent.

Already other insensitive redevelopment proposals have been submitted by opportunist developers in the conservation area.

Artwork: Axel tel 0181-8885038

was significant and their architectural features and character were of importance to the area.

The Planning Department approved the demolition but rejected the developer's replacement scheme of 26 flats and a much reduced commercial provision. The developers appealed to the Department of the Environment. A public local inquiry was held in July 1996 at the Town Hall. Local residents were handicapped on two counts. The Council failed to give residents proper notice of the inquiry and secondly the Council did not make public the full contents of the only thorough and comparative study of the Primrose Hill Conservation Area – the GLC study of 1975.

To everyone's surprise the Department of the Environment inspector ruled in favour of the developer. The campaigners decided the fight must go on. They now needed a good barrister and money. Concerts and readings were organised, including one evening at St Mark's Church where Alan Bennett read from his diaries.

Christopher Katkowski agreed to represent the residents. He proved to be a very good choice. Other barristers had been approached but had all been too pessimistic about the residents' case.

In January 1997 the case was heard in the High Court. The residents lost but refused to let up. They still believed that their ability to represent themselves at the Public Inquiry had been severely compromised by the actions of the Council.

In December 1997 the campaigners won their case in the Court of Appeal. Four months later the councillors on the development control sub-committee rejected the planning officers' advice and voted in favour of retaining the chapel buildings, believing they did indeed contribute to the Conservation Area.

The strain of running such a campaign was such that no one person oversaw it all. Bob Starr, David Roberts and Gervais Williams all chaired the group at various times. Jane Fulford, whose contribution was crucial, has the lasting honour of the Appeal Court ruling bearing her name.

Cecil Sharp House
Vic Godrich

Cecil Sharp was a musician and teacher and also a collector of folksongs and dances at the turn of the twentieth century. The Industrial Revolution in England and the resultant break up of rural communities together with the influence of the Church which saw many customs as 'pagan' and the dances as licentious, meant that the folksongs and dances of this country were fast receding into oblivion. The Folksong Society, of which Cecil Sharp was a member, was formed to collect the folksongs before they all disappeared. In 1889 Cecil Sharp saw the Headington Quarry Morris Men at a now historic meeting on Boxing Day. The result of this was that he was to collect dances as well as songs and in 1911 he formed the English Folk Dance Society (EFDS). His aim was to return to the people of England their dances as well as their songs and, being a teacher, he used the education system to pursue this aim, and was responsible for the inclusion of English folk dance in the curriculum of schools at the beginning of the twentieth century.

Cecil Sharp was always on the lookout for a suitable headquarters for his society but his search was unsuccessful, and when he died in1924 it was felt that the most suitable memorial to him should be a purpose-built headquarters. A committee was formed headed by Lady Mary Trefusis, the first president of the EFDS and the secretary was Winifred Shuldham Shaw, who also started a special fund to provide furniture and equipment for the Cecil Sharp Library, the collection of books which Sharp had bequeathed to the Society with the proviso that they be made available to the public.

For the building £25,000 was needed and after much campaigning £31,780. 6s. 4d. was collected, including a personal donation of £5,000 from Mrs J. J. Storrow, President of the Federation of American Branches of the EFDS, and a grant from the Carnegie United Kingdom Trust, although most of the donations were small amounts. There was a scheme for members of the public to 'buy a brick'. A number of sites were inspected and the present site chosen in the summer of 1927. The foundation stone was laid in June

1929 by Miss Maud Karpeles assisted by William Kimber, the leader of the Headington Quarry Morris Men whose dancing had led Cecil Sharp into the collection of dance. William Kimber was a bricklayer by trade and laid a course of bricks in the new building. The architects were H.M. Fletcher and Godfrey Pinkerton. Cecil Sharp House was formally opened on Whit Saturday 1931 by the Rt. Hon. H.A.L. Fisher. The lower hall in the building was named Trefusis after the Society's president and two other rooms were named Storrow and Carnegie.

In 1932 the Folk Song Society was on the point of being wound up. Members felt that all the folksongs that could be collected had now been found and that the Society had no further function. Ralph Vaughan Williams, the Secretary of the Folk Song Society, disagreed and conferred with Douglas Kennedy, the Director of the English Folk Dance Society with a view to amalgamating the two societies. This was done in 1932, the resulting organisation being named the English Folk Dance and Song Society. The new society was an incorporated body and as such able to hold the freehold of Cecil Sharp House. This had previously been held by trustees consisting of the original committee. The freehold was therefore transferred to the EFDSS which was an educational charity in its own right.

War came in 1939 and during hostilities Cecil Sharp House was hit by a bomb and a large part of the structure destroyed. After the war the Society was once again in the business of appealing for funds, this time to rebuild the damaged part of the building. A grant of £10,000 was offered by the Ministry of Education and £12,000 was recoverable from the Government for war damage. However, £36,000 had to be spent on the refurbishment as a condition of the Education Ministry's grant. The rebuilding started in 1950, and a new floor was added to accommodate additional administrative offices. The main hall lost its musicians' gallery in the bombing, and this was not restored as it had proved an unfavourable location for musicians. Instead the wall was decorated with a mural. Ivon Hitchens accepted the Society's commission

Maud Karpeles laying Cecil Sharp House foundations stone 1929; Willliam Kimber and architects in attendance *EFDSS*

to paint what proved to be the largest picture of his career.

During the sixties and seventies folk music and dance became very popular, partly due to the visit to Canada by Princess Elizabeth, now the Queen, who acquired a taste for square dancing there, and brought the craze back with her. Both the Royal Princesses had been introduced to English folk dance by the Girl Guide movement, and HRH Princess Margaret became a patron of the Society and is now the Society's President. Folk song clubs also proliferated and Cecil Sharp House became the scene of a great deal of activity. On a Saturday night in the sixties you could not gain entrance after 8 p.m. because the hall was full.

During the 1980s public interest in English folk music began to diminish somewhat. In 1986 the National Executive Committee of the EFDSS decided to sell Cecil Sharp House. This caused an uproar from the Society's membership and a battle commenced to save the building. The Charity Commission was involved and for two years the building was in danger of being lost. Indeed it was actually put on the market at one stage. In the end the membership held sway and the sale was halted. A new National Executive took over and, since that time, have worked hard to husband their resources and to keep the building maintained in good condition. Cecil Sharp House is now a Grade II listed building.

Cecil Sharp House today is still the headquarters of the English Folk Dance and Song Society. When the building is not in use for folk music and dance, then halls are available for hire to produce income to pay for running costs. It houses the Vaughan Williams Memorial Library, the heir to the Cecil Sharp Collection left to the Society in the 1920s, which has become the foremost collection of English folk material in the country: this is available to anyone who wishes to research it, just as Cecil Sharp wanted.

The Civic Society & Darwin Court

Diana Gurney

A local planning issue made me aware of the need for a group dedicated to the aesthetic interests of the borough. I knew there was a Marylebone Society and they advised me to get in touch with the St Pancras Borough Librarian. He told me that other people had expressed a similar need and put me in touch with them. They were Tammo de Jongh, John Hulton, Hugh Morris, Jenny and Philip Marriott, Tim Sturgis and others who had formed a group that was already meeting.

In the summer of 1963 the inaugural meeting of St Pancras Civic Society was held; a committee was formed and began its work. Much later when the three boroughs were merged it became the Camden Civic Society.

By 1970 it became necessary to get Primrose Hill declared a Conservation Area because of the imminent destruction of some of the best houses in the area – nos. 2–24 Gloucester Avenue. They were owned by the Railway which had bought them when they had extended the track. There were four large detached houses with their own stable accommodation; the rest were semi-detached. One gap caused by a bomb had been filled by garages. All were bigger than those elsewhere in the area and were very impressive, even though some had been multi-occupied and though handsome were neglected. British Rail were willing to sell and planning permission had been given for replacement by a number of smaller houses.

When I subsequently saw the file at the Town Hall it contained the comment that the houses were more suitable for preservation and conversion than demolition, but it had been disregarded. Once permission had been given for redevelopment the site was sold on and a new plan submitted for a much larger development of flats; more money could be made that way. The Council was in favour because the rateable value of the site would increase in proportion to the potential number of dwellings to be built. It was a tragedy because these were the most distinguished houses in Primrose Hill.

The new plans were horrible and a fight

THE VICTORIAN SOCIETY

From the Chairman
12 Bloomsbury Square
London wc1
Telephone 01-405 2520

The national society responsible for the study and protection of Victorian and Edwardian architecture and other arts. Registered as a charity.
Chairman Professor N B L Pevsner CBE PhD FBA FSA

17 April 1970

Sir,

As Chairman of the Victorian Society, I wish to plead for the preservation of nos. 4, 6, 8 and 10 Gloucester Avenue, four houses which could easily be converted and which represent the best that is left of a group once larger. Even so, these four remain very impressive, and they belong to a kind too rapidly jettisoned. They are doubly impressive owing to their position at the junction of Gloucester Avenue and Regents Park Road.

Yours faithfully,

Sir Nikolaus Pevsner

The Chairman,
Planning Committee,
Camden Council,
Old Town Hall,
High Holborn,
W.C.1.

Letter from Sir Nikolaus Pevsner, The Victorian Society

Diana Gurney

4 Gloucester Avenue, one of the villas demolished 1970/71 *Diana Gurney*

began to save at least the four largest houses. These were attributed (by John Summerson) to Henry Bassett, a Royal Academy Gold Medallist who, he thought, had also built the upper quadrant of Gloucester Crescent. We lobbied John Summerson, Nikolaus Pevsner and the Victorian Society, all of whom endorsed our opinion of the houses and could not understand why they had not been listed or why Primrose Hill had not been made a Conservation Area. The Act which authorised such areas had been passed in 1967 and it was now 1970.

In Camden we had a planning officer who thought many of the old neighbourhoods should be pulled down and he succeeded in destroying some of the nicest areas. So in spite of a lengthy struggle and eminent support we lost this battle, but we did succeed in modifying the plans for the new Darwin Court flats which are considerably better than they would have been. And in 1972 we achieved our long-term objective; Primrose Hill was designated a Conservation Area.

Opposite Darwin Court is a hard red block of flats by James Stirling which replaced another large detached house and doesn't fit well with its neighbours, even though the flats inside are good. The original plan would have used the whole rear garden for car parking which would have ruined the green garden triangle behind three busy roads. The Civic Society supported the objections of the residents and as a result the car park was built underground.

Chalk Farm Baptist Church

Revd David Shosanya & Sandra Nicholas

The Baptist Church today is one of the largest Protestant Free Church communions, extending to every continent. A survey, *The Religious Life of London* (Mudie Smith: 1904) shows that overall they were the only denomination not in decline at the beginning of the last century. The survey noted 'the Baptists, at 4,732, ...were second only to the Established Church': and Berkley Road came fifth among the 11 Baptist Churches in St Pancras, with Sunday attendance at 257.

The history of Berkley Road Chapel has its origins in the 1860s. Members of Bloomsbury Baptist Church, who had moved northwards to Camden Town and the Chalk Farm area, found a Sunday's journey back to their Bloomsbury church unpleasant and even dangerous. They therefore began to meet in the house of a Mr Hawes, and then founded a church in King Street, now Plender Street. Soon after, they purchased a barn in the Lower Chalcot area, and on this site was built the 'Peniel Tabernacle', a substantial brick structure, apparently still visible in 1965, set back from the Chalk Farm Road. This purchase and later building costs involved the Church in 'substantial financial obligations ... ground rent, interest charges and mortgage repayments'.

Membership and the congregation increased and in 1867, the Revd G.T. Edgeley undertook the pastorate, encouraged by the Revd Charles Haddon Spurgeon, perhaps the most famous of nineteenth century preachers of any denomination.

The church continued to flourish and in 1870 the building of a new and larger chapel was begun on the present site in Berkley Road. It was opened on 15 February 1871, and was capable of seating 500 in the church, with a Sunday School for 600 children below.

The years of the Revd F. Hodgson's ministry were perhaps the brightest in the history of the church. Taking up his appointment during the 1914–18 war, he served until failing health forced his retirement in 1931. During this period church and Sunday school attendances were high, and there were many conversions. He was ably supported by his wife 'Sister Lizzie' who combined her work in the Hammersmith South Street Mission with service as a Borough Councillor. Throughout its history the church has been kept alive by the faith and determination of many men and women – in particular, the Read family, the Bucknells, and George Moon and his wife.

During the war the church was damaged by a bomb that fell in Regent's Park Road and it was not until later that the site was redeveloped and a new building provided. This involved the rebuilding of the front elevation, and eventually planning permission was granted for redevelopment to provide a new church at ground floor, and hall below with the addition of flats above. The Million Penny Fund was raised in 1952 by Mrs G. Moon, to provide funds to help the re-establishment of the church during and after the rebuilding.

From 1987 to March 2000, Chalk Farm Baptist Church was led by Pastor Kate Coleman. She was the second woman minister at the Church, the Revd Violet Hodges (1953–57) being the first.

Now the church leadership consists of the Revd David Shosanya and two elders. This differs from the ecclesiastical structure of a traditional Baptist church, which usually consists of the Pastor, Elders and a Diaconate. The Revd Shosanya and the two elders are assisted by Departmental heads and a large number of practical helpers.

The Church conducts a ministry based on the nurturing of relationships in family life; work with children and young people; healing; counselling; teaching; preaching and worship. In particular the Chalk Farm Baptist Church is committed to working with people from many different nationalities and backgrounds. It has links with many different parts of the world, and people from the Church have gone on missions to various countries in Africa, Eastern Europe and the Middle East.

The Shalom Eastern European Church has been meeting in the church for more than four years. They are a group made up of people – mainly refugees – from the nations of the former Yugoslavia. There are meetings jointly with the Baptist Church members.

This worldwide interest was particularly illustrated by an international evening when people came in national costumes and provided entertainment from their 'homelands'. There was also a joint weekend away when, among 40 adults taking part, 18 different nationalities were represented.

Although the attendance at the regular Sunday morning services is now much lower than it used to be, the Church continues to attract a devoted following from a wide area both in and around Primrose Hill.

Hopkinsons Place: Installing The Old Piano Factory Gates, 1996 *Jo Killip*

The Community Centre
David Gray

The piano factory, which sits rather nonchalantly and improbably in the midst of terrace housing in Fitzroy Road, was in the mid-seventies earmarked for conversion into flats. (This was the post-Schlaffenberg age and we were all by now concerned with preserving our heritage, and this stoutly built building had been one of the outposts of the local piano-manufacturing industry.) It had an ancillary building, two storey, separate from the main building, perhaps a materials store. Some said it was in this building that the piano frames were cast, but these must have been imported. Anyway, the ancillary building was at first proposed for conversion into four or five dwellings, but it made an awkward alteration.

Our local councillor, at that time Jonathan Sofer, started a campaign locally for its adaptation as a community association building, in effect our village hall, and I surveyed the building and drew up a feasibility scheme. At first we negotiated a club room above four (extravagantly large) garage spaces, but eventually the Council was persuaded to let us have the whole building, and the space below the main club room was assigned to further activity space. This level was eventually converted to a bar space with cellarage below. The feasibility scheme drawings formed the basis for the eventual conversion in 1978, which was detailed and its building supervised by Camden Architects Department, and the building has been used energetically by the local community ever since.

(Bruno Schlaffenberg was Camden Borough Planner in the sixties. To him we owe the substitution of the Oldfield Estate Blocks for what had been a pleasant nineteenth-century terrace, set back behind trees and overlooking Primrose Hill; and also the replacement, by the Darwin Court Blocks, of a row of handsome Victorian villas beside the railway cutting, in Gloucester Avenue. This last 'improvement' provided the incentive for the formation of the Primrose Hill Conservation Area.)

Primrose Hill Community Centre, Hopkinsons Place, early 80s *CLSAC*

Primrose Hill Conservation Area Advisory Committee

Richard Simpson

The Primrose Hill Conservation Area Advisory Committee is a community watchdog, keeping a close eye on development in our conservation area.

Conservation areas were first designated under a new Act of Parliament of 1967. This law reflected public revulsion against both commercial redevelopment, especially of historic town centres like Bath, and against the 'comprehensive redevelopment' schemes adopted by some councils – the complete redevelopment of areas like Chalcot Square and the Manley Street and Kingstown Road areas were just two local examples considered in the 1960s. Government response to this disquiet sought not only to protect localities, but also to ensure public engagement in the conservation process, and local councils were recommended to set up Conservation Area Advisory Committees.

These Advisory Committees were given specific tasks under central government guidance, and the nature of their membership was also laid down. An important function has always been to provide local knowledge and expertise, and to engage the active participation of the community – residents, commercial interests, local groups, and amenity societies – in the operation of the planning process as it applies to all aspects of the environment of conservation areas.

Several local councils were very reluctant to offer local communities such a mechanism for influencing the planning process, but Camden was among the first to set up Advisory Committees, the first being in Bloomsbury and Hampstead and Highgate in 1968. There are now 32 conservation areas in Camden, 20 of them covered by 12 working Advisory Committees: new committees for areas not yet served by a committee are under active consideration.

The Primrose Hill Conservation Area was designated in 1972, and an Advisory Committee established in the same year. Membership, decided by Camden, was to include the nominees of a number of local residents' and tenants' associations, local amenity groups, like the Camden Civic Society, the three main political parties, the professional associations most concerned with the built environment, and business interests. The list of participating bodies was extended later to include two of the national amenity societies. The committee consists only of nominees of these groups and cannot appoint any of its own members. As a result, the Committee's 15 members – all volunteers – are the nominees of a wide range of interested bodies, with a broad set of local knowledge and technical skills. The Committee has maintained an archive of applications, its advice, decisions, and of photographs, to help in its work.

The Committee currently meets twice each month to consider every planning application made within the conservation area, or on its borders. We then provide formal advice to Camden Council on each application, and to the Department of the Environment if necessary. Our primary task is to consider whether each application would 'preserve or enhance' the character and appearance of the conservation area – the legal duty on planners in conservation areas – and we interpret this broadly. For example, we see keeping jobs in the area as vital to its character, and have successfully opposed a number of attempts by developers to provide flats by destroying work places. Primrose Hill never became merely a residential suburb: the areas beside the railway and behind the houses and their gardens provided an opportunity for a rich mixture of living and working accommodation, and this in turn has enabled the lively mixture of cafés, restaurants, and specialist shops to survive and prosper. Keeping small flats, and ensuring that there is 'affordable' housing in the area are also priorities. In seeking to conserve the area, the Committee has also taken an active part in encouraging good modern design: we look forward to seeing design of our own times which is consistent with the scale and texture of the area, and which recognises the need to be a good neighbour to the old. The need to meet new standards in sustainable development – from reusing our existing buildings, to making sure that new provision is well-planned and energy efficient – is also a vital consideration.

As locals, using our streets, open spaces,

shops, cafés and restaurants, we are in a position to monitor the results of new development, and try to make sure that one person's lively activity is not another's nuisance. Successful new development relies on neighbourliness, and confidence that no one will be damaged by change.

The Committee also takes a larger view. We are consulted by a wide range of authorities on a wide range of issues – from plans for Camden High Street to licencing issues. We are all aware that although the use of cars has devastated some areas of London, neglect of the transport infrastructure has made it hard for people to identify practical alternatives. We are not isolated from the effects of these larger issues, and give advice on how they affect our area too.

The Committee has enjoyed some important successes – the housing in Hopkinsons' Place, and the Community Association building were the consequence of early victories. More recently, the Committee played a crucial part in support of local residents who won in the Court of Appeal over the developers who sought to destroy the former Boys' Home Chapel. We helped local people in blocking plans to give London Zoo ten acres of Regent's Park.

People enjoy living in Primrose Hill, and many more want to do so, in part because of the successful protection of our environment. We try to understand what makes the area attractive, so that success can protect the area we love, not destroy it.

The Friends of Regent's Park & Primrose Hill

Valerie St Johnston

Primrose Hill – the grassy outcrop that provides the raison d'être for the residential area of the same name – is in need of constant protection. We have to be vigilant to ensure that it is well maintained. We have to fight against any sort of commercial development, against dangerous cyclists, skate boarders and now scooter riders, against motor vehicles and against dog litter. Some of these battles have been won by the Friends, but others are ongoing problems which need the concerted efforts of local residents who want to keep the Hill as a tranquil green area for rest and play.

The Friends of Regent's Park was founded in 1991, following a study by the London Business School which established the need for such a group to safeguard the interests of those visiting the Park and living in or around it. At that time the Zoo was trying to annex 10 acres of Regent's Park with the alleged intention of introducing a theme park, which would increase its revenue. This rallied intense local opposition and the Friends were created to prevent any further attempted inroads.

I joined the Friends as Secretary in 1993 since when I have been immersed in what you might call Park politics. In those early days, what the Royal Parks' Agency called 'consultation' meant informing the Friends after a plan was effected. This led to fairly abrasive relations with the Royal Parks' Agency and with the Park Manager. Since then we have gradually developed a better working relationship based on the notion that we must be consulted before a policy is decided. I can discuss our views with the Park Manager, David Caselton, in a frank but friendly atmosphere and we usually arrive at a consensus.

One of the first things I changed was the name of the Friends so that it would incorporate Primrose Hill. An increasing number of our members come from the area in which I too live, and it is important that Primrose Hill is not seen as a poor relation to Regent's Park. The Park Manager really gives consideration to the Hill. In 1994 he employed a master hedge-layer, Mr Tunk, to cut back and re-lay the old hedge on Prince Albert Road. At first there were outcries that the hedge had been destroyed, but those who watched Mr Tunk at work, intricately weaving the base of the hedge, knew that it would grow again in a few years and provide a thicker habitat for wild life. Now we have a fully restored hedge, though it still shows scars at three points, where cars have run into it.

For the last 10 years the grass on the front of the Hill has been allowed to grow long. This has raised some criticism but it does give a more natural and less manicured effect. It is unfortunate that cyclists still race down the Hill, carving a new narrow path down its centre. During the winter of 1996–7 the Friends planted two oaks just behind the summit of Primrose Hill, in addition to six we planted in the Broad Walk in the Park. About six of us neatly shovelled earth into the holes that the Park staff had already prepared using the dainty spades which are specially made for royal plantings. Oaks do not grow easily on the Hill and their first years have been slow, but it is important that we should support tree planting as older trees die, and we strongly favour indigenous English species.

Many members ask why we can't have primroses on Primrose Hill. In the first place, the primroses of the past grew in ditches to the south of the Hill. The Hill itself is too dry for moisture-loving plants. The Park Management has tried to encourage primroses under shrubs and along the edge of the Hill, but too often the plants are lifted and taken away.

A year ago the Park Manager proposed to landscape the top of the Hill with a sunken paved area above the old Second World War gun emplacement. This plan united the people of Primrose Hill in a way that I had not seen since the two old battles – to keep the gates on the Hill open at night and to prevent an ugly toilet building in the south-east corner. We inundated the Park Manager with letters of protest. In the old days of

The Shakespeare Commoration in London; planting an oak on Primrose Hill *The Illustrated London News, 30 April 1864*

confrontation, the scheme might have gone ahead but in the newer climate of co-operation, the plan was withdrawn and we have retained the simple natural summit that we all appear to prefer.

The Royal Parks' Agency is always trying to raise money from exploiting the Parks commercially. Filming on the Hill is a contentious issue because it can mean cars parked on the Hill and sometimes the top of the Hill is closed to us, the public. But we on Primrose Hill are much more fortunate than other parts of Regent's Park. The Friends fight hard to prevent the Agency holding inappropriate events in Regent's Park. Three years ago we led the protests against a Prince's Trust pop concert on Cumberland Green, which was scheduled to attract an audience of 100,000. In the end this was transferred to Hyde Park. Our own big event, the November Fireworks Display, is a much more suitable affair, which we wholly support. About 30,000 people come from all over London, giving voluntary contributions at the gates, which in 1999 raised £23,000 for Crisis at Christmas. There is a tradition of fireworks on Primrose Hill as early as the celebrations for the ending of the Crimean War.

The Broadwalk, Regent's Park, January 2001 *Ivòr Kamlish*

The Friends encourage sport in Regent's Park and try to keep it accessible to all against the trend of rising charges for the hiring of facilities. There is more sport in Regent's Park than on Primrose Hill, but we do have the petanque area introduced in the late 1970s as a result of a petition from elderly local people. The primary schools in the area sometimes use it now.

The open air gymnasium has been completely modernized. Installed in 1847, for the use of men and boys only, it was immensely popular. Detailed by-laws had to be drawn up such as restricting the time spent on one piece of equipment and forbidding anyone from standing on top of the apparatus. Even so, there were many falls and injuries. From the 1920s up to 100 men and boys attended a PE class on Friday evenings. One young enthusiast reported 'When I left school seven years ago I was 4'5". My height is now 5'6" thanks to that gym on Primrose Hill'. Now of course people go to indoor gyms and the one on Primrose Hill is less popular.

Working for the Friends, first as Secretary and then as Chairman, is a mixture of frustration and reward. The responsibility is broader than that of a residential association, because Regent's Park and Primrose Hill are enjoyed by London's workers and tourists as well as local residents. So it is not a 'Not in my back yard' role. Moreover, the Chairmen of the eight Royal Parks join together in the Royal Parks' Forum to put pressure both on the Royal Parks' Agency and the Government on matters that concern all the Royal Parks. These include declining government funding of the Royal Parks and the resultant commercial activities. By and large, Primrose Hill is not yet threatened by these activities, but we have to maintain our watch. One of our safeguards is that the authorities respect the proven truculence and determination of Primrose Hill residents in all the protest campaigns that we have waged. I only have to mention the possibility of the Friends in Primrose Hill taking to the barricades and negotiations re-open!

Knights of Rizal

Barry Bowman

Dr José Rizal, freedom fighter and National Hero of the Philippines once lodged in Chalcot Crescent while he gathered the lost history of the ancient Filipinos from the archives in the British Museum. Through his writing he helped free the Philippines from the Spanish.

The Embassy of the Philippines and the Philippine Society of London unveiled a commemorative plaque on 19 June 1955, the birthday anniversary of Dr Rizal: 'Let this plaque, finally, attest that, whatever men may say about the British Empire, there was always, and always will be, room and welcome in London to men of every race and clime who believe – as José Rizal believed – in human freedom.'

Saviour of The Philippines, José Rizal has become the fourth world hero to have a bust unveiled in Camden in his honour.

The three-foot bronze sculpture is on display in Chalk Farm Library, Sharpleshall Street, Primrose Hill, just yards from 37 Chalcot Crescent, where Rizal lived between 1886 and 1888. As a mark of co-operation between the Philippine community and Chalk Farm Library, the garden at the rear now houses the Rizal Memorial Garden and is maintained by the Knights of Rizal, an organisation dedicated to promoting the memory of Dr Rizal. Councillors Bob Hall and Heather Johnson and the Ambassador of the Philippines unveiled the plaques in the library and in the Rizal Garden.

Dr Rizal wrote many books and by all accounts he is quite comfortable in our library. Visitors from the Philippines are attracted to the library since it now features in the *Philippines National Heritage Trail*. The Knights of Rizal and Maclariz here in London stood shoulder to shoulder with the Friends of the Library and everyone else involved in the campaign to Save the Library.

After unveiling a plaque to Dr. Rizal in Chalk Farm Library: HE the Ambassador of the Philippines, and his wife; Mayor of Camden, Cllr. Bob Hall and his wife, with two Filipino dancers *Sir Barry Bowman*

Primrose Hill Action Group
David Birkett

Parking difficulties in Primrose Hill had already been a topic of informal discussion at a meeting of a group of local residents when, in late 1990, a brief questionnaire was received from Camden Council. This was in no way a formal document and its purpose seemed to be to take preliminary soundings of public opinion: we therefore decided to make a collective response.

At that time there were no restrictions at all on parking: every bit of curb-side space was parked, and cars were double-parked for much of the day in most of the shopping section of Regent's Park Road.

Some people favoured a laissez-faire approach: the situation could not get any worse: once saturation point had been reached, further parking would be physically impossible. Most people, however, thought that some action should be taken, and that this should be tailored to the unique character of Primrose Hill.

Our reply to Camden expressed our preference for a scheme that would remove the commuters – those who parked their cars in the area for the day and completed their journey by other means – but leave residents unaffected. To achieve this, we suggested a two-hour restriction between 8 a.m. and 10 a.m. only.

Soon after, we heard that our local ward councillors had called a meeting to discuss this issue at Primrose Hill School, Princess Road. We went along in the hope of a balanced debate, but it soon became clear that residents' views were not to be heard, and the evening ended in angry frustration: the battle lines had been drawn.

Within days the Primrose Hill Action Group had been formed – PHAG – a name we never then expected to hear repeated in the High Court in the Judgement of a Learned Judge! As convenor of the previous ad hoc group, I became co-chairman with Pattie Caldwell – and we circulated a questionnaire, and leaflet with the title 'We can say NO!' – to the parking restrictions Camden intended to impose.

We had enormous support for our view, but this was not the whole story. Another group – the Regent's Park Road Residents' Association – favoured restrictions, and their speedy implementation – a course of action PHAG believed would aggravate the problems, and solve nothing.

Demonstrations: banners in the Council Chamber: night traffic counts at 3 am: acrimonious correspondence in the local press: nothing moved Camden from its chosen scheme: eventually we sought legal advice from Mark Cran, QC, a Regent's Park Road resident.

As a result in November 1994 a nervous group of 10 local residents found themselves in the High Court taking action against Camden Council. The hearing before Lord Justice McCulloch lasted almost three weeks.

Finally we received judgement on 11 January 1995. We had won. The traffic orders were quashed and Camden was told to begin the process again. The costly four-year struggle had been justified.

In his final comments, the Judge defined the proper procedure:

...Whatever the eventual outcome, the process of consultation must start again and the differing views and suggestions considered and evaluated in a spirit of respectful mutual cooperation. May I express the hope that this judgment will not be seen, for too long at least, as one producing winners and losers, but rather as something that provides a new beginning.

Later that year a steering group was established by the Council. This was made up of representatives of various local groups and led by an independent facilitator. It met for about two years, and hammered out the details for a parking plan and traffic management scheme that could be put before local people. In 1997 consultation took place and the scheme was finally implemented in 1998.

It is fair to say that most people approve of the parking restrictions and believe they work well. True, you cannot always park exactly where you want, but there is usually a space nearby. Some people want further restrictions at weekends or in the evenings. Maybe one day these will come, but I think Camden will consult the residents of Primrose Hill next time!

Primrose Hill neighbours help
Sharon Ridsdale

The history of the Primrose Hill community would not be complete without telling the story of Primrose Hill Neighbours Help.

In the early seventies the area known as Primrose Hill began to change rapidly. Many dwellings were being 'gentrified' and many writers, artists, journalists, publishers and other professionals moved into the renovated houses. Some of the large Victorian house changed from bed-sitter occupation back into family houses.

In 1974 a group of local people noticed that older people in particular had lost their 'neighbourly' neighbours. Some members of the community became isolated and many young mothers with small children were unaware of what facilities the community offered.

The London Borough of Camden Social Services set up a public meeting inviting local people to become involved in setting up a 'Good Neighbours' scheme. This initiative led to a group of volunteers meeting regularly and eventually becoming Primrose Hill Neighbours Help with links to Camden's social services.

In 1976 with a small grant from the Social Service Department an organiser was appointed to co-ordinate the befriending element of the volunteers. These volunteers visited people in their homes to offer neighbourly help. Many of these clients were housebound and the volunteers helped with shopping, odd jobs, transport, etc. The volunteers visited on a regular basis. This service was particularly useful to the many pensioners housed on the Oldfield Estate, a sheltered housing scheme for vulnerable people.

During these early years many events were organised for this client group by PHNH enabling them to mix socially and to participate in a number of local events.

The other element of PHNH was opening a 'drop in' information service held at the Circle 33 shop at 33 Chalcot Road. This was run by the Social Services with PHNH volunteers in attendance. The local social services were responsible for vetting and taking up references of volunteers.

In 1980 Durham University's Sociology department did a pilot study of 'Good Neighbour' schemes in England. It was published in 1981, *Action for Care*: Philip Abrams, Sheila Abrams, Robin Humphrey and Ray Smith.

This study highlighted the strengths and weaknesses of such schemes, particularly that groups of volunteers were often from a middle-class background while the client group consisted of people of very modest means. These clients were often pensioners on a fixed income and young families on low incomes.

The study led to PHNH becoming a properly constituted group and the adoption of a more professional profile. The volunteer group was encouraged to participate in 'workshops' and training sessions. A campaign was undertaken to recruit volunteers and to try and secure some measure of long term funding.

In 1989 PHNH moved into Chalk Farm Library and set up the information desk as

An origami workshop *CFL*

a 'drop in' service. Volunteers ran the desk on a rota basis. The move enabled the volunteers to access more easily the Camden Index (CINDEX) information service and allowed for clients to be guided to the service that they needed.

PHNH went from strength to strength and ran their own workshops, undertook counselling, took part in local community events and even ran a stall at the Chalcot Square Festivals. Volunteers attended public meetings and were visited by local Councillors, MPs and were supported by the local Mayor.

The move into Chalk Farm Library was very successful as this gave access to a wider client group: it also meant that the PHNH desk had a higher public profile and a more permanent base. The clients were able to access up-to-date information and were offered the appropriate service for their needs.

In the early nineties Chalk Farm Library was threatened with closure and this would have meant the end of PHNH as a thriving and very necessary service to the local community. The local community lobbied and campaigned vigorously to keep the library open and to maintain the uniquely 'local' service that PHNH offered of real 'care in the community'.

A partnership was established with Camden's Vulnerable Older People's Project (an initiative proposed by a local Councillor, Harriet Garland) and Age Concern, Camden. The group set up a management committee and was able to acquire funding for a co-ordinator to run the befriending service. The committee ensures that a rolling programme continues to attract volunteers and maintains casework and follow-up of the problems encountered by the client group.

In 1998 again Chalk Farm library was under threat of closure and again the local community fought a long and often contentious campaign to keep the library, and thus the service offered by PHNH.

During the past 20 odd years both the library and the PHNH scheme have become a valued and inseparable part of this community. It has helped the client group, to retain an independent and social interest in their local community; and the volunteer group to achieve personal growth and an understanding of 'community care' and all the complex issues involved.

Today PHNH has, through Camden Library Service, Information Technology (IT) access and information. It is able to offer its clients information that gives them real choice and empowers them to overcome, not only their problems, but also their isolation. So from small beginnings in the local community, clients and volunteers can all access the World Wide Web, surf the Internet, join the Superhighway club, and reach out to a wider world community.

Primrose Hill School, 1995 *Ron Sidell*

Primrose Hill Primary School

Irene Demetriou & Jean Rossiter

On 2 February 1885 Princess Road Board School was opened with accommodation for 988 pupils. The date 1884 is carved into a stone above one of the entrances – presumably the date that building began. Then, as now, it was a state school, publicly funded first by the London County Council, then under the Greater London Council by the Inner London Education Authority and now (since 1990) by Camden Local Education Authority.

Initially, the management of the school was closely controlled by the local council but gradually more and more authority has been devolved and the school is now managed by a triumvirate of Local Education Authority, Head Teacher and senior staff, and voluntary Governors.

The school was built on land that had been used as paddocks for the horses of the Riding Department of His Majesty's Ordnance. The local blacksmith had his smithy in Kingstown Street and the barracks were in Gloucester Avenue until they moved to the Ordnance Hill site on the other side of Primrose Hill.

The school was so close to the lines of the LMS railway that the smuts from the steam engines often marked the girls' white pinafores and the school walls became covered with black grime. It eventually became known as 'The Old Smoke School'. It was designed as a 'three-decker' school, on three floors, each with its central hall, the classrooms opening off the hall on either side; and was built in red brick with grey stone slabs high-lighting its traditional design. It is now a listed building.

As you walk round the school there is still evidence of the Victorian building's gas lighting and open fires and of a 'dumb-waiter' type lift between the three floors. Children sat in tiered rows of double desks, complete with inkwell, facing the teacher at the front of the class – and the chalkboard. There was a row of outside toilets in the upper, girls' playground. The boys played in the lower playground. The children entered and left school by separate entrances – Boys, Girls and Infants. It housed children up to the age of 14 with the older children, the seniors, in classrooms on the top floor where there were kitchens for housecraft lessons.

In between the wars, during the 1920s, the small house in the lower playground was used for school meals. Cookery classes were held in there with a class of children learning to cook alongside the cooks who were preparing the schoolchildren's meals. The house, which was one large room, was the school dining room and children would come for their meals in relays. School dinners cost 4d. and all children were given one third of a pint of milk to drink every day. Some of the food cooked during the cookery lesson would supplement the school meal but sometimes children could take the meal that they had prepared home for the family to eat. Children then left the school at 11 to transfer to secondary school.

During the Second World War, the Regent's Canal was used as a landmark by German bombers when they attacked the railway lines of King's Cross, St Pancras and Euston Stations. A branch of the canal that ran down parallel to Park Village East was filled in and covered with allotments to disguise the area and beneath the school, the open area known as the arches was sandbagged and children and teachers took cover there when the sirens sounded.

Some time in the late fifties or early sixties the school changed its name to Primrose Hill Junior Mixed and Infant school. Boys and Girls were no longer segregated but the Infants and Juniors were organised as two separate schools within the one building, each with its own Headteacher and staff and each with its own budget and resources. When, in 1991, the Headteacher of the Infants school retired, the opportunity was taken to amalgamate the two schools and since then it has been known as Primrose Hill Primary School with unified and integrated policies, staff, resources and facilities.

The classroom layout gradually became more informal, with tables instead of desks, as teaching policy and practices changed, with more individual and group learning. Education became 'child centred'.

At this time, the house in the lower playground provided tutorial accommodation for children with special educational needs from all over the Borough and children from other schools would come to the Tutorial for morning or afternoon sessions. When this shared facility was reorganised by the Local Education Authority, the small building stood empty until, in 1995, it was imaginatively converted into a nursery to house children from three-and-a-half years until they entered the reception class in the main building at the age of five. The nursery has its own enclosed garden and play area.

In 1984 the school celebrated its centenary. A garden was built in the upper playground and opened by David Bellamy. The older children and their teachers dressed in Victorian clothes and old double desks were brought back into the classrooms together with slates for writing. The wall displays were as they would have been in Victorian times. Parents and visitors came into school to view the Victorian lessons which were also filmed for television. A gallery of photographs spanning the 100 years was mounted in a lower corridor which brought back fond memories to the many ex-pupils who were invited to an all-day Saturday party.

In the playground there is a plaque commemorating a teacher, a magnolia tree with seating around it in memory of a school secretary and three wooden animals in the nursery playground donated by the family of an ex-pupil, all three of whom died tragically.

The school now has an annual intake of up to 75 children and, with a total of about 450 pupils, is the largest primary school in Camden. There are more than 40 languages spoken by the children as their first language; it is a socially-mixed, multicultural school. It is widely acclaimed for its musical achievements and justifiably proud of the happy, harmonious and, as two OFSTED inspections have shown, academically sound environment. Proud, too of its long and illustrious history, the school has plans to improve the building still further. One day there will be a central entrance befitting its size and position, a lift to carry disabled children and equipment from one floor to the next, and, dream of dreams, a hall large enough to take the whole school for Assembly and for the wonderful dramatic productions the children put on each year.

Primrose Hill Studios
Elizabeth Bordass

The Primrose Hill Studios are so well concealed behind the terraces of Fitzroy Road that a stranger to the area would have difficulty in finding them. There are twelve studios and a lodge, all facing onto a rectangular court. They are very typical of their period and were designed and built by Alfred Healey, a local builder and property developer around 1877.

Alfred Healey's father, a Yorkshire builder, started the family business in London in 1820 by taking out building leases on Crown Lands to the east and north of Regent's Park. The firm became involved in the development of the Primrose Hill area. Alfred Healey didn't appear to have had any formal architectural training, but was certainly used to working closely with the well-known architects of the day.

In 1860 Alfred became a partner in the firm and seems to have been an enlightened and caring landlord. An elderly resident can still remember him calling on a regular basis to consult her parents about maintenance to their home. The Healeys lived in the area and had their offices in Princess Road, only a few blocks from the site of the Studios. Healey purchased the plot in Fitzroy Road, with a view to building a row of superior terraced houses, one of which would be occupied by his own family. One can only speculate about his reason for building the Studios. The space behind the proposed terrace was the only buffer between them and the small terraces of railway workers' homes which once occupied the site where Auden Place now stands. What could have been better insulation than a small colony of artists?

Art and artists had achieved a new status in this period of Victorian society. The increasing number of second generation middle-class, of which the Healeys were a part, had growing affluence and social aspirations. They sought to rid themselves of their industrial connections and to throw off the label of 'philistine'. They patronised the arts and in so doing made it possible for artists to make a good living. This improved status made 'Art' a respectable occupation. Salon entertainment was fashionable and the artist interpreted this into the studio. The wealthier artists employed architects to design them studio homes while the poorer sought studios to rent. Within a small radius of Primrose Hill there were a number of studios built at this time, and Alfred Healey would have been aware of this fashionable trend. His addition of a lodge was unusual but neatly answered the problem of providing servants' quarters. Healey seems to have been willing to make adjustments to suit the individual requirements of the original tenants. For instance he constructed a small south-facing skylight to enable Joseph Wolf to test the durability of his colours by exposing them to sunlight. Frank Mason, a marine artist, left his mark on studio 3 by having portholes fitted in the front door and in the wall of his gallery so that he could sit up in bed and look into his studio.

Artists have continued to paint in these Studios, among them Arthur Rackham, Matthew Maris, Frederick Millers, Maurice Greifenhagen, Talbot Kelly, Montague Smyth, Pauline Boumphrey (sculptor), Lord Methuen, Patrick Caulfield and John Hoyland.

Its residents have also included actresses Martita Hunt and Margaret Webster, impressario Percy Pitt and authoresses Clo Graves [Richard Denham] who wrote *Dop Doctor* and Caroline Ramsden.

Primrose Hill Studios *Elizabeth Bordass*

Regent's Park Road Association

Caroline Cooper & John Emanuel

This association was founded in 1972 – as the Regent's Park Road Residents' Association – in order to represent local interests in discussion with Camden Council over the closure to traffic of the railway bridge at Chalk Farm – a closure which adds much to the comparatively secluded atmosphere of Primrose Hill village. Over the next few years the association monitored the gradually increasing flow of traffic through the area.

It became fully active again in the early nineties when it was felt that something had to be done about the parking situation. Commuter parking had become intolerable: residents all over the Primrose Hill area were infuriated every morning by the sight of commuters parking outside their homes, getting briefcases (and even a folding bicycle) out of their cars and setting purposefully off to work. Locals returning home were often forced to park several blocks away from where they lived – very difficult for the elderly, or for those with small children or shopping. The village was a much less attractive place than it is now, with what seemed like permanent double parking, frequent blockages, angry motorists trying to weave their way through, and poor vision for pedestrians crossing the road. For these reasons the majority of residents in the area were pleased when the council proposed the introduction of controls – though some objected to having to pay to park outside their own homes. Some of the shopkeepers were understandably anxious that parking restrictions might cause a loss of trade and, for a while, the community was unfortunately divided. However a co-operative steering group eventually ensured that the parking issue was satisfactorily resolved, and all of us would probably now agree that the Controlled Parking Zone has immeasurably improved the quality of life in the area.

The association recently dropped the 'residents' from its name, becoming RPRA. This was because residents of various smaller streets without their own associations had asked whether they could join. Also, since about a third of Regent's Park Road happens to pass through the shops, RPRA is naturally concerned about matters which involve the village and the community as a whole, not just those who happen to live in one street. It is anxious to support and co-operate with such essential local facilities as Chalk Farm Library and Primrose Hill Community Centre, and is currently working to erect a community notice board which could be shared by these three bodies.

Its main concerns in 2000 are persuading the Council to introduce further measures to curtail the speed and volume of traffic along Regent's Park Road, co-operating with the new Neighbourhood Watch scheme (a police initiative), and promoting smaller but nevertheless valuable projects such as the restoration of the little Victorian fountain on the corner of Albert Terrace.

Virginia Smith

Fountain & Dog Trough

just outside Primrose Hill, junction of Albert Terrace with Regent's Park Road

This fountain, made of polished granite, was erected in August 1872 by The Metropolitan Drinking Fountain and Cattle Troughs Association. In their Thirteenth Annual Report, 1872 [p.10] the Committee

...beg to assure their friends that ....their business is not to make an architectural display, but to provide as many free supplies of water for man and beast as possible. They never, under any circumstances, erect elaborate or expensive Fountains, except where the entire cost is defrayed by those who desire to erect such structures for Memorial or other purposes. Of such Fountains there are now in course of erection, three in central London, and a Fountain at Primrose Hill in memory of the late Judge Payne, the cost of which will be borne by a number of his admirers and friends.

The cost of £200 was raised by The Band of Hope, an association of young people who took vows of lifelong abstinence from alcohol; it was founded in 1847.

Deputy-Assistant Judge Joseph Payne was one of the Vice-Presidents of this association, indeed 'a most faithful and consistent advocate of Bands of Hope' whose 'presence at our public meetings was always hailed with delight'.
The fountain bore the inscription (now lost)

IN MEMORY OF
JOSEPH PAYNE, ESQ
DEPUTY-ASSISTANT JUDGE.
A ZEALOUS TOTAL ABSTAINER,
AND A FAITHFUL FRIEND OF
BANDS OF HOPE
DIED MARCH 29, 1870

ERECTED BY THE COMMITTEE
AND FRIENDS OF THE
UNITED KINGDOM
BAND OF HOPE UNION

Caroline Cooper

10 Regent's Park Road
Erwin Kronheimer

When, shortly before the outbreak of World War II, the Hungarian-born architect Ernö Goldfinger, an impassioned leader of the Modern Movement, built himself a house in Willow Road overlooking Hampstead Heath, he so enraged his neighbour, Ian Fleming, a no less impassioned member of the Old Hampstead Protection Society, that in 1959, having nursed his grudge for twenty years, Fleming bestowed the architect's name on a quite exceptionally determined megalomaniac – the eponymous protagonist of one of his most successful novels – with the consequence that 'Goldfinger' has become a household word in a million households in which architecture is seldom, if ever, a subject of engaging interest.

10 Regent's Park Road: exterior *AD*

The post-war years were a period of severe housing shortage, with the use of building materials primarily restricted to repair and reconstruction; and it was not until 1952 that conditions had eased sufficiently for Goldfinger to undertake, as he wished, another domestic project. The Festival of Britain had raised the profile of modern architecture; but the memory of the Battle of Willow Road (and, perhaps, Goldfinger's not wholly baseless reputation as a man who, in his strength of will and purpose, if in no other respect, could be thought to resemble his yet-to-be-created namesake) made some private clients who might otherwise have engaged his services shy of doing so. He therefore mustered a handful of typically ill-housed but impecunious friends and instructed them to form themselves into a co-operative housing society with ten shareholders and commission him to build them a block of ten flats on a bomb site in the Borough of St Pancras, whose Council was likely to look sympathetically on an application for a mortgage from such a source. The story of this venture, which in any other hands would have been doomed, is, not surprisingly, a long one; but the end result – four small and six large flats and three garages, all on the site of a single Victorian house – can be seen at 10 Regent's Park Road. The building of this began in 1954 and was almost complete when a workman leaping down the stairs two at a time cracked one of its fifty-two cantilevered concrete treads, thereby revealing that all fifty-two of them had been faultily cast and would have to be removed, remade and replaced and putting the whole work nine months behind schedule. In the event, the members of the Regent's Park Housing Society moved into their new homes in January 1956.

The house in Willow Road is now cherished by English Heritage and has become, if not a jewel, then a small pearl, in the crown of the National Trust, who periodically open it to the public. Going round the house, one becomes aware of its very close resemblance – a consistency both in detailing and concept – to the Regent's Park Road flats, notwithstanding the fifteen years that separate their construction. That resemblance extends to the initial – but perhaps by now attenuated – dislike the two buildings inspired in their respective neighbourhoods: both now Conservation Areas. And by way of postscript, to the fact that, four decades after its completion, 10 Regent's Park Road, too, has been listed by English Heritage.

It is still not, however, in the possession of the National Trust.

10 Regent's Park Road: interior *Ideal Home*

St Mark's Church

Valerie Taylor

(The writer has drawn extensively and gratefully on *A Short History of St Mark's*, a talk given in 1978 by a former parishioner, Jean Scott Rogers who died early in 2000.)

The history of St Mark's starts in the middle of the nineteenth century: in 1851, on 25 April, St Mark's Day, the Foundation Stone of the church was laid: in 1853, the nave and aisles were consecrated, and in 1891, the chancel.

The opening of the twentieth century saw Dr William John Sparrow-Simpson as Vicar. He was a renowned preacher and a follower of extreme High Church practices and during his time as Vicar 'large crowds were drawn to hear his sermons between Matins and Sung Eucharist'. Sparrow-Simpson resigned the living in 1904 and was succeeded by Maurice Bell, a talented musician and composer who had much to do with the compilation of the *English Hymnal*, which came into St Mark's in 1906 and whose editors were Percy Dearmer (vicar at that time of our sister church, St Mary the Virgin, Primrose Hill) and Ralph Vaughan Williams. In 1908 Bell had the Victorian galleries removed from the church and he did much to brighten up St Mark's, which had been said to be 'a rather dismal place'.

Three vicars followed Bell in quick succession, and then in 1928, with Britain in the throes of the Depression, began the incumbency of Hugh Stuckey, which was to continue until 1964, when he died in office after 36 momentous years, in which he was to face, as a bishop described it, 'the most grievous disaster that can befall a parish priest – the destruction of his church'.

Turning back to the thirties, Stuckey saw a social revolution in his parish, as it was at this time that many of the larger houses were divided into flats or bed-sitting rooms, and people began to go to second homes in the country at weekends – with obvious effects on the size of the congregation. But there was one instant weekend success story at St Mark's, when in 1930 Hugh Stuckey started tea parties in the church grounds on summer Bank Holiday Mondays. Many visitors to Regent's Park Zoo would come to St Mark's for refreshment – earning St Mark's the name of 'The Zoo Church' – and amongst the supporters of the teas were 'Gert and Daisy' (Elsie and Doris Waters) who at that time lived at 16 Prince Albert Road, opposite the church. Their brother, Jack Warner, was married to Mollie Peters in St Mark's in November 1933. Today at St Mark's the regular and popular summer Sunday teas bear witness to the success of Hugh Stuckey's innovation.

Many improvements were made to the interior of the church during the 1930s. In 1931 the Willis organ was dismantled and cleaned – but sadly to go up in flames nine years later, as did the magnificent High Altar reredos designed and executed by Sir Ninian Comper and dedicated in 1938. The reredos had been described as 'one of the most beautiful modern altar-pieces in London'.

On 23 August 1940 an all-night raid on London was the start of the Blitz and from then on for many weeks air raids were a nightly occurrence and on 21 September, St Mark's was set alight by incendiary bombs. The first bombs fell near midnight, but by the time the fire hoses were brought into action most of the nave roof was blazing. Strenuous efforts were made to save the vestments, vessels and registers – but nothing could save the reredos, which collapsed in ruins. Five nights later the church was again hit – by a high explosive bomb, which fell in the chancel, 'and the ruin was complete'.

But worship at St Mark's did not stop. Within eight hours of the first bombing, the Sunday morning Communion Service was held at Turner House in Chalcot Square. Turner House was then a home for blind women, run by the Church Army. Sister Richards gave St Mark's the use of their chapel for three services each Sunday, and four weekday services until July 1941. After that the services were held in the ruined porch of the church and later in the enlarged Choir Vestry, which had escaped the fire. Then, in 1943, a temporary church – a hut – was opened in the grounds of St Mark's where services were held, suffering greatly from the vagaries of the elements. In 1953, the Centenary of St Mark's was celebrated within the ruins of the church and *The Centenary Book of St Mark's Regent's Park* was compiled (a copy of this is now held in Camden's Local Studies Library).

On 5 October 1957, the restored St Mark's was consecrated by the Bishop of London. Jean Scott Rogers writes: 'Those of us who were at the service will never forget that lovely Saturday afternoon. The church was packed to capacity .... Sir Ninian Comper, although by then over 93 years old, attended, and took part in the procession. His new High Altar Reredos was to be completed two years later. Dr Harold Darke was at the new organ.' A former Assistant Priest at St Mark's observed: 'If we are honest, the old St Mark's was not a beautiful church, although its Victorian atmosphere might have satisfied John Betjeman. It was an example of the apparently strange workings of God's providence that it has taken Hitler to give us the opportunity to make it really beautiful.' The cost of restoration amounted to close on £80,000.

In 1964 Hugh Stuckey died and Michael Dean was appointed Vicar. 'The work since then has' says Jean Scott Rogers, 'been to enhance the beauty of the restored church and its surroundings and build up a new spiritual life in the parish, based on the church.' There were many additions to the building itself, including a stained-glass window in memory of Hugh Stuckey.

Michael Dean retired in 1981 and was succeeded as Vicar by Tom Devonshire Jones who for 18 years continued to give inspiration to the worship and life of St Mark's. The congregation was to benefit from his particular talents in the fields of music and of art history, and many a sermon was laced with the symbolism of religious artists. This period saw the establishment and flourishing of St Mark's Sunday School; the re-shaping of the Carol Services; the introduction of a monthly Healing Service; the expansion of the summer Sunday teas, the Autumn Fair and of concerts in the church. The music of St Mark's has continued to be a cherished part of its life.

On 12 November 1994, the eve of Remembrance Sunday, St Mark's was again set alight. This time the fire was started by a (never identified) arsonist who, from the evidence of his treatment of the Crucifixes, appeared to have a serious grudge against religion. Mercifully the Fire Brigade was able to put out the fire before any serious structural damage was done, but the damage caused by the smoke was considerable, and the heart of the fire in the All Saints' Chapel destroyed that altar, a quantity of furniture, and the organ and electrical system were badly damaged. The many of us who worked with our then Curate, Joanna Yates, the next morning to make it possible for the Remembrance Day service to be held will not forget the black river running down the nave, the acrid smell – and the sense that history was repeating itself.

The next year saw the work of restoration, the total cost of which amounted this time to £220,000. Services were held in the crypt for a period of time, and then on 1 October 1995 – Dedication Sunday – a splendid Sung Eucharist celebrated the reopening of the restored church. The Vicar preached to a packed and even more beautiful St Mark's which had once again risen Phoenix-like from adversity.

In March 2000 Tom Devonshire Jones retired and St Mark's moved into the care of Priest-in-Charge Tony Andrews, whose ministry has brought to St Mark's amongst his attributes the experience of a Hospital Chaplaincy and the membership of the Franciscan Order. St Mark's awaits its tenth Vicar.

St Mark's Church, St Mark's Square *Virginia Smith*

Church of St Mary the Virgin
Christopher Kitching

St Mary the Virgin traces its origin back to the Boys' Home which moved from Euston Road in 1865 to the junction of King Henry's Road and Regent's Park Road. This was then an area of new housing developments. Local residents began to attend services in the Home's chapel, conducted by the chaplain, the Revd Charles James Fuller. It was then decided to set up a new mission church nearby, a temporary iron building seating 400 adults and children in Ainger Road. Following a mission campaign in 1869, the congregation decided to build a new parish church on a site donated by Eton College in the angle of King Henry's Road, Elsworthy Road and Primrose Hill Road. Building began in 1870 and the first phase was completed in 1872. A congregation attracted to the (then still controversial) Catholic rituals inspired by the Tractarian Movement began to grow.

Nobody today has direct links with early days of the parish but first issues of the parish magazine provide an account of the services and social activities; the Eucharistic liturgy, the guilds formed to maintain the church and its social activities, the church school, fundraising events including music and drama. Some of the earliest members of the congregation wrote their recollections for a golden jubilee booklet, *St Mary the Virgin Primrose Hill After 50 Years* (Mowbrays, 1920). This includes a report on the events of the 1870s when the Bishop of London refused to consecrate the church because of its Catholic practices and eventually banned most of its ornaments and ceremonial.

St Mary's was not finally consecrated until 1885, by the new Bishop, Frederick Temple, but the reintroduction of ceremonial thought too elaborate even by many of Fuller's supporters brought a decline in the congregation. Fuller's health deteriorated, forcing him to retire in 1889. He died soon afterwards. The second vicar Revd Albert Spencer had to inject new life into the parish. His heroic efforts were successful; he

Church of St. Mary the Virgin *Virginia Smith*

extended the building, raised funds for stained glass, and established new church societies. He also re-launched the magazine, last published in 1879, and built a parish hall (now demolished) on land behind Oppidans Mews.

Percy Dearmer, third vicar 1901–1915, combined knowledge of the history of the English Church, both before and after the Reformation with an appreciation of the part played by art and music in creating an environment conducive to worship. He set a new pattern for the liturgy and ambience not just for St Mary's but for a large section of the Church of England.

St Mary's preserves to this day, the spirit of the Dearmer tradition, though adapted to the present generation and new evolving liturgies of the Church of England. Dearmer, his organist Martin Shaw, and Ralph Vaughan Williams, collaborated in compiling *The English Hymnal, Songs of Praise* and *The Oxford Book of Carols*. Succeeding clergy of St Mary's have maintained this tradition.

St Mary's therefore, is famous for its music. The quality of its acoustics has made it a popular choice for concerts, especially by unaccompanied choirs. The long running series of concerts, under the patronage of the late Sir Peter Pears and Sir Georg Solti, was sponsored by Music at St Mary's. Camden Choir and Camden Chamber Choir have given many concerts here and a resident amateur choir continues to give the liturgy its distinctive musical character under the direction of Michael Willford.

A drama group flourished from the 1920s and from the 1950s to 1970s under E. Martin Browne and Helen Lowry.

Past issues of the parish magazine are a source of local history: Geoffrey Dearmer who lived to be over 100, wrote there of his recollections of a hansom cab rank and the crossing sweeper who cleared a path to the church doorway.

Those interested in the church's history are referred to an article on the Boys' Home in the *Camden History Review No.2, 1974* by Kathleen Beck who died recently just before her hundredth birthday. Long a member of St Mary's congregation, she was one of the group of local historians who compiled *Primrose Hill to Euston Road*, published by the Camden History Society in 1982.

St Paul's Primary School

Goug Wilcox

St Paul's School emerged 125 years ago, from a Sunday School attached to St Paul's Church in Avenue Road. It occupied rooms in a house in King's College Mews off King's College Road. (The mews was demolished in 1968.) An admissions register for 1871 records the occupations of the parents; they included Bell Hanger, Oilman, Sweep. Blacksmith, Cheesemonger, Sawdust Dealer, Ostler, Brakesman, Farmer, and Charwoman.

In 1872 a 99-year lease was granted on a piece of land in Winchester Road: the idea was that the school should have its own building, and it was planned to charge 'three pence per week each child'. Built in 1873, the Old School had separate rooms for boys, girls and infants. Ages ranged from 5 to 13 for both boys and girls.

The school, then as now, wasn't big enough, and in 1913 was placed on the Board of Education's Black List: it was to be either improved or replaced. War intervened and nothing happened until 1924, when the then headmaster, Mr Walker, integrated the boys' and girls' areas. At this time St Paul's was an all-age school, with older boys going to Harben School for woodwork and girls to Haverstock for domestic science.

During World War II the School – together with All Souls School in Loudon Road – was evacuated to the Scouts' and Guides' Hut in Abbotts Langley, Hertfordshire. Mr Walker remained at Abbotts Langley throughout the war, though the Winchester Road site reopened for around a hundred pupils, with one of its classrooms strengthened for use as an air raid shelter.

When the war was over, all the children returned to Winchester Road, together with the children from All Souls, whose school had been bombed.

Another casualty of the war was St Paul's Church itself, bombed and not replaced. In 1952, after the death of its vicar, the Revd Leycester Mallet the Parish of St Paul's was joined with the Parish of St Mary the Virgin.

Following the 1944 Education Act, St Paul's received Voluntary Status, and became an

Elementary School, Mixed Infants and Juniors.

In 1954, Hampstead Borough Council bought the freehold of the Winchester Road site from Eton College, and Sir Basil Spence began designing a new civic centre which was to cover the whole area.

In 1961, the managers of the school were told that a new school for 280 children was to be built in Elsworthy Road. This good news did not last long. When the Borough of Camden was created out of Hampstead, St Pancras and Holborn, only part of Sir Basil Spence's plan went forward, and thus only the library and swimming baths were built.

The old school, dilapidated, buttressed and blacklisted, still remained in Winchester Road. The need for a new school grew desperate, since nobody wanted to improve the old one, the lease of which was due to expire in 1971.

In March 1967, the hoped-for 280-place school was reduced to 200 places, the London Diocesan Board having declined to pay for more places than they were legally obliged to, despite the Inner London Education Authority agreeing to 280 places.

By September 1969, St Paul's was so full that many children had to be turned away – though even the nearby, newly built tower blocks were then only one third full.

In 1972 a partial move was made to the new school in Elsworthy Road. Mrs Sylvia Taylor, an auxiliary helper at the school has described how for a while half the school was in Winchester Road while the other half was in Elsworthy Road. The then Headmaster, Mr Simons, did not feel happy about the school's arrangements until its official opening in 1976, which coincided with his own retirement after 42 years at St Paul's, 26 of them as Headmaster.

The new school, however, still only had six classrooms, and it was not until 1991, under the current Headmaster, Mr Wilkinson, that a seventh was added, giving each year its own classroom.

St. Paul's C.E. Primary School *Julie Blackshaw*

Utopia Village
Shirley Neale

If you walk along Chalcot Road from Princess Road, you will notice that on the right-hand side, as you approach Egbert Street, the numbers run from one to 13, but number seven is missing. Where it would have been is a house-wide gap. Number seven has never existed. Now it is the entrance to a courtyard complex of small businesses – Utopia Village.

The Rate Books for 1863 show that number seven, flanked by individual houses, was listed as 'workshop and stabling'. Those for 1864 reveal that number six was occupied by Thomas Rogers, while Mark Manley was down for both number seven and number eight. The proximity was very significant, for Manley and Rogers were the builders of St George's Road, (now Chalcot Road) terraces, so that 'workshop and stabling' could well have been the original builders' offices and stores.

The name Manley persists until 1887 when it seems that the rates (£250 for two houses and the workshops) had not been fully paid. By April 1888 the name Manley is crossed out and in 1889 it is replaced by 'John Spencer & Co. Sole Makers of the Spencer Piano'.

A new era began for number seven and, from the insurance plans for 1900, it was clear that all the processes of piano manufacture took place there. Eventually the piano factory swallowed up the small square of, apparently, public ground at the end of Egbert Street. Insurance was essential where there was much wood and veneered material. The former inhabitants of Gloucester Road have noted the persistent noise of the mechanical saw, for which they were given sacks of piano wood offcuts for firewood, in compensation.

It was from this company that the site eventually became known as Spencer Court, though not, ironically, until the pianos had gone. Oddly too the piano company had not been run by John Spencer but by a John Gloag Murdoch, and later his two sons, John and James. John Murdoch, a formidable Scotsman and entrepreneur, had followed an apprenticeship in the cotton trade in Scotland by the successful manufacture of family bibles, photograph albums, musical boxes and, eventually, organs and pianos. At number seven he established the forerunner of the light industry that exists there today.

The piano factory existed until 1939, by which time St George's Road had become Chalcot Road and Beltona clockwork gramophones were also made in the factory. Then came the Second World War, and the premises were occupied by the 'Scientific Communications Company, electrical engineers', but the narrow track for trundling completed pianos out to the road remained. Little is known about what this company did, and older inhabitants remember a certain anxiety about this – there was even a rumour that mentioned mustard gas! Nothing is clear until 1946 when Westminster Laboratories, manufacturing chemists, took over and stayed for 20 years.

In this period, further building took place. In 1957 the startlingly out-of-character extension at the end of Egbert Street was built, and a small chapel, already deconsecrated and used as a canteen, was demolished. This chapel could possibly have harked back to Joseph Gondar, a Muggletonian (a Commonwealth religious sect) who built and lived in part of Gloucester Avenue.

Westminster Laboratories' products included Sennacot, Ex-Lax, and Brook-Lax, named after the Chairman, Simon Brook, father of the theatre director, Peter Brook: after a take-over by Reckitt and Colman, in 1967 the factory moved north,

Post-war technology now arrived at number seven with Modern Telephones, the first company to install private telephone systems. Further rebuilding and reorganisation in 1970-71 transformed the cobbled courtyard into a complex of 16 small units. Some light industry remained - Medico, the medical and electrical instrument company - but a new era had begun, and new tenants included architects, interior-design consultants, graphic designers, and recording studios - enterprises now typically associated with Primrose Hill.

Spencer Court was renamed after the current managers, Utopia Records, and so the last link with the original industry was broken, and Utopia Village was born.

An Architectural Postscript
Peter & Joanna Eley

We came to live in Primrose Hill in 1969. It was Chalk Farm then, an interesting area 'with a park attached'. It had everything a village needs , including one of London's first health food shops, and I wanted to live near an open space, a lung to the city, where I could walk to work. It had been a very run down area, made grimy, until electrification, by steam trains noisily and smokily snuffling along one boundary and down into Euston, and the stuccoed houses were in poor repair, with 'sitting tenants on every floor', and washbasins on the landings.

We made a bid for our house on Fitzroy Road, without even looking at it or doing a survey, but had looked at the house next door, and seen a good big open space at the back, not filled with a mews or industrial development. It had eight good sized rooms, a 17 foot wide by 25 foot deep plan, with two party walls, built in the 1850s or 1860s. Four wider rooms, 200 foot square each at the front, and four narrower ones, 120 foot square, at the back alongside the staircase. A very useful set of spaces allowing flexibility of use. The floor to ceiling heights are graduated, with the rooms getting higher from basement to first floor, and the top floor a bit lower to complete the proportioned façade. Generally large sash windows, with single pane glazing. The roof as a typical central valley gutter hidden behind a less standard but intriguing parapet wall frieze of eight full and two half-open linked stucco circles.

The road had been built in the way traditional from the 17th to the 19th century, with the house set half a storey into the ground. The excavated spoil was put in the middle of the road, covering the drains and the supply pipes. The terraced houses are therefore set so that the access to the main front door on the 'ground floor' is up a varying number of front steps. This allows development on sloping land, like the lower edges of Primrose Hill, with access from a pavement of York stone slabs. Cast iron circular coal covers are set within the pavement to allow the delivery of fuel to three vaults under the pavement. Long gone servants could fill up coal buckets from these vaults off the front basement area, where the 'area' door allowed another independent access to the whole house.

This is how we found the original stacking plan, the way that 'they' (who were they?) had lived in the house 100 years ago. In the basement at the back was the kitchen – the imprint of the dresser, and the recess for the range still very evident – with a scullery and loo, and a servant's bed-sitting room at the front. A narrow servants' stair led up to the entrance ground floor. The parlour was in the front, and dining room at the back, with a small conservatory adjoining it, but with no room underneath it. This may have been added about 10 years later, perhaps because the houses didn't immediately sell. Our proof is the window with its external sill, and the drainpipe from the roof, both inside the conservatory. The only other loo in the houses was off the ground floor corridor. First floor piano nobile, with drawing room in front-double windows, and study, or maybe a bedroom at the back, and the top floor bedrooms, with no bathroom. More recently let off as a lodging house with very minimal facilities.

Joanna did not want to spend all her life in a basement kitchen – though this was the then fashionable thing to do, with an opened-up grand 'farmhouse kitchen' modelled on the *Guardian* pied à terre country set. Not for us: we abstained. We couldn't get a mortgage, as Building Societies 'wouldn't lend on this type of property'. We were well served by the valley gutter during our first winter. Laths and plaster from the top floor ceiling came crashing down on to our bed, within a month of settling in. With unswept coal fires, we camped on the top floor, eating meals from a borrowed electric frying pan, before we did a bit of renovation, re-roofing, rewiring, and re-plumbing. We also put in water filled radiators, driven by a gas-fired boiler. My mother was amazed, 'We never had heating in the bedrooms – there was a war on'. We also resisted the current minimalist/modernist tendency, and did not take out the chimney breasts to gain more space, because we liked the architecturally unfashionable ornate ceiling friezes, and kept the stained glass, even where the frames were softish and starting to rot. We re-used the fireplace alcoves, but I've never been able to square my feelings over what to do with the original room focus.

One of the attractive features of the house was that it was built as one of a set of six, set up like a palace (not that I wanted a palace), but the speculative mid-Victorian builders followed on from earlier architectural styles, and after Nash's ideas with grand Terraces, circling round nearby Regent's Park, designed a terrace of houses as a unit, so that the whole appeared greater than the parts. Our neighbours have all now succumbed to modern fashion, and painted their stucco different pastel shades – we are holding out. Is Brighton right for Primrose Hill?

The blocks of six houses were grouped as four sets of terraces in each quadrant, located round the intersection of Chalcot and Fitzroy Roads, a development of about 48 to 50 houses, though sadly without satisfactory (externally that is) specially designed corner houses. One of the interesting aspects of this arrangement is that from many points in the street, and from within the houses, a single view can take in both front and back elevations. With one glance you can appreciate all the elevations of the house. The classical 'Queen Anne' front, with all the windows with large sheets of glass, in line with the 'Mary Ann' back, with its crest of central valley gutters, and its slipped staircase windows, with the old-fashioned (Georgian) many small cheap panes, on the half-landings, with the flat-roofed garden extensions. You see across the street a reflection of your own façade, a permanently built three dimensional projection of a theatrical flatted stage set. When the sun shines through the rings on the houses opposite, for a short time their moving shadows are projected on to the blinds of our rooms.

I've seen earlier Victorian builders' speculative plans for this area, where the proposed four quadrant sites were laid out with four large semi-detached houses, with only eight dwellings and large gardens, like the ones on Regent's Park Road. Here, as in other parts of London, the building booms were quickly followed by busts, and housing density layout needed to be increased to keep pace with inflation, and the dwelling demand of the gents, clerks and business folk, commuting each day to their workplaces in the City.

The stack of rooms demonstrates a useful model of zoning to respond to the demands of a growing family. The houses have flexibility, and can adapt to changing needs, responding to changing late-20th century family patterns – the need to separate and join together or to work from home. Other neighbours have all converted their homes slightly differently. The eight rooms are interchangeable, the smaller rooms wide enough for a bed length and space to walk past, and they can also be opened up between each other, en suite, with outside (passage circulation), another useful model. A convertible sofa in most rooms allows them all to be sleeping places to service a fluctuating population.

The ground floor has always been our family floor, with kitchen and eating, and communal round table, and softer- sitting space. We started with the top floor for children, with our bedroom and study on the middle floor. Then when they were teens, they moved to the basement, and we moved up to sleep at the top, away from loud beat music. The self-contained rooms have always been useful for visiting relatives and friends. Now, though some have flown the nest, there seem to be lots of acquaintances and family that want to stay.

Our experience of living here over the last 30 years perhaps indicates some of the attributes of – in 1990s jargon – a sustainable house – easy to live in, to adapt, to repair and enjoy. . . and in a London village. I think the Victorians got the density, form and pattern right. What are we building today?

Acknowledgements

The Reminiscence Group would like to thank the following for their invaluable advice and help:

Pauline Baines
Kevin Bucknall
Charmian Cannon
Angela Cole
Mel Art
Nick Powell
Karen Ross
Gervais Williams
Joyce Williamson

Illustrations have been generously loaned by individuals and organisations. Accreditation is given with each illustration.

The following abbreviations have been used for organisations:

CFL	Chalk Farm Library
CHS	Camden History Society
CLSAC	Camden Local Studies and Archives Centre
EFDSS	English Folk Dance and Song Society
HP	Historical Publications Ltd.
PHCAAC	Primrose Hill Conservation Area Advisory Committee
PHS	Primrose Hill School

The following individuals have kindly loaned drawings, paintings or photographs for illustrations:

Sylvia Ballerini
Betty Bird
Julie Blackshaw
Elizabeth Bordass
Peter Bond
Sir Barry Bowman
Jonny Bucknell
Tony Coghan
Caroline Cooper
Winifred Coulter
Irene Demetriou
Simon Dobbs
John Donat
Malcolm Fowler
Harriet Garland
John Grosse
Philip Gundry
Diana Gurney
Peter Haxton
Nora Holder
Ronald Hooberman
Timothy Jaques
Marian & Ivor Kamlish
Christine Kay
Celia Kelly
Jo Killip
Alison Langan
Andolie Luck
Normski (Norman Anderson)
Caroline Read
Jean Rossiter
Philip Sanderson
Ron Sidell
Virginia Smith
Derek Sprange
Peter Toms
Jenny Wallis
Gwyneth Williams
Adam Wolfit

The following have kindly given permission to use copyright material:

Express Newspapers plc to use Sidney Strube's cartoon

Hulton Getty to use the photograph of the 1947 Opening of Chalk Farm LIbrary

David Higham Associates for permission to use an extract from Louis MacNeice's *Autumn Journal VII*

Gered Mankowitz © Bowstir Ltd. 2001. for Rolling Stones photograph

Morning Star to reproduce the photograph of the unveiling of Engels plaque

The William Roberts Society to reproduce the drawing of the artist and his family, c.1950-5

Some illustrations have been reproduced less successfully due to the condition of the original.

Myra Newman 'I remember it well'

'I REMEMBER IT WELL' was the title for reminiscence talks held at Chalk Farm Library. You didn't need to join up, nor was there any age barrier. Colleagues, Tony Adams and Helen Pollock of Camden Libraries offered much encouragement having produced *Kentish Town Library Millennium Memories* and Dorothy Starling, a long-time resident of Primrose Hill suggested the title for the talks. In the late nineties the Chalk Farm Library Reminiscence Group came into being with the support of Camden Libraries, and regular meetings took place.

Heartfelt thanks to all who joined in, however small their contribution. For all involved it has been a hugely enjoyable experience.

Further reading

Camden History Society, *From Primrose Hill to Euston Road: A Survey of Streets, Buildings and Former Residents* (1995)

Carpenter, Bob, A *Heritage Trail around Chalk Farm and Primrose Hill* (Camden Leisure Services Department, 1993)

Cline, Roger, *Regent's Park and Primrose Hill* (unpublished thesis, 1991). Available in Camden and Westminster Libraries

Holmes, Malcolm J., *Hampstead to Primrose Hill* (Alan Sutton Publishing in association with Camden Leisure and Community Services, 1995). (*Britain in Old Photographs)*

Richardson, John, *Camden Town and Primrose Hill Past* (Historical Publications, 1991)

Webster, A.D., *The Regent's Park and Primrose Hill* (Greening, 1911)

Whitehead, Jack, *The Growth of Camden Town: AD 1800-2000* (Jack Whitehead, 2000)

Andrews, Hazel, *The Role of a Public Library in a Local Community: The Case Study of Chalk Farm Library, North London*, (1998). Available through the Friends of Chalk Farm Library

The Record: Newsletter of Chalk Farm Residents Association, 1954-62

A wide range of publications and maps is available at the Camden Local Studies and Archives Centre

Wells, H.G., *The War of the Worlds* (Heinemann, 1898)

Farjeon, Eleanor, *A Nursery in the Nineties* (Gollancz 1935)

Ramsden, Caroline, *A View from Primrose Hill* (Hutchinson, 1984)

Thomson, David, *In Camden Town* (Hutchinson, 1985)

Lurie, Alison, *Foreign Affairs* (Joseph, 1985)

Smith, Dodie, *The Hundred and One Dalmatians* (Heinemann, 1987)

Amis, Kingsley, *The Folks that Live on the Hill* (Hutchinson, 1990)

Brown, Molly, *Invitation to a Funeral* (Gollancz 1995)

Rendell, Ruth, *Keys to the Street* (Gollancz 1995)

Weldon, Fay, *Big Girls Don't Cry* (Hutchinson,1997)

Charles, Paul, *Last Boat to Camden Town* (Do-Not Press, 1998)

Falconer, Helen, *Primrose Hill* (Faber, 1998)

Craig, Amanda, *In a Dark Wood* (Fourth Estate, 2000)

Author index

The printing of this book has been made possible by generous donations from the following people:

Mrs Diana Adler
Stuart & Finola Andrews

Mrs P Baines
Marian Baraitser
Amber Barnard
Dr A Berger
Mrs M Beusch
Bibendum Wine Ltd.
Dick & Sue Bird
Susan Blum
Brace Family
Mrs V Brinton
Bucknells Ltd

Dr & Mrs Cannon
Fliff & Steve Carr
Stuart Cathcart
Paul Charles
Aenne & Claude Chene
Mrs Angela Cole
Mrs B Colloms
Caroline Cooper
J & U Cornish
Veronica Cotgrove
Claire Crocker & Adam Lurie
Winifred Coulter

Teddy & Ramona Darvas
Dr Paul Davies
Liz de Kerbrech
Pam Dempster
Les Dennis
Phyllis Dobbs
Ms Jacqueline Doherty
Mrs I Dowie

Jane Echlin &
Virginia Edwards
Nicholas & Gillian Eeley
Robin Ellis

Lorna Fowler
Steve Frost

Jocelyn Gamble
Harriet Garland
Mr & Mrs J M Garner
Miss M Garnham
Victoria Gath & Mark Echlin
Liz Gerschel
Chris Glen
David & Ilse Gray
Graham & Green
Dr P M Gundry

HTA Architects Ltd
Theresa & Tony Hallgarten
Yvonne Harper-Scholar
Chris Harrald
V V Hartshorn
Lady Selina Hastings
Mrs M Hawes
Peter Haxton
Elizabeth Horder
Dominic Hicks
Roy Hidson
Malcolm Holmes
Philippa Huins
Bernard & Florence Hunt
Avis Hutt
Nicholas Hytner

Michael Jackson
Philippa Jackson
James Jacovides
Helen Janacek
Moira Jenkins
Peter Jessop
P R Johnson
Stanley Johnson
Bernard & Pamela Jolles
Patricia Jones

Marian & Ivor Kamlish
Mrs Sam Katz
Christine Kay
Jo Killip
L Kipping
Patricia Kruijer

Janet Lang
Alison Langan
Mrs S Lassen
Vicky Lee
Gail Levy
Henry Lewis
M Lightbown
Colin Luke
Jo & David Lyall

S Magan
Dr & Mrs R F Mahler
Ian Mankin Ltd
Priscilla McBride
Mr & Mrs L Marks
Alec Marmot
Rick Mather Architects Ltd
Mel Art Graphics
Andrea Mendelson
Sam Mendes
Robin Michaelson
James Miller
Andrew Moor
Martin & Joyce Morton
Kate Moses
Jean Muir

Helen Newnham
Mrs S M Nicholls
Mr & Mrs H C Nottman
N A Nowell

Gael O'Farrell
Oregano Restaurant

Cindy Palmano
Susanna Pancaldo
Paxton Locher Architects Ltd.
Lois Phillips
Michael Pickering
Mr Edward & Mrs Denise Pincheson
Reg Pleeth
Jacques Portier
Stephen J Prior

Paula Quirk

Ms M G Robshaw
Mrs L Romano
Jean Rossiter
Cecil Rowe

Sainsbury's
Lady St Davids
Valerie St Johnston
P J Sanderson
M S Scott
Meriel Serjeant
Mrs Linda Seward
Mrs Y Shane
Sybil Shine
M J Smith
Ethna Smyth
Patricia Snell
Sparky-Mullarkey
Anne Sofer
J Stanger
Mrs Dorothy Starling
Ann Marie Starr
Gill & Peter Stern
Emily Stewart
Carol & Michael Storey
Mr & Mrs Edward Stork
Caroline Strachan

Valerie Taylor

Dr Gillian M Vanhegan
Mrs R Vaughan Williams
Anita Venezia & Patrick Yau

Lady Wade-Gery
A Webb
Jessica Weiss
Patrick Whelan
P Whitaker
Peter White
David H Whyte
David Widdicombe
Gervais Williams
Miss G A Williams
Edward Williams
B Winkleman
Dr F Peter Woodford
Gregory & Patricia Wright

H Zazzara

Index and glossary

An italicised number indicates an illustration in the text.

'f' or 'ff' indicate further entries on following page or pages.